ON LITURGICAL ASCETICISM

DAVID W. FAGERBERG

ON LITURGICAL ASCETICISM

THE CATHOLIC
UNIVERSITY OF AMERICA PRESS
Washington, D.C.

The paper used in this publication meets
the minimum requirements of American
National Standards for Information Science—
Permanence of Paper for Printed Library
Materials, ANSI Z39.48-1984.
∞

Library of Congress
Cataloging-in-Publication Data
Fagerberg, David W., 1952–
On liturgical asceticism / David W. Fagerberg.
p. cm.
Includes bibliographical references (p.)
and index.
ISBN 978-0-8132-2117-5 (pbk. : alk. paper)
1. Asceticism. I. Title.
BV5031.3.F34 2013
248.4'7—dc23 2012038228

To Samuel Suter,

a living witness to Orthodoxy, who

never refused a fruitful discussion,

with gratitude for our personal

ecumenical dialogue

CONTENTS

PREFACE

This book identifies the third leg of a stool that is wobbly without it. Why I think that third leg is necessary might be most easily explained by giving a brief narrative of how it pressed itself upon my understanding.

I am honored to be mentioned as belonging to a school known as the Schmemann-Kavanagh school of liturgical theology. The shared supposition in this approach is that liturgy is primary theology, and that the *lex orandi* of the Church establishes her *lex credendi*. Fr. Alexander Schmemann, former dean of St. Vladimir's Orthodox Seminary, died before I had the chance to meet him, but I was introduced to his work by Fr. Aidan Kavanagh in my first semester at Yale. I begged Kavanagh for a directed readings course, and since he was just completing the lectures that would make up his book *On Liturgical Theology*, he agreed on the condition that we read together everything we could by Schmemann. (The title of this present work is meant to echo Kavanagh's book, gratefully and as a tribute.) I tell people that the rest of my graduate education was spent trying to get the number of the bus that hit me in those directed readings. Schmemann opened a new front in liturgical studies by saying that liturgy is the ontological condition for theology. He took the liturgy seriously as a theological matrix, and said liturgical theology is the reintegration of liturgy, theology, and piety. Kavanagh further elaborated this understanding by taking *lex orandi statuat lex credendi* seriously, as meaning exactly what it says, and concluding that if Mrs. Murphy has been formed by the Church's *lex orandi* then she can be called a primary theologian. We do not create our own *lex orandi,* we are created by the *lex orandi* of the Church, and that makes us theologians.

The combined approaches of Schmemann and Kavanagh gave me an entirely new way of looking at liturgical theology. I had arrived at graduate school as a systematician planning to dissect liturgical subjects, but this approach supposed that the liturgy should be looked at in motion. Schmemann and Kavanagh asserted that the true primary theologian in the Church is the liturgical assembly. Thus the task was not for me to add liturgy to theology, or theology to liturgy. The task was for me to follow the contours of liturgical theology, two words joined as an organic phrase to name but one thing: the action of the Church at liturgy. Liturgy is theology at the primary level, it is not just pious straw for an academic Rumpelstiltskin to spin into supposedly real theological gold. My dissertation was an attempt to work that out, and was published in 1992, bearing the same title: *What Is Liturgical Theology?*[1] I had two legs of the stool in place: liturgy and theology were connected.

However, in the years that followed I watched the puzzlement some people had with that Schmemann-Kavanagh definition, and wondered why. Why was it difficult to grasp? What was the objection to calling Mrs. Murphy a theologian? Why treat liturgy under the thinnest ceremonial category, and as something of interest only to historians and not theologians? I began to sus-

1. David Fagerberg, *What Is Liturgical Theology?* (Collegeville, Minn.: Liturgical Press, 1992).

pect that some other ingredient had been assumed not only by Schmemann and Kavanagh, but even in my own thinking, and it needed to be made more explicit. In the process of a long reflection, I came to the conclusion that people have misunderstood liturgical theology because they have overlooked its ascetical dimension. This book attempts to remedy that—to identify the third leg. It clarifies liturgical theology by integrating the ascetical dimension into it, connecting the three in a kind of conceptual perichoresis.

I was given the opportunity to experiment with the thesis in 1996 by the University of Durham, U.K., as a Richardson Fellow. My lecture was simply entitled "Liturgical Asceticism" and it contained this book within it as the oak is contained within an acorn. (A modified version of that lecture was accepted by the journal *Diakonia* in 1998, as "A Century on Liturgical Asceticism," and is reprinted at the end of this book.) I owe the University of Durham a public word of acknowledgment, and a private word of thanks for their patience, as I finally publish the fruits of the seminal lecture I gave there.

I discovered that writing about asceticism proved to be a slow process because it is so humiliating. There are countless stories warning against the temptation to teach about the virtues instead of acquiring them.[2] Just when an academic author is getting up his head of steam, he comes across someone like Abba Nestoros, who tells John Cassian that his lips should maintain strict silence "lest your pursuit of reading and the intensity of your desire come to naught because of empty pride.... For it is impossible for a person who pursues reading persistently with the intention of winning human praise to deserve the gift of true knowledge.... Nor should anyone presume to teach in words what he has not previously done in deed.... Be careful, therefore,

2. Some of these warnings I gathered together in a light-hearted treatment in "Caveat Lector: On the Reading of Theological Books," *Touchstone* 17, no. 3 (April 2004): 30–35, available at http://www.touchstonemag.com/archives/article.php?id=15-06-049-f.

that you not jump to teaching before you have acted."[3] Or someone like Dorotheos of Gaza, who reproves the man who does not humbly confess his own weakness but instead "speaks about the virtues with praise and admiration as if he had long acquired and practiced them."[4] Or John Climacus: "The insensitive man is a foolish philosopher, . . . a scholar who contradicts himself, a blind man teaching sight to others. . . . He talks profoundly about death and acts as if he will never die. . . . He has plenty to say about self-control and fights for a gourmet life. He reads . . . about vainglory and is vainglorious while he is reading."[5] Or Diadochus of Photiki: "Opening the door of the steam bath lets heat escape; likewise the soul, in its desire to say many things, dissipates its remembrance of God through the door of speech. . . . Ideas of value always shun verbosity."[6] There were reminders like this wherever I stepped in the ascetical literature, so it was very slow going and I had an incomplete manuscript on my computer for seven years (a biblical number for patience).

Then came an opportunity to publish a second edition of my book *What Is Liturgical Theology?* through Liturgy Training Publication's new imprint, Hillenbrand Books. This series comes out of the Liturgical Institute at the University of St. Mary of the Lake/Mundelein Seminary, where I had just arrived. My understanding of liturgical theology had continued to evolve in my mind; could the book not also evolve? It is an amusing fantasy to think of a scholar revising one book ten times in his life instead of writing ten different books in his life: it would all depend upon whether the subject matter could bear deeper scrutiny. So in addition to a thorough revision, and deleting or combining some

3. *John Cassian: The Conferences,* 14.9.4 (Mahwah, N.J.: Newman Press, 1997), 512–13.

4. Dorotheos of Gaza, *Discourses and Sayings* (Kalamazoo, Mich.: Cistercian Publishing, 1977), 161.

5. John Climacus, *The Ladder of Divine Ascent,* Step 18, "On Insensitivity" (New York: Paulist Press, 1982), 192. Or see *The Ladder of Divine Ascent* (Boston: Holy Transfiguration Monastery, 2001).

6. Diadochus of Photiki, "On Spiritual Knowledge," *The Philokalia,* edited by G. E. H. Palmer, Philip Sherrard, and Kallistos Ware (Boston: Faber & Faber, 1979), 1.276.

chapters that had originally only been included for the benefit of the doctoral committee, I wrote a new head chapter for the second edition. I transferred the opening chapter intended for *On Liturgical Asceticism* to make it the first chapter in *Theologia Prima: What Is Liturgical Theology?*[7] The reader thus holds a corpus with two heads and may read either the first chapter here, or the first chapter there. Both of them conclude that liturgical theology, as conceived by Schmemann and Kavanagh and my own humble self, cannot be understood without the element of asceticism because of the mutual interplay of these three factors.

John of Kronstadt traces the direct connection from participation in liturgy to the felt desire for ascetical purification and praxis:

> In church I am truly as if in heaven upon earth; here I see the images of the Lord, of the Most Pure Mother of God, of the holy Angels; here is God's throne, here is the life-giving Cross, here is the eternal Gospel.... This is truly heaven on earth: here I know that I am, and feel myself indeed a member of Christ and of His Church, especially during the celebration of the most holy Liturgy, and the Communion of the Holy Mysteries of the Body and Blood of Christ. O, how I ought to live, think, feel, speak, in order to worthily be in this heaven on earth! I ought to live worthily of the high calling to which I am called by the grace of the much-endowing God. How I ought to live, in what meekness, humility, purity, abstinence, in order to worthily name my Lady, the Most Pure Mother of God, my Master, the Lord of glory! Lord, make me worthy of such an abode! I desire to live worthily of the Christian calling, but I find no power in myself to attend this; sin unceasingly tempts and wars against my soul.[8]

This book is about that connection. Every Christian should feel liturgy awaken and command asceticism. This book is therefore *not* about the liturgical practices of monks, as if they are the only ascetics; it does not ask about the way eucharists were cel-

7. David Fagerberg, *Theologia Prima: What Is Liturgical Theology?* (Chicago: Hillenbrand Press, Liturgy Training Publications, 2003).

8. John of Kronstadt, *My Life in Christ* (Jordanville, N.Y.: Holy Trinity Monastery, 2000), 325–26.

ebrated in the Egyptian desert; it does not compare the schedule and severity of monastic fasts to the liturgical fasts incumbent on the whole Church during the Church year; its title does not propose liturgies of such sparse and austere character that sitting through them can be a meritorious act. Rather, this book proposes that the category of asceticism, essential to the Christian life, is also essential for understanding liturgy and theology. What does asceticism add? First, to liturgy it adds the awareness that the liturgical mysteries have a formative power upon the liturgist (the subject who celebrates liturgy). This worked its way into Kavanagh's background from his studies on ritual activity, and although Schmemann did not engage modern ritual studies he naturally assumed that liturgy was at the ground of a Christian's life. Living the liturgy forms a Christian. Second, to theology it adds the awareness of the broader definition the term once possessed. It places theology within a different context, an older context: before the term was limited to a university faculty, *theologian* meant someone who arrived at the end of an ascetical struggle. Apart from this larger use of the term, it seems difficult to understand how Kavanagh can call Mrs. Murphy a theologian.

To my surprise, once my radar had been attuned to the ascetical dimension I found mention of it in numerous places in Kavanagh's book. I recount them in the first chapter of this work in order to observe how a teacher can plant a concept in a student's mind without the latter realizing it until years later.

In that same sense, I should acknowledge the agency of another mentor, Paul Holmer. I have come to realize that his work has conditioned how I value asceticism. Holmer thought about the cost exacted from the subject who knows. This was not subjectivism, as it is commonly defined. It did not mean that the subject determines the truth of a proposition, or that truth is different for each subject, or that there are different truths for different subjects. Rather, Holmer focused on the insight that "what we know depends upon the kind of person we have made of ourselves."[9] He pursued this idea through a variety of philosophers, but especially through Kierkegaard and Wittgenstein. True, certain kinds of knowledge can be stored up and handed down as repeatable propositions, but certain other kinds of knowledge must be attempted if they are to be understood. In class he would often say, "You cannot peddle truth or happiness; what a thought cost in the first instance, it will cost in the second." Whatever it cost Augustine to understand grace, it will cost us to understand grace, if we would really understand it and not just repeat what the textbooks have said about it. We had to be capacitated to understand—he introduced *capacitate* as a verb to me.

In Holmer's world of discourse, "capacity" did not mean a vacant space, like the empty stage behind the curtain; rather it meant potential, like staging the set on which you will act out your life. He spoke of being capacitated to grow into a complete person by means of practicing the virtues. Being capacitated means cultivating a form of life. Capacities are woven into the texture of a life, and they construct a life. He would make his point by distinguishing a capacity, on the one hand, from an activity or skill, on the other. Playing basketball is an activity, playing basketball well is a skill, but hoping is a capacity. And one of the signs that distinguishes a capacity from the others, Holmer would say, is that skills and activities are done by the hour, but a capacity is constructed over a lifetime. It would not be odd for me to say I will be reading in the library between 2:00 and 3:00, but it would be odd for me to say that I will be hopeful between 2:00 and 3:00. Hopefulness is a capacity, not an activity, and capacities have to operate steadily and persistently below the surface—they do not start and stop the way activities do. Our identity develops according to how we live, and the task of our life is the acquisition of those capacities that will become a deep-seated and controlling disposition in us. I came to think of this in ascetical

9. Paul Holmer, *C. S. Lewis: His Life and His Thought* (New York: Harper & Row, 1976), 90.

terms, and the formation of a person became connected to the capacity to understand.

In his book *The Grammar of Faith,* Holmer says "[a] leading thought of this book suggests that quite primitive instances of the language of faith and the life of faithful believers answer to one another. Both belong to a single grammar."[10] As Wittgenstein said that language fits the world, Holmer is saying that the language of faith must fit the world of faith. "Theology is that discipline in which the believers declare what the facts are, what the hopes, fears, and loves are, what the beliefs are, for those who find God in Christ Jesus. Believers are clearly in a life-and-death game of salvation.... Theology is that interpretation and that game which we all must play if we are to refer our lives to God."[11] One must be schooled in the human heart, in a logic of life, indeed, schooled in a grammar of holiness. One concluding thought by Holmer, then:

> If theology is like a grammar, and certainly it is, then it follows that learning theology is not an end in itself.... In so far as Christianity can be "said" at all, theology and Scripture say it. But what is therein said, be it the words of eternal life, be it creeds, or be it the words of Jesus Himself, we must note that like grammar and logic, their aim is not that we repeat the words. Theology also must be absorbed, and when it is, the hearer is supposed to become Godly.[12]

Allusions in my work to theology being a "grammar" come out of this framework, a framework in which a subject is formed, capacitated, shaped, enabled, and empowered toward Godliness. And insofar as liturgy does that forming and capacitating and deifying, it seems proper to speak of a liturgical asceticism.

That is the story of how this book came to be, and what it hopes to accomplish. The first chapter defines liturgical asceticism; the second describes the passions (*pathe*); the third con-

10. Holmer, *The Grammar of Faith* (San Francisco: Harper & Row, 1978), ix.
11. Ibid., 8–9.
12. Ibid., 19

siders the prescribed strategies for resisting them (*askesis*); the fourth marvels at what a righteous and dispassionate person would look like (*apatheia*); the fifth asks whether this asceticism is for monks alone; and the sixth sees the face of the sanctified ascetic in the icons and apprehends Mary as the supreme liturgical person.

Successful writers might warn me off making apologies in a preface, but there are nevertheless two to make, both in the sense of explanation and in the sense of begging pardon.

First, the material about asceticism is so vast and rich that it was a temptation to lose myself in an act of organizational cross-referencing. I was tempted to compare what one certain desert father says about fasting with what another later theologian would say about it, or to catalogue the various definitions of *nous* and *metanoia,* or to collect all my favorite quotations on a certain vice or virtue. But if I were to include every favorite beautiful and insightful saying, where would I stop? Such an approach would result in a multivolume glossary, and such is not the assignment I had given myself. My desire was instead to discover the theological rationale behind liturgical asceticism, and the ascetical cost of being capacitated for liturgical theology. How do these three terms—liturgy, theology, asceticism—interrelate and interpenetrate? How can we explain liturgy as a substantially theological enterprise, asceticism as a product of and prerequisite for Christian liturgy, and see the mutual integration of all three?

Second, I feel some trepidation in writing about Eastern Christian categories when I am a Roman Catholic, and more trepidation in taking lessons from the monks when I am not one. I wish to say to both communities that I am open to their correction. Concerning monasticism I can only take recourse to those Orthodox thinkers who say that the monk is a special expression of the ascetical life, but does not have a monopoly on it; indeed, that a sort of "interiorized monasticism" is incumbent on every baptized Christian. Concerning Eastern Orthodoxy, I make the endeavor because in *Unitatis Redintegratio* my Church tells me that I will benefit from the attempt: "Catholics therefore are earnestly recommended to avail themselves of the spiritual riches of the Eastern Fathers which lift up the whole man to the contemplation of the divine" (15). I can only hope that the contours of an object might be felt from both the inside and the outside, and that though I am not inside Eastern Orthodoxy, I can nevertheless feel the contours of their theology without altering its shape. Though I think the case for liturgical asceticism could also be made with Western sources, I have here primarily confined myself to Orthodox authors, ancient and modern, since they are the ones who awakened this awareness in me. About the tacit Michael Polanyi says, "we know more than we can say." Although I am aware that Mrs. Papadopoulos and Mrs. Ivanov know more about liturgical asceticism than I can say, academics have the urge to write, nevertheless.

I have already pointed out that in most of the ascetical tradition this urge to write is not encouraged.

> Once a brother came to Abba Theodore of Pherme, and spent three days asking him for a word. But the Abba did not answer, and he went away sadly. So Abba Theodore's disciples asked him, "Abba, why did you not speak to him? Look, he has gone away sad." And the old man said: "Believe me, I said nothing to him because his business is getting credit by retailing what others have said to him."[13]

And St. Gregory of Sinai records that according to Maximus the Confessor

> there are three motives for writing which are above reproach and censure: to assist one's memory, to help others, or as an act of obedience. It is for the last reason that most spiritual writings have been composed, at the humble request of those who have need of them. If you write about spiritual matters simply for pleasure, fame or self-display, you will get your deserts, as Scripture says, and will not profit from it in this

13. Systematic Sayings, 8.6. This translation is from Owen Chadwick, ed., *Western Asceticism* (Philadelphia: Westminster Press, 1958), 98.

life or gain any reward in the life to come. On the contrary, you will be condemned for courting popularity and for fraudulently trafficking in God's wisdom.[14]

Stern words, ones that could easily tempt another delay. But if the reader will pray for me, a sinner, I will take heart from a leniency expressed by John Climacus:

Do not be a harsh critic of those who resort to eloquence to teach many important things, but who have few actions to match their words. For edifying words have often compensated for a lack of deeds. All of us do not get an equal share of every good, and for some the word is mightier than the deed ... and vice-versa for others.[15]

The Feast of the Assumption of Mary, August 15, 2011

14. St. Gregory of Sinai, in *The Philokalia* (London: Faber & Faber, 1995), 4.251.
15. John Climacus, *The Ladder of Divine Ascent*, 251.

ON LITURGICAL ASCETICISM

1 WHY LITURGICAL ASCETICISM?

It is a fair question to ask what reason there is to slap the adjective "liturgical" in front of the noun "asceticism" and try to open up a new field of discussion. Why not let liturgy slumber peacefully in the world of ritual and rubric, and let asceticism snuggle comfortably in the world of spirituality and monasticism? Why *liturgical asceticism*? The answer to this question will require us to think about liturgy in more profound terms than being just one more elective activity a Christian might choose, and instead see liturgy as foundational to Christian identity. "To swim" is a verb, "swimmer" is the noun; "liturgy" is a verb, "Christian" is the noun. Liturgy is the verb form of "Church" and "Church" is the noun form of "liturgy." To pursue this idea, we will start by molding some bricks out of which we will build our functional definition of liturgy, one that will demand liturgical asceticism and explain liturgical theology. The first step in creating these building blocks is to permit ourselves a fresh appreciation of liturgy, and we will attempt this by posing the question this way: Who originates liturgy?

In his "Four Hundred Chapters on Love" Maximus the Confessor counsels, "Seek the reason why God created, for this is true knowledge."[1] He answers his own query elsewhere in this same work. "God who is beyond fullness did not bring creatures into being out of any need of his, but that he might enjoy their proportionate participation in him and that he might delight in his works seeing them delighted and ever insatiably satisfied with the one who is inexhaustible."[2] And he elaborates on this explanation in another place.

> God made us so that we might become "partakers of the divine nature" (2 Pet. 1:4) and sharers in His eternity, and so that we might come to be like Him (cf. 1 John 3:2) through deification by grace. It is through deification that all things are reconstituted and achieve their permanence; and it is for its sake that what is not is brought into being and given existence.[3]

The reason for creation was so that creatures might delight in the Creator insatiably, not from a distance but by participation in the divine nature. Such union with God has been called "deification" by the tradition; *theosis* in Greek.[4] Insofar as a gratuitous action has a reason, deification is the reason for God's acts of creation and redemption. The liturgy celebrates the Christian mystery, by which we mean not only the paschal mystery (Incarnation, Crucifixion, Resurrection, and Ascension of Christ), but the whole mystery this brought to fruition. It must not be forgotten that the Word who was incarnated and crucified is also the *Logos* who was with God, and who was God, and through whom all things came to be, and without whom nothing came to be (John 1). The Christian mystery is not only the cross, but extends from creation to

1. Maximus the Confessor, *The Four Hundred Chapters on Love,* 4.5, in *Maximus Confessor: Selected Writings* (New York: Paulist Press, 1985).

2. Maximus, *The Four Hundred Chapters on Love,* 3.46.

3. Maximus the Confessor, "The First Century," in "Various Texts on Theology, the Divine Economy, and Virtue and Vice," in *The Philokalia,* edited by G. E. H. Palmer, Philip Sherrard, and Kallistos Ware (Boston: Faber & Faber, 1981), 2.173.

4. See Norman Russell's survey of the term in *The Doctrine of Deification in the Greek Patristic Tradition* (Oxford: Oxford University Press, 2004).

eschaton. Maximus is reminding us that creation is the beginning of redemption, and redemption is the fulfillment of creation. To fulfill the mysterious plan for creation, God had to take the Fall into account, but he did not change plans when he did so. As Vladimir Lossky puts it, "After the Fall, human history is a long shipwreck awaiting rescue: but the port of salvation is not the goal; it is the possibility for the shipwrecked to resume his journey whose sole goal is union with God."[5] Union with God, or deification, is the North Star we are following in this definition of liturgy.

Liturgical theology explores the economy of the Holy Trinity as it is manifested in the liturgical mysteries. The liturgical mysteries invite our participation in this divine economy, accomplished in us by the Holy Spirit. Recognition of the inseparability of the three persons in this economy led Fr. Virgil Michel, O.S.B., a pioneer of the liturgical reform in the twentieth century, to describe the liturgy as an action of the whole Trinity.

> The liturgy, through Christ, comes from the Father, the eternal source of the divine life in the Trinity. It in turn addresses itself in a special way to the Father, rendering him the homage and the glory of which it is capable through the power of Christ. The flow of divine life between the eternal Father and the Church is achieved and completed through the operation of the Holy Ghost.
>
> The liturgy, reaching from God to man, and connecting man to the fullness of the Godhead, is the action of the Trinity in the Church. The Church in her liturgy partakes of the life of the divine society of the three persons in God.[6]

This suggests that liturgy begins in a place where we don't normally look. People look for the origin of liturgy in ancient history, in religious purity rituals, in human need, in communal fellowship, but apparently we do not begin the liturgy, the Trinity does.

5. Vladimir Lossky, *Orthodoxy Theology: An Introduction* (Crestwood, N.Y.: St. Vladimir's Seminary Press, 1978), 84.

6. Virgil Michel, O.S.B., *The Liturgy of the Church, according to the Roman Rite* (New York: Macmillan, 1937), 40.

The bulb from which the liturgical tulip grows is not a human decision, it is a divine decision intertwined with the reason why God created in the first place. We join a liturgy already in progress. The liturgy is not the activity of the Jesus Club, liturgy is rather coming to be connected into God's own life. The Father unveils the mystery of his will by giving his beloved Son and his Holy Spirit for the salvation of the world and for the glory of his name, and these two purposes are the classically named purposes of liturgy: the sanctification of man and the glorification of God.

Fr. Jean Corbon sees liturgy in terms of kenosis and ascension. In the first kenosis by God, which is the gift of being that is creation, the Blessed Trinity is still hidden from sight. "The Father gives himself, but who receives him? His word is given, but who answers? His Spirit is poured out, but not yet shared."[7] So begins a long history of salvation, says Corbon, preparing for a second kenosis. The drama in which this unfolds to its climax (the hypostatic union) is called history. "If it be true that the drama of history is the interplay of God's gift and human acceptance of it, then the drama reaches its climax, and its eternal beginning, on this day [the day of the Resurrection], because these two energies are now joined together forever.... The liturgy has been born; the resurrection of Jesus is its first manifestation."[8] With Christ's paschal mystery, eucharistic life was restored to humanity, and this accomplished what had been intended from the beginning. This is why Christ is called the "second Adam," or properly, the "eschata Adam." Creation and redemption are not "Plan A and Plan B," as if when the first creation failed then God went on to try something else. Creation and redemption are not two different plays; they are two acts in one play, with the protological act oriented toward the conclusion, and the eschatological act fulfilling all that has gone before. Gregory Palamas sees the whole picture.

7. Jean Corbon, *The Wellspring of Worship* (New York: Paulist Press, 1988), 17.
8. Ibid., 32–33.

The world was founded with this in view from the beginning. The heavenly, pre-eternal Counsel of the Father, according to which the angel of the Father's Great Counsel made man (Isa. 9:6) as a living creature in His own likeness as well as His image, was for this end: to enable man at some time to contain the greatness of God's kingdom, the blessedness of God's inheritance and the perfection of the heavenly Father's blessing .... Even the indescribable divine self-emptying, the theandric way of life, the saving passion, all the sacraments were planned beforehand in God's providence and wisdom for this end, that everyone who is shown to be faithful in the present shall hear the savior say, "Well done, thou good servant."[9]

Maximus has asked what God's purpose was in creating. Dante suggests an answer that can be considered a liturgical cosmology. "Not to gain any good for Himself, which cannot be, but that His splendor, shining back, might say *Subsisto,* —in His eternity, beyond time, beyond every other bound, as it pleased Him, the Eternal Love revealed Himself in new loves."[10] The God who is Being is also Love and Goodness, and when these three attributes compound, then other creatures get willed into existence. God's loving goodness shares being so that there are other creatures to love—meaning not only that there are other creatures whom God can love, but also that there are other creatures who are themselves capable of loving. Creation is a generous overflow of the indwelling love that moves between the Father and the Son and the Holy Spirit. Once there was nothing besides God, and then the Uncreated made created beings beside himself. If we dare say so, creation is God being beside himself with love. Dorothy Sayers thus interprets Dante to be asking why these different things exist.

9. Gregory Palamas, Homily Four, in "On the Gospel Passage Describing Christ's Second Coming," in *Saint Gregory Palamas: The Homilies* (Waymart, Pa.: Mount Thabor, 2009), 28–29.

10. Dante, *The Divine Comedy 3: Paradise,* this translation by Dorothy Sayers in "Dante the Maker," *The Poetry of Search and The Poetry of Statement* (London: Victor Gollancz, 1963), 32.

Why are these different things? In order that the divine splendor, shining back in innumerable facets from the face of the finite creation, should be able to stand up before its Creator and say, "look! this is me. I really exist. I am something. I am myself. *Subsisto.*" It can add nothing to the source from which it derives—God gets nothing out of it; but it has pleased Him that every creature—angel, man, beast, beetle, or buttercup—should be able, in its small way, to enjoy itself, to enjoy being a self of some sort, dependent on God and yet distinct from Him.[11]

An earlier poet made the same point with a concept that required a neologism to express. The famous hierarchies of Dionysius are the result of God saying *subsisto* to different levels of being. Although the word *hierarchy* has poor connotations due to its sloppy misuse these days, it seems only fair that the person who coined the neologism should have the privilege of defining it, and Dionysius says in *The Celestial Hierarchy* that "[t]he goal of a hierarchy, then, is to enable beings to be as like as possible to God and to be at one with him."[12] Again, "Hierarchy causes its members to be images of God in all respects, to be clear and spotless mirrors reflecting the glow of primordial light and indeed of God himself."[13] And again, "The aim of every hierarchy is to imitate God so as to take on his form. . . ."[14] Man and woman, as the image of God, are to grow and mature into the likeness of God.

Dionysius's hierarchical notion attributed an innovative move to God, unimagined by ancient philosophers, and one that could only have been the result of the transformation of their philosophical categories by a biblical doctrine of creation. We might call it the novelty of a "downward ecstasy," with the assistance of Fr. Alexander Golitzin's study on the Areopagite. The philosophers knew that if the created mind encountered the divinity in darkness, it was no longer as a creature *qua* creature, because to have any contact with the Creator, the creature must go outside

11. Ibid.

12. Dionysius, *The Celestial Hierarchy*, 3.2, in *Pseudo-Dionysius: The Complete Works* (New York: Paulist Press, 1987), 154.

13. Ibid.

14. Ibid.

of himself (*ekstasis*). What was unthinkable to the philosophers is that God could go outside himself to the creature.

> If the creature may only encounter God as the latter is in his transcendence through "passing out" of its proper being, then conversely God may enter into relationship, including the act of creation, only through a kind of "self-transcendence." Moved to create ... God "leaves" in a sense that state of being, or "super-being," proper to him. He goes "outside" his hidden essence. It is this divine "out-passing" that is the foundation or subject of the *Divine Names* and, in so far as they are the mirrors of God, of the Celestial and Ecclesiastical Hierarchies as well. God as he is known in his names and in his creation is God "outside," as it were, of his essence.[15]

If we may be excused a spatial metaphor, it is as if in creation the Trinity turned itself inside out, and being was poured through the hierarchies as a golden chain from the Uncreated to the created. Or Fr. Louis Bouyer uses the metaphor of a beating heart.

> Across this continuous chain of creation, in which the triune fellowship of the divine persons has, as it were, extended and propagated itself, moves the ebb and flow of the creating *Agape* and of the created *eucharistia*. Descending further and further towards the final limits of the abyss of nothingness, the creating love of God reveals its full power in the response it evokes, in the joy of gratitude in which, from the very dawn of their existence creatures freely return to him who has given them all. Thus this immense choir of which we have spoken, basing ourselves on the Fathers, finally seems like an infinitely generous heart, beating with an unceasing diastole and systole, first diffusing the divine glory in paternal love, then continually gathering it up again to its immutable source in filial love.[16]

Maximus interprets Dionysius to be saying that the divine is an erotic force that goes out of itself to rouse creation by an attracting, attractive love.

15. Alexander Golitzin, *Et Introibo ad Altare Dei: The Mystagogy of Dionysius Areopagita, with Special Reference to Its Predecessors in the Eastern Christian Tradition* (Thessaloniki, Greece: George Dedousis, 1994), 48–49.

16. Louis Bouyer, *The Meaning of the Monastic Life* (London: Burns & Oates, 1955), 28–29.

> One must also in the name of truth be bold enough to affirm that the Cause of all things, through the beauty, goodness and profusion of His intense love for everything, goes out of Himself in His providential care for the whole of creation. By means of the supra-essential power of ecstasy, and spell-bound as it were by goodness, love and longing, He relinquishes His utter transcendence in order to dwell in all things while yet remaining within Himself. Hence those skilled in divine matters call Him a zealous and exemplary lover, because of the intensity of His blessed longing for all things and because He rouses others to imitate His own intense desire.[17]

Father, Son, and Holy Spirit turned their mutual indwelling love outward, and that action gave being to other nondivine creatures. The Trinity turns outward in an economy of creation and redemption that will lead to the moment when God will appear in the midst of creation, his ecstatic product. The world will become a habitat for divinity. And at the end, the Trinity will draw back into itself everything in creation that is attracted to its truth, beauty, and goodness, in the wake of the ascension that Christ launched from Sheol.

The Church Fathers called this dynamic activity within God *perichoresis,* from *peri* ("around") and *choresis* ("to dance"). Perichoresis means a co-inherence, a dance of love, a mutual indwelling by the three persons of the Trinity. (*Graphe* means "to write," and a record of dance steps is a *choreo-graphe*; liturgy is the divine choreography encoded in the sacramental mysteries to train our feet for this dance.) The extension of the Trinity's love in an act of creation and the return of that creation to its source in God is a *kenosis* and an *ascension* (an *exitus* and a *reditus*). True, an adjustment had to be made to overcome sin and the effects of the Fall. If creation's purpose was to make beings capable of union with the Trinity's perichoretic love, then Christ would have to overcome our alienation in order to complete creation. So he descended in kenosis all the way to Sheol where he found Adam

17. Maximus the Confessor, "The Fifth Century," in "Various Texts on Theology, the Divine Economy, and Virtue and Vice," in *Philokalia,* 2.281.

and Eve shackled by mortality, then he broke their chains, trampling down death by death, and raised human nature to ascend with him. This doctrine is written in icon, too. When Christ ascended as the first fruits of humanity, he blazed a trail for all to follow. Grace has sought us out, and grace will lead us home, but a Christian must follow Christ to the throne of the Father. This involves co-operation with the operation of the Holy Spirit; we synergize with divine energy. *Syn-ergeia* means "to co-operate," and in a synergistic relationship there are two powers unequal in importance but equal in necessity. "The incorporation of man into Christ and his union with God requires the co-operation of two unequal, but equally necessary, forces: divine grace and human will."[18] Synergy is a response to an initiatory action that nevertheless requires our answer, and grace is not demeaned by acknowledging that an agent created with free will must make this response.

To summarize, we have been gathering together the terms needed for the functioning definition of liturgy in this work, which is: *Liturgy is the Trinity's perichoresis kenotically extended to invite our synergistic ascent into deification.* In other words, the Trinity's circulation of love turns itself outward, and in humility the Son and Spirit work the Father's good pleasure for all creation, which is to invite our ascent to participate in the very life of God; however, this cannot be forced, it must be done with our cooperation.

This definition of liturgy, I submit, begs asceticism. One would not need asceticism if the liturgy under consideration was merely church services; one would not need asceticism if the theology under consideration was merely study in the library. But if liturgy is heaven on earth, and *theologia* is deified union with God, then asceticism is demanded. Why call the asceticism liturgical? Because its cause and effect is liturgical. The term *askein*, from

18. A Monk of the Eastern Church, *Orthodox Spirituality* (Crestwood, N.Y.: St. Vladimir's Seminary Press, 1987), 23.

which *askesis* comes, means "to work," and "the word 'asceticism' derives from the Greek term for physical exercise, such as athletic practice."[19] There are many reasons to undergo a discipline, but the Christian reason is different. This can be seen by taking one ascetical practice as an example: fasting. People fast for health reasons (when their cholesterol is too high), for medical reasons (before a blood test), for reasons of vanity (which the magazines encourage), for athletic purposes (the coach insists), for moral reasons (in protest of animal husbandry practices), for religious reasons (all religions use fasting as a tool), and there is even restraint from food that comes from mood swings (from depression or the sad illness of anorexia). But just as the fast of the hospital patient is different from the fast of the supermodel by reason of motive and end, so, too, the liturgical fast is different from all other fasts by its purpose and *telos*.[20]

We struggle in this book for an understanding of liturgy that considers its theological and ascetical dimensions, called liturgical theology and liturgical asceticism. These three—liturgy, theology, and asceticism—interpenetrate each other, and co-inhere in a way that is almost a kind of conceptual perichoresis. One term must be understood in light of the other two in order to grasp the full content of any one of them. *Liturgy* without asceticism and theology is a species of ritual studies; *asceticism* without liturgy and theology is athletic or philosophical training; *theology* without liturgy and asceticism is an academic discipline in higher education.

Each of the following statements attempt this co-inherence, and each may be taken as a thesis statement of this book.

- Liturgical asceticism is the cost of being made more Christoform in order to commit liturgy.

19. John McGuckin, "Monasticism," in *The Blackwell Dictionary of Eastern Christianity* (Oxford: Blackwell, 1999), 321.

20. Cf. David Fagerberg, "On Liturgical Fasting," *Logos: A Journal of Eastern Christian Studies* 48, nos. 1–2 (2007): 83.

- If liturgy is the ontological condition for theology, as Schmemann said, then liturgical asceticism is asceticism that has liturgy as its ontological condition.
- Liturgy is participation by the body of Christ in the perichoresis of the Trinity; asceticism is the capacitation for that participation, called deification; theology is union with God, making the Church's liturgy a theological act.
- There are many other motives for practicing an asceticism, but if the motive is to become by grace what Christ is by nature, then this asceticism is liturgical because it relies upon the sacramental bestowal of the grace of Christ through the working of the Holy Spirit.
- The whole aim of asceticism is to capacitate a person for prayer, and the highest experience of prayer is theology.
- *Theologia* is knowing the Trinity, but in the biblical sense of "knowing"; which, observes Paul Evdokimov, gives us "[t]he patristic definition of theology: the experiential way of union with God."[21] This theology is a kind of knowing that requires a deep change in the mind *(nous)* of the knower, and such a change is ascetical, and it capacitates for liturgy: so we call it liturgical asceticism.
- A person is a block of marble within which lies an image of the image of God (the Son), and each strike of mallet and chisel by the Holy Spirit frees that image from stone-cold vices in order to create out of women and men a liturgical son who shares the Son's filial relationship with God the Father.[22]

21. Paul Evdokimov, *Ages of the Spiritual Life* (Crestwood, N.Y.: St. Vladimir's Seminary Press, 1998), 130. An earlier English publication was entitled *The Struggle with God* (Glen Rock, N.J.: Paulist Press, 1966).

22. The metaphor comes from John Behr. "We are a work in progress; our blueprint, the statue lying in the block of marble waiting to be sculpted, is already in the image of Christ, though for now hidden with him. We are being worked on, so that when he appears, we will appear with him." From "The Eschatological Dimensions of Liturgy," *Assembly: A Journal of Liturgical Theology* 36, no. 1 (January 2010): 3.

- Liturgical asceticism increases the measure by which we become theologians, and being a theologian involves seeing all things in the liturgical light of Mount Tabor.
- If liturgy means sharing the life of Christ (being washed in his Resurrection, eating his body), and if *askesis* means discipline (in the sense of forming), then liturgical asceticism is the discipline required to become an icon of Christ and make his image visible in our faces.

The above statements outline the territory we hope to explore in this book. The tradition held liturgy, theology, and asceticism together naturally and necessarily, and we wish to understand how and why.

This liturgical asceticism comes out of an anthropological maximalism: it looks at what man and woman were meant to be, sees the command to grow from the image of God into the likeness of God, and prudently examines what it will cost any particular person to attain this liturgical state of deification. *Askesis* is simply the reconstruction of the *imago Dei*. Even if the ascetical tradition has borrowed some terminology from the philosophers, its grammar is Christian, and it is different from dualism because Christian asceticism does not condemn the body. Vladimir Solovyof affirms the point by saying, "the purpose of Christian asceticism is not to weaken the flesh, but to strengthen the spirit for the transfiguration of the flesh."[23] Liturgical asceticism does not seek to free the spirit from the body, it seeks to use body and spirit together for liturgical purpose. This positive origin of asceticism needs to be established at the outset, or else the idea of asceticism will continue to have pessimistic and distasteful overtones.

On the one hand, corporeal but unintelligent creatures, like the sun in its orbit or matter serving as substructure for life, offer a sort of cosmic liturgy to God by their obedience to natural

23. Vladimir Solovyof, "The Jews," in *A Solovyof Anthology*, edited by S. L. Frank (London: SCM Press, 1950), 120.

law; on the other hand, incorporeal but intelligent creatures, like seraphim and angels, offer their liturgy to God by surrounding the throne in constant praise; however, with the appearance of human beings a new kind of liturgy is possible, a response that is both corporeal and intelligent. It is a liturgical response made with both body and spirit. For this reason Gregory of Nazianzus describes man as a hybrid.

> The great Architect of the universe conceived and produced a being endowed with both natures, the visible and the invisible: God created the human being, bringing its body forth from the pre-existing matter which he animated with his own Spirit.... [T]hus in some way a new universe was born, small and great at one and the same time. God set this "hybrid" worshipper on earth to contemplate the visible world, and to be initiated into the invisible; to reign over earth's creatures, and to obey orders from on high. He created a being at once earthly and heavenly, insecure and immortal, visible and invisible, halfway between greatness and nothingness, flesh and spirit at the same time ... an animal en route to another native land, and, most mysterious of all, made to resemble God by simple submission to the divine will.[24]

Enrolled as citizen in both realms, man and woman were given a particular place in the cosmos. It was a liturgical place. This hybrid royal priest was to rule over matter under the spiritual light of God. Asceticism deals with the relationship of body and spirit because this liturgical place in creation depends precisely upon being both body and spirit. Had man and woman remained obedient to this cosmological priesthood, they would have mediated God's descending blessings to matter, and would have woven the ascending praise of material creation into the celestial song of praise, and all would have been right with the world. Matter would have been experienced sacramentally, and as raw material for eucharist.

But, alas, the combination of spirit and body that was supposed to bless the world and conduct creation's symphonic wor-

24. Gregory Nazianzen, *Oration 45, For Easter, 7*; cited in Olivier Clement, *The Roots of Christian Mysticism* (New York: New York City Press, 1996), 77.

ship of God proved to be a combination all too easily corruptible by a fallen angel, jealous of this new being who was endowed with liberty and created to be ruler over earth's creatures. Bouyer says the devil wished to seduce Adam and Eve into joining his rebellion, and knew how to go about it.

> In the sphere of all this physical reality of the flesh in which man's very spirit has emerged, the devil has all too much room in which to tempt him, however incapable he may be of touching the deep springs of man's intelligence and freedom.... [T]he Tempter interweaves specious enticements to sensual delight.
>
> Man will yield. The potential redeemer of the earth will be the supreme conquest of the rebel spirit. Satan, incapable of repressing, will prove himself, alas, only too capable of seducing that liberty which he had felt surge up beneath him [man], as a possible taking back by God of the empire which the demon had stolen from him.[25]

Christians read the book of Genesis with an eye to understanding how the body affects the spirit, but this is not dualism, it is realism. Liturgical asceticism must be distinguished from gnosticism, dualism, or modern forms of spiritualism because it does not see the body as the problem, yet it does acknowledge that sin has affected both the body and the spirit, and ruined their right relationship. As is often the case, G. K. Chesterton can point out the difference with penetrating insight.

> Nothing is more common ... than to find such a modern critic writing something like this: "Christianity was a movement of ascetics, a rush into the desert, a refuge in the cloister, a renunciation of all life and happiness; and this was part of a gloomy and inhuman reaction against nature itself, a hatred of the body, a horror of the material universe, a sort of universal suicide of the senses and even the self." Now the most extraordinary thing about this is that it is all quite true; it is true in every detail except that it happens to be attributed to the wrong person. It is not true of the Church; but it is true of the heretics condemned by the Church.[26]

25. Bouyer, *The Meaning of the Monastic Life*, 29.

26. G. K. Chesterton, *The Everlasting Man*, in *G. K. Chesterton: Collected Works* (San Francisco: Ignatius Press, 1986), 2.354.

> The early Church was ascetic, but she proved that she was not pessimistic, simply by condemning the pessimists. The creed declared that man was sinful, but it did not declare that life was evil, and it proved it by damning those who did.... It proved that the primitive Catholics were specially eager to explain that they did *not* think man utterly vile; that they did *not* think life incurably miserable; that they did *not* think marriage a sin or procreation a tragedy.[27]

So even if the liturgical ascetic works with the same external methods as a Stoic philosopher (fasting, celibacy, sleeplessness, solitude, poverty, etc.), what each is doing—and what each is capable of doing—is quite different.

The purpose of asceticism is not to free the spirit from the body, as some philosophers would have it, but to free both the spirit and body from the passions. Being body-spirit creatures, the remedy has to be applied to the spirit through the body, by the body, along with the body. Asceticism is not a reproof of the body, it is a response to love, and the first responsive act is to turn one's face unflinchingly against anything that would disorient this love. Satan dangled his specious promise before the woman's eyes, and in Genesis 3:6 one finds appetite, eros, and hubris all together in one piece of fruit: "The woman saw that the tree was good for food, pleasing to the eyes, and desirable for gaining wisdom." But the sin was not taking the fruit, the sin was taking it prematurely, and taking it as anything other than a gift.

This is often overlooked because the words that stick with us in Satan's whispered temptation are "you will be like gods," and we conclude that Yahweh, like Zeus, does not want human beings to become too powerful, like Prometheus. But the Fathers of the Church would not think this interpretation of Genesis could be squared with Psalm 82:6, which they understood to describe the true state of mankind: "I said, you are gods, and all of you sons of the Most High."[28] Or 2 Peter, which joyously declares that

27. Ibid., 356.

28. In Norman Russell's comprehensive compendium of uses of the word *theosis*,

the work of divine power is to give man and woman everything needed for life and godliness, so that through God's promises they "may participate in the divine nature" (Peter 1:3–4). Deification is our created human end, and Satan cannot change that; he cannot change the ontological will of God, he can only distort its presentation to us. It is God's will that man and woman be deified, and all Satan could do was corrupt the terms of the promise. When he whispered "you can be your own gods," he turned promised deification into a temptation to idolatry. Satan's deceit was to use a true end for a false purpose. Idolatry is a liturgical category: it is misplaced worship. Christian anthropology, with its assessment of what it means to be human, and what is human responsibility, and the doctrine of human corruption, is best done as a liturgical anthropology, because the temptation for Adam and Eve was to forfeit their liturgical career.

Reparation of this chaos will require restoring human beings both within and without. On the inside, right order among the passions must be reestablished; on the outside, right relationship to God must be reestablished. The whole person has fallen, not just the body, and not just the spirit, therefore asceticism will not deal with one or the other, but with the body-spirit relationship. The remedy must be applied to the body as well as to the spirit so that both will operate in harmony. Whereas the new creature described as a body-spirit hybrid by Gregory Nazianzus is a liturgical priest, this asceticism may be called liturgical. Whereas it is the essence of a sacrament to use visible matter to accomplish a spiritual healing, and this asceticism will apply healing to the spirit through the body, it may be called liturgical asceticism. But, to assert our premise one more time, this means that liturgical asceticism arises from the most positive anthropology ever seen. Olivier Clement describes it this way:

---

the reader notices that the Scripture passage most often referenced to support the idea of deification was this Psalm 82. It is a striking instance of how Old Testament and New Testament are read as one Scripture; no Marcionitism here.

Ascesis then is an awakening from the sleep-walking of daily life. It enables the Word to clear the silt away in the depth of the soul, freeing the spring of living waters. The Word can restore to its original brightness the tarnished image of God in us, the silver coin that has rolled in the dust but remains stamped with the king's likeness (Luke 15:8–10). It is the Word who acts, but we have to co-operate with him, not so much by exertion of will-power as by loving attentiveness.[29]

Paul Evdokimov also approaches asceticism from this positive angle. In his work *Ages of the Spiritual Life,* he speaks to Christians in the world and uses ascetical categories throughout. "According to the definition of the Sixth Ecumenical Council, sin is a sickness of the spirit,"[30] and "Christian asceticism is only a method in the service of life."[31] Asceticism only appears as a negation because it is clearing something away: it clears away anything that prevents us from giving full-hearted response to God. "The initiative of God who knocks is answered by the eagerness of the human being who waits with all his heart for this to happen.... If this positive form is not present at the very beginning, St. Macarius teaches, if it does not precede negative, normative and disciplinary asceticism, the latter is of no use."[32] Asceticism does not wall us in, it is the prerequisite to opening horizons. "This is exactly the aim of asceticism: to transcend every limit, to expand souls by the audacity of love, and to develop the person by means of gifts and charisms."[33] Asceticism does not drag us down, rather "[w]hen humanity had sunk below itself, monastic asceticism raised it above its own nature."[34] During the ascetical struggle the person develops into the image and likeness that God intended. "Asceticism is practiced in order to return us to God's idea of us, to make us 'very similar' to him."[35]

As we will see in the chapters ahead, the ascetical tradition

29. Clement, *The Roots of Christian Mysticism,* 130, 131.
30. Evdokimov, *Ages of the Spiritual Life,* 62.
31. Ibid., 64.
32. Ibid., 69.
33. Ibid., 187.
34. Ibid., 134.
35. Ibid., 184.

used the language it inherited from Greek philosophy to speak about human faculties, understood to be three in number: first, a human being is able to think—this is the *intellective* faculty; second, a human being can be moved to action by having his ire stirred up—this is the *irascible* faculty; and third, a person has appetites that generate desire—this is the *concupiscible* faculty. But the ascetical tradition put that philosophical language to a theological use, instead. And this included a theological anthropology maximum in scope if they maintain their relation to God. The intellective must rule the irascible and concupiscible faculties, and the intellective faculty must be ruled by God. These faculties were created good, as all creation is good, but the faculties are capable of corruption if their hierarchy is upset. Break the exterior relationship with God and the interior relationship between the faculties is affected and they become passions. Satan's lie was to distort the hierarchical relationship. Adam and Eve were created as royal priests, but Evdokimov urges us not to forget that "[t]he royal dignity is of an ascetic nature; it is the mastery of the spiritual over the material, over the instincts and impulses of the flesh, the freedom from all determination coming from the world."[36] In light of his physical makeup and dependencies, the hybrid creature might be called an animal, but in addition to animal body he is immortal spirit, and spirit could have communicated immortal life to the whole person had the connection to the Immortal One remained intact. That is why Evdokimov concludes that asceticism is spiritual mastery over the material: "asceticism constituted a very exact science and a vast culture that renders the body and the soul transparent and submissive to the spiritual."[37] And where else are we cracked open to the mystery, to the invisible, more than in liturgy? "The purification of the heart comes above all from liturgy where rite, dogma and art are closely bound together. The images of the Liturgy are

36. Ibid., 238.
37. Ibid., 155.

symbols that lift our gaze to the level of the invisible presence of God."[38]

Liturgical asceticism does not arise from despair over the human character, but from hope—greater hope than the world knows, a supernatural hope for a supernatural end. This accounts for the deep joy the ascetic knows and the world cannot understand. Chesterton saw it in Francis of Assisi.

> It may seem a paradox to say that a man may be transported with joy to discover that he is in debt.... It is the key of all the problems of Franciscan morality which puzzle the merely modern mind; but above all it is the key of asceticism. It is the highest and holiest of the paradoxes that the man who really knows he cannot pay his debt will be forever paying it. He will be forever giving back what he cannot give back, and cannot be expected to give back. He will always be throwing things away into a bottomless pit of unfathomable thanks.... We are not generous enough to be ascetics; one might almost say not genial enough to be ascetics.[39]

Chesterton makes this point again at the end of his biography of Francis, where he treats the story of Claire running away at the tender age of seventeen to become a nun. He suggests seeing it as a case of Francis helping Claire to *elope* into the cloister, since the scene had many of the elements of a regular romantic elopement: she escaped through a hole in the wall, fled against her father's wishes, and was received at midnight by the light of torches. "Now about that incident, I will here only say this. If it had really been a romantic elopement and the girl had become a bride instead of a nun, practically the whole modern world would have made her a heroine... [because] modern romanticism entirely encourages such defiance of parents when it is done in the name of romantic love. For it knows that romantic love is a reality, but it does not know that divine love is a reality."[40] Perhaps the reason we find it so difficult to comprehend the extremes to

38. Ibid., 194.

39. G. K. Chesterton, *St. Francis of Assisi*, in *G. K. Chesterton: Collected Works* (San Francisco: Ignatius Press, 1986), 2.76.

40. Ibid., 99.

which the Fathers went in the desert is because we do not know divine love as a reality: we have become callused to our lover's touch.

Any attempt to understand liturgical asceticism will end in failure unless one admits the possibility of a wild, bracing, divine love exactly like this. Any search for practical reasons for acts of liturgical asceticism will be disappointed, because acts of liturgical asceticism are not done for practical reasons. Chesterton says that if ever romance fell out of fashion, we should have the same difficulty understanding behaviors caused by motivations then alien to us. "We should have the same sort of unintelligent sneers and unimaginative questions" about the lengths to which lovers go, that will appear unconscionable. "Men will ask what selfish sort of woman it must have been who ruthlessly exacted tribute in the form of flowers, or what an avaricious creature she can have been to demand solid gold in the form of a ring: just as they ask what cruel kind of God can have demanded sacrifice and self-denial."[41]

Purification of heart, synergy with eternal life, redirection of appetites, and reorientation of spirit are all ways of speaking about a transformation effected in the Christian when he or she lives from the mysteries of Christ in the liturgy by means of the Holy Spirit. Liturgical theology is coming to rest in God. However, the purity of heart required for this is an ascetical accomplishment, and one consequence of liturgy would be to create more ascetics. I believe that the main reason people have misunderstood the concept of "liturgical theology" as Schmemann defined it, Kavanagh clarified it, and I, in some small way, have added to it, is because this ascetical dimension was overlooked. When I wrote about liturgical theology, I was assuming liturgical asceticism but not consciously enough to account for it, and it is both a surprise and a pleasure to review the pages of Kavanagh's

41. Ibid., 77.

book, and discover that the teacher had planted the concept in his student without my realizing it until years later, after reading further about the ascetical tradition. To credit Kavanagh, as well as to show what kind of theology he was thinking of as he worked out his description of liturgical theology, I would like to look at some specific passages that mention asceticism.

In the opening pages of *On Liturgical Theology*, Kavanagh describes his place on the academic map by using four coordinates. First, he confesses to be a creature of a deeply sacramental tradition of orthodoxy, the latter term meaning "right worship;" second, as a liturgical scholar he is more at home in the iconic East than in the pictorial West; third, he teaches in an interconfessional, university-based school of divinity, which brings challenges that he then enumerates; and fourth, "the author takes Christian asceticism seriously."

> Far from being something esoteric to Christianity, asceticism is native to the Gospel and is required of all. Specifically monastic asceticism was generated, it seems, in that same process by which living the Gospel began to take on ecclesial form in the earliest Jewish-Christian churches.... One must therefore take the continuing fact of organized asceticism in Christian life as a given which provides access to whole dimensions of Christian perception and being. The existence, furthermore, of specifically monastic asceticism is a theological datum which lies close to the very nerve center of Christian origins and growth. One cannot study Christianity without taking monasticism into account. One cannot live as a Christian without practicing the Gospel asceticism which monasticism is meant to exemplify and support. A Christian need not be a monk or nun, but every monk and nun is a crucial sort of Christian.[42]

Although asceticism was brought to perfection in the sands of the desert, it originates in the waters of the font, and one cannot live as a Christian without practicing liturgical asceticism. Liturgical asceticism is the art of maintaining the life bestowed

42. Aidan Kavanagh, *On Liturgical Theology* (New York: Pueblo, 1984), 6.

in baptism. Fr. Jeremy Driscoll observes that the dogmas of the monastic Fathers "are put in direct relation to baptismal faith, indicating that Evagrius thought of his and other monastic teachings as a way of life which develops out of this baptismal faith."[43] When Driscoll says no monk was ever advised to thrust off the spiritual seal he received at baptism, he is referring "to the sealing which occurs at Christian initiation, and with this expression Evagrius wishes to refer specifically to the Holy Spirit. This faith and the Holy Spirit are necessary for the monk to come to true knowledge, here expressed as the Lord coming into the soul."[44]

In his own article on Evagrius, Kavanagh writes, "[a]scetics blaze the trail all must follow, but they do not walk it alone."[45] Kavanagh seems to think of structured, monastic asceticism as something that gives external, visible form to the baptismal reality of grace (almost like a sacrament, which many in the ancient Church considered the monastic vow to be). This asceticism is connected to the Church's pastoral theology, which, Kavanagh reminds us, is the setting in which Christian theology was done in the early Church. "The ambience of their work was immediately pastoral, the purpose of their work was pastoral, they themselves were almost invariably pastors (i.e., bishops) and as often as not practicing ascetics who had to be forced into pastoral ministry against their wishes."[46] Evdokimov will speak of an "interiorized monasticism" or "the monk within" in order to make similar observations about the relationship between the monk in the desert and the secular Christian in the world.

Kavanagh returns to asceticism when he interprets Evagrius's dictum, "the true theologian is he who prays." He objects to the

43. Jeremy Driscoll, *Evagrius Ponticus: Ad Monachos,* Ancient Christian Writers 59 (New York: Newman Press, 2003), 141. Originally published by Pontificio Ateneo S. Anselmo (Rome, 1991).

44. Ibid., 142.

45. Aidan Kavanagh, "Eastern Influences on the Rule of Saint Benedict," in *Monasticism and the Arts,* edited by Timothy Verdon (Syracuse, N.Y.: Syracuse University Press, 1984), 56.

46. Kavanagh, *On Liturgical Theology,* 18.

treatment this statement has usually received, which has been to encourage a doxological quality in the academic, when Kavanagh believes it was actually recognizing the theological quality of the ascetic in prayer.

> The dictum, so far from endowing a doxological quality upon the second-order activity of theology, in fact confers a theological quality upon the first-order activity of people at worship. More specifically, the *theologos* in this Eastern dictum is not the scholar in his study but the ascetic in his cell, and the *theologia* implied is not secondary theological reasoning but contemplation on the highest level, the roots of which are sunk deep in the ascetic's own fasting and prayer, particularly in the recitation of the psalter. The "theologian" in this Eastern view is a contemplative whose life is suffused with the *leitourgia* of a cosmos restored to communion in its trinitarian Source. "Theology" is the contemplation of God in and for his own sake. Prayer is the condition of this, and prayer, as Evagrius of Pontus said, is the rejection of concepts.[47]

We will see in a future chapter that asceticism is the condition for prayer, but for now we can point out the hermeneutical key contained in this quote that enables us to understand Kavanagh's very idea of liturgical theology. He does not seek to endow a doxological quality on the work of an academic theologian, but rather to confer a theological quality upon Mrs. Murphy, his famed personification of a liturgical theologian. And the reason he can assume this is because asceticism leads to prayer, and prayer leads to *theologia,* and readers will misunderstand the identity of Mrs. Murphy as a liturgical theologian unless they realize that Kavanagh also considers Mrs. Murphy a liturgical ascetic.

When noting how intertwined asceticism is with the Church, Kavanagh points out how systems of rite have not only produced particular worship patterns, canonical laws, structures of evangelism and catechesis, and styles of theological reflection, they have also produced ascetical and monastic structures.

47. Ibid., 124.

By asceticism here, one does not mean giving up candy during Lent, or flagellants and hair shirts. One means something broader, deeper, and harder; a kind of Zen in the art of maintaining a life of "right worship" as the only way to live in the real order....

The ascetic's fundamental contribution to Christian *orthodoxia* as a life of cosmic normality is thus not education or good works, but an exemplary existence kept clean, clear, and free of this world's intense and warping abnormality. It is a life of lucid and abiding clarity which goes with the grain of reality at every point. Charity emerges from such an unbeholden life, a charity which is absolutely requisite in coming to true knowledge of even the created universe by natural reason. Only from such knowledge can there then arise knowledge of God, *theologia*, and the supreme beatitude of seeing and knowing God face to face.[48]

We do not do nature naturally anymore, and so the knowledge of God that our natures were made to possess requires a repair of our current state. *Theologia* is knowledge of God, but this is not a matter of liquidating ignorance; it is not knowledge that can be had at a distance; it is knowledge that requires a change in the knower. Mrs. Murphy is a theologian insofar as she has this knowledge of God.

The practice of liturgical asceticism is more important than its study, but if this study can offer any help, it will come from being attentive to what is required of the human subject to know God. And that is something expected of every Christian, says Kavanagh.

This is a life expected of every one of the baptized, whose ultimate end is the same supreme beatitude. It is a life all the baptized share, a life within which the professed ascetic is nothing more or less than a virtuoso who serves the whole community as an exemplar of its own life. The ascetic is simply a stunningly normal person who stands in constant witness to the normality of Christian *orthodoxia* in a world flawed into abnormality by human choice.[49]

Theology is a unique kind of knowing: it is a knowing that depends upon a character restored in baptism and cultivated in an

48. Ibid., 161–62.

49. Ibid., 161–62.

ascetical life. Evdokimov said the Fathers understood theology to be a way of union with God that comes from direct experience; it is empirical theology. To call Mrs. Murphy a liturgical theologian is to say she may experience this union with God through the liturgical life, and asceticism is its cost. This is the proper interpretation of Kavanagh's notion of rite as the "convergence, meeting, entwining, and melding of Christian worship and belief."

> Rite involves creeds and prayers and worship, but it is not any one of these things, nor all of these things together, and it orchestrates more than these things. Rite can be called a whole style of Christian living found in the myriad particularities of worship, of laws called "canonical," of ascetical and monastic structures, of evangelical and catechetical endeavors, and in particular ways of doing secondary theological reflection. A liturgical act concretizes all these and in doing so makes them accessible to the community assembled in a given time and place before the living God for the life of the world. Rite in this Christian sense is generated and sustained in this regular meeting of faithful people in whose presence and through whose deeds the vertiginous Source of the cosmos is pleased to settle down freely and abide as among friends. A liturgy of Christians is thus nothing less than the way a redeemed world is, so to speak, done.... A liturgy is even more than an act of faith, prayer, or worship. It is the act of rite.[50]

It comes as no surprise when Kavanagh's next line acknowledges that "this understanding of rite is hardly common today." It is hardly common because of the anemic sense of rite we now possess. Our Christian identity should be shaped by living the liturgical rite, by the rhythm of the Church year, by the procession to the altar every eighth day, by seeing moral questions about human beings in light of their being an image of God, by the intellectual grasp of the content of faith and the bodily enactment of that same content, by fasting and feasting, by obedience to canonical authority, by stepping under the priestly hand of absolution, by catechetical witness that is sometimes uncomfortable in prophetic circumstances, by actualizing the domestic Church

50. Ibid., 100–101

within the family, and by the hundred other concretized instances of liturgical life. Attaining *apatheia* in ascetical battle with the passions produces a stunningly normal person, a liturgical person, a saint. An angel stands with a fiery sword at the gate to Eden from which our parents were expelled, but the baptistery is decorated with paradisiacal imagery because the font is the gate back into Eden, and liturgical asceticism is lifting one's foot to cross that threshold, because from there—*O felix culpa!*—the shipwrecked are accompanied by Christ in his humanity on their resumed journey to deification.

I suggest the term "liturgical asceticism" as a way of describing the disciplined obedience we are talking about because ultimately that discipline recapitulates the royal and priestly liturgical dignity of man and woman. Kavanagh frequently said in class that "liturgy is doing the world the way it was meant to be done." But to do the world properly will require us to control the passions and regain our eschatological reorientation. Liturgical asceticism is the path to stunning normality. Liturgical asceticism names Christ's purity of heart become our own. "This will be the case," Abba Isaac tells John Cassian, "when every love, every desire, every effort, every undertaking, every thought of ours, everything that we live, that we speak, that we breathe will be God, and when that unity which the Father now has with the Son and which the Son has with the Father will be carried over into our understanding and our mind."[51] In the twenty-seventh step of *The Ladder of Divine Ascent* John Climacus writes, "It is risky to swim in one's clothes. A slave of passion should not dabble in theology."[52] This is the starting point for our investigation into what I have called liturgical asceticism. I have elsewhere defended the claim that liturgists are theologians, and if it is risky for a theologian to swim in his or her clothes, then it behooves liturgists to be ascetics.

51. John Cassian, 10.7.2, in *The Conferences,* Ancient Christian Writers, translated by Boniface Ramsey, O.P. (New York: Newman Press, 1997), 375–76.

52. John Climacus, *The Ladder of Divine Ascent* (New York: Paulist Press, 1982), 262.

2 THE MALADY

Pathe

At the opening of the anaphora in the Divine Liturgy of John Chrysostom, the deacon bids the Church, "Let us stand aright; let us stand with fear; let us attend, that we may offer the Holy Oblation in peace." This is an effective expression of the definition we are trying to establish for liturgical asceticism: the goal of the process is for us to again stand aright, through ascetical conformation to Christ accomplished in the Holy Spirit, in order to fulfill our liturgical vocation of standing in union with Christ before the Father and as Christ's body in the world. Liturgical asceticism is the struggle to imitate what we see in the liturgy, namely, a human being in filial communion with God the Father. Liturgical asceticism is embracing by grace what Christ is by nature. It is rooted in the expectation that the hypostatic union does not affect our Lord alone, but somehow its effects are prolonged in us, the members of his Mystical Body. The divine life we receive is the eternal life given in all plenitude to Christ's human nature, and extended through him—as mediator—to us. The Savior's humanity possesses such an abundance of supernatural life that the divinization of the human race is made possible.

> The decisive orientation appears with St. Athanasius. The idea of life is emphasized more and more, and one by one the other points of doctrine are organized round this concept. When St. Cyril [of Alexandria] teaches that the life of the Church is none other than the communication to the Christian of that supernatural fullness of life which the hypostatic union had given to Christ, the second Adam, he is merely completing a process that had been going on for centuries.[1]

By Christ as the renewed Adam, the human race receives a new Head; it is recapitulated; Christ finally does what *anthropos* was created to do. Schmemann says the Eucharist "is the movement that Adam failed to perform, and that in Christ has become the very life of man: a movement of adoration and praise in which all joy and suffering, all beauty and all frustration, all hunger and all satisfaction are referred to their ultimate End and become finally meaningful."[2] When this mystery is celebrated in the liturgy, every human being sees what he or she is to become if only something did not stand in the way of fulfilling that vocation. The name the tradition uses to identify that which debilitates our liturgical identity is *the passions,* and so liturgical asceticism may be said to consist of overcoming the passions in order to attain the liturgical posture that *anthropos* has forfeited.

It is tempting to sidetrack on the following pages into a detailed description of all the passions, how they interrelate and interact, their multiple causes, tracing the way they were understood by various spiritual writers. However, that is not our purpose here. This is not a study of the passions, but of liturgical asceticism. Therefore this chapter will deal more generally with the passions (*pathe*), taken as a problem, so that in the next chapter we can consider the discipline of overcoming them (*askesis*),

1. Emile Mersch, *The Whole Christ: The Historical Development of the Doctrine of the Mystical Body in Scripture and Tradition* (Milwaukee: Bruce, 1938), 357–58.

2. Alexander Schmemann, *For the Life of the World* (Crestwood, N.Y.: St. Vladimir's Seminary Press, 1973), 35.

and after that the state of dispassion (*apatheia*) which is the goal of asceticism. We are trying to keep our eye on the relevance of this philokalic tradition to liturgy.

It is first important to understand the particular use the ascetical tradition is making of the term "passion." There are other contexts in which the word can have a morally neutral meaning. The Latin *passio,* used to render the Greek *pathos,* mixes the notion of strong feeling with involuntariness. The latter element is seen in the sense of suffering something (hence "the passion of Christ"), the former element accounts for why one must add a qualifier in order to distinguish a good passion (for learning) from a bad passion (for adultery). However, in the majority of cases when the Eastern ascetical tradition uses the word "passion" it has a negative meaning because it refers to a disoriented and discordant and diseased heart. "For the Eastern Fathers, the passions could be neither good nor indifferent. The soul is by nature the image of God. As the result of sin, it has been cloaked with various passions. The aim of *praxis* is to strip the soul of these *pathe*."[3] A passion, with a few exceptions, refers to a state contrary to the divine purpose for a human being. It designates whatever distorts the image of God in *anthropos*. Adam and Eve were created with emotions and faculties, but not with passions such as these; Jesus was innocent of them, and Mary's pure heart is the dispassion ascetics seek. In Fr. John Behr's illuminating study of a very early treatment of this subject, he quotes Clement of Alexandria as saying

> Appetite (*orme*) is the movement of the mind (*dianoias*) to or from something. Passion (*pathos*) is an excessive appetite, exceeding the measures of the word (*ton logon*), or appetite unbridled and disobedient to reason (*logo*). Passions then are a movement of the soul contrary to nature in disobedience to the Word.[4]

3. Tomas Spidlik, *The Spirituality of the Christian East* (Kalamazoo, Mich.: Cistercian Press, 1986), 268.

4. Clement, *Stromata* 2.13.59.6, quoted in John Behr, *Asceticism and Anthropology in Irenaeus and Clement* (Oxford: Oxford University Press, 2000), 147.

A regular mark of the definition remains this note of contrariety between what one intends and the state that one suffers, between what is natural and what is unnatural. Maximus the Confessor defines a passion as "a movement of the soul contrary to nature.... Vice is the mistaken use of ideas from which follows the abuse of things."[5] As with everything, misuse is sin. Augustine knew the interior tension well. Passions can therefore be distinguished from emotions.

[I]t is crucial to notice that the emotions corresponding to these words do not have to be "passions" to be emotions. Passions are pathologized versions of these emotions, such that they are experienced as "disturbances" (*perturbationes*) to use Cicero's expression for what, Augustine says, are called by the Greeks "passions" (*passiones*). The hallmark of a "passion" or "disturbance" is that it is a movement of the soul, an "emotion," contrary to reason or "irrational." Animals may have strong movements of the soul but they do not have passions because they do not have reason. Passions have a life seemingly independent of ourselves as reasoning beings. As such they are disturbances, they are like "storms and tempests," properly compared to a sea in a storm [*City of God,* 8.17], and so they seem to come from somewhere else other than the rational mind, which they disturb, which can be said to "suffer" them as passions.[6]

There is another word in Scripture that has an original positive meaning but a subsequent pejorative meaning due to a corruption that has occurred. The term "world" can mean the good cosmos, or it can mean one of the forces of rebellion against God. Isaac the Syrian says, "When we wish to give a collective name to the passions, we call them *world.* And when we wish to designate them specifically according to their names, we call them *passions.*"[7] This is why Maximus says, "[t]he one who has self-love has all the passions."[8] The passions prevent us from doing the

5. Maximus the Confessor, *Four Hundred Chapters on Love,* 2.16–17.

6. John Cavadini, "Feeling Right: Augustine on the Passions and Sexual Desire," *Augustinian Studies* 36, no. 1 (2005): 198–99.

7. Isaac the Syrian, Homily 2, in *The Ascetical Homilies of Saint Isaac the Syrian* (Boston: Holy Transfiguration Monastery, 1984), 14–15.

8. Maximus the Confessor, *Four Hundred Chapters on Love,* 3.8.

world as it was meant to be done (liturgically), and from receiving matter the way it was meant to be received (sacramentally), and from governing creation the way it was meant to be administered (sacrificially). Gregory of Nyssa observes that man and woman were created in the image of God, and that according to Scripture our prototype has wings. Hence, he concludes, human nature was also created with wings, and that to suffer the passions is to be stripped of them.

> It is clear, of course, that the word "wings" here will be interpreted on an allegorical level suitable for the divinity. Thus the wings would refer to God's power, his happiness, his incorruptibility, and so on. Now all these attributes were also in man, so long as he was still like God. But then it was the inclination towards sin that robbed us of these wings. Once outside the shelter of *God's* wing, we were also stripped of *our* wings.[9]

So this is what the passions look like: an eagle trudging, a falcon shuffling along, a person stripped of his wings. A human being ruled by the passions looks like Pegasus crawling on his belly like a great Komodo dragon. A person under the rule of the passions doesn't look right any more, and doesn't love right.

We shall not look right again until we stand aright and stand with fear, offering our holy oblation in peace. And the process of uprighting our posture is called asceticism. Man and woman's vocation in the world is liturgical priest, but fulfilling that vocation takes ascetical discipline in our current sinful state, and that is the point of deep connection between liturgy and asceticism. What cripples our liturgical posture is no material flaw, but a spiritual fall. This must be insisted upon emphatically or else Christian asceticism will be mistaken for Manichaeism, particularly when the modern investigator is startled by some of the practices of the more zealous Christian ascetics. Put bluntly, it

9. Gregory of Nyssa, *From Glory to Glory: Texts from Gregory of Nyssa's Mystical Writings*, edited by Jean Danielou, S.J. (Crestwood, N.Y.: St. Vladimir's Seminary Press, 1979), 284.

was never money, sex, or beer that the ascetic opposed, it was avarice, lust, and drunkenness. Maximus says, "The whole war of the monk against the demons is to separate the passions from the representations. Otherwise he will not be able to look on things without passion."[10] No material thing is a problem, the problem is our misuse of material things. "It is not food which is evil but gluttony, not the begetting of children but fornication, not possessions but greed, not reputation but vainglory. And if this is so, there is nothing evil in creatures except misuse, which stems from the mind's negligence in its natural cultivation," says Maximus.[11] Another list, compiled by Peter of Damaskos, further reinforces that what an ascetic combats is a passionate attitude.

For it is not food, but gluttony, that is bad; not money, but attachment to it; not speech, but idle talk; not the world's delights, but dissipation; not love of one's family, but the neglect of God that such love may produce; not the clothes worn only for covering and protection from cold and heat, but those that are excessive and costly; not the houses that also protect us from heat and cold ... but houses with two or three floors, large and expensive; not owning something, but owning it when it has no vital use for us; ... not friendship, but the having of friends who are of no benefit to one's soul; not woman, but unchastity; not wealth, but avarice; not wine, but drunkenness; not anger used in accordance with nature for the chastisement of sin, but its use against one's fellow-men.

Again, it is not authority that is bad, but the love of authority; not glory, but the love of glory and—what is worse—vainglory; ... not the world, but the passions; not nature, but what is contrary to nature.[12]

He also concludes, like Maximus, by saying that "[i]t is not the thing itself, but its misuse that is evil," making the battleground of asceticism the human heart, not created matter. Virtue has been called *ordo amoris*—rightly ordered love—and liturgical asceticism is the process of overcoming disordered love by restoring in our hearts the hierarchy designed by God, who is Love.

10. Maximus the Confessor, *Four Hundred Chapters on Love,* 3.41.

11. Ibid., 3.4.

12. St. Peter of Damaskos, "A Treasury of Divine Knowledge," in *The Philokalia* (Boston: Faber & Faber, 1984), 3.156.

Whenever the ascetics speak about a material thing, they have their eye on its potential spiritual effect if misused, that is, the passion that can be caused by the thing if it is manipulated by the demons and received by a willing spirit. The mystery of iniquity involves a tension between voluntariness and involuntariness that John Climacus captures by saying we are "voluntary epileptics."[13] The reason for managing material things, says Mark the Ascetic, is to protect the spirit. "He who hates the passions gets rid of their causes. But he who is attracted by their causes is attacked by the passions even though he does not wish it.... We cannot entertain a passion in our mind unless we have a love for its causes."[14] We suffer the passions, but we are also to blame in our complicity with the Tempter.

If we could but remember this, it would result in a significant advance in precision in the way we speak about the world. Colloquial speech may be innocent in sometimes using a sort of verbal shorthand and calling money, sex, and beer the culprits, but to start believing that things themselves are flawed would turn us into Manichaeans or Cathars or teetotallers, and not ascetics. Things have not gone wrong; we have used things wrongly, and in so doing we have wronged things. Christians do not practice asceticism because they think things in the world are corrupted, but because human beings are corrupted in spirit, and only by a properly ordered use of the world—that is, by sacramentally directing matter to a spiritual end—can the world become an encounter with the anticipated Kingdom, as Evdokimov affirms. "Liturgy elevates matter to its real dignity and destiny, and we understand thereby that matter is not some autonomous substance but rather a function of the Spirit and a vehicle of the spiritual.... In the final analysis we are talking of the ascetical rehabilitation

13. "An angry person is like a voluntary epileptic who, through an involuntary tendency, breaks out in convulsions and falls down"; see Climacus, Step 8, in *The Ladder of Divine Ascent*, 147.

14. Mark the Ascetic, "No Righteousness by Works," in *The Philokalia* (Boston: Faber & Faber, 1979), 1.135.

of matter as the substratum of the resurrection and the medium in which all epiphanies take place."[15] To understand that there is nothing wrong with the world, but that we must leave the world and bless the Kingdom of God is what Schmemann calls the great liturgical paradox. Assembling as the Church presupposes separation from the world, but "this exodus from the world is accomplished in the name of the world, for the sake of its salvation. For we are flesh of the flesh and blood of the blood of this world. We are a part of it, and only by us and through us does it ascend to its Creator, Savior and Lord, to its goal and fulfillment. We separate ourselves from the world in order to bring it, in order to lift it up to the kingdom, to make it once again the way to God and participation in his eternal kingdom."[16]

Vladimir Solovyof makes the connection between ascetical work and the liturgical transfiguration of the world even more explicit.

> In order to realize the Kingdom of God on earth, it is necessary, first, to *recede* from earth; in order to manifest the spiritual idea in the material world it is necessary to be free and detached from that world. A slave of the earth cannot possess it and consequently cannot make it the foundation of God's Kingdom....
>
> The highest aim for Christianity is not ascetic detachment from the natural life but its hallowing and purification. But in order to purify it, one must, in the first instance, be pure from it. The purpose of Christianity is not to destroy earthly life, but to raise it towards God who comes down to meet it.... Only he who is free from the world can benefit it. A captive spirit is unable to rebuild its prison into a temple of light: he must first of all free himself from it ... the purpose of Christian asceticism is not to weaken the flesh, but to strengthen the spirit for the transfiguration of the flesh.[17]

15. Paul Evdokimov, *The Art of the Icon: A Theology of Beauty* (Redondo Beach, Calif.: Oakwood, 1990), 28.

16. Alexander Schmemann, *The Eucharist* (Crestwood, N.Y.: St. Vladimir's Seminary Press, 1987), 53; see also *For the Life of the World*, chapter 2, in which he describes the liturgy under the metaphor of journey: it is departure from and return to the world.

17. Solovyof, *A Solovyof Anthology*, 119–20.

All Christians are commanded to be free from the world; some Christians freed themselves from the world by literally fleeing from it. But the monk left the world in order to serve its transfiguration, not for the purpose of abandoning it.

Beginning in the fourth century, some Christians began going into the desert to carry out an experiment upon the human heart. Now, as everyone knows, a prerequisite for conducting any experiment is to isolate the object being investigated by removing whatever external factors might affect the object. This is called a controlled environment. The Desert Fathers also sought a controlled environment for their experiment, but they removed the external factors by removing themselves from those factors. They relocated their hearts to the desert, away from city, family, wealth, and property, not because they thought these things were bad, and not because they lacked love for their neighbor, and not because they sought something that did not concern Christians in the world; rather, they left the world to search for the tranquility required to notice the heart's deeper movements, and they recorded the heart's tremors like a seismograph records movements deep in the earth. Makarios of Egypt writes, "If a man is entangled in the things of this world, caught by their many shackles, and seduced by the evil passions, it is very hard for him to recognize that there is another invisible struggle and another inner warfare. But, after detaching himself from all visible things and worldly pleasures, and beginning to serve God, he then becomes capable of recognizing the nature of this inner struggle and unseen warfare against the passions."[18] As a person might shut down other causes of noise in order to hear a soft sound, the Desert Fathers sought tranquility in order to give "the soul the opportunity to look at the impressions previously stamped on the mind, and to struggle against each one and eliminate it."[19]

18. Makarios of Egypt, "The Freedom of the Intellect," *The Philokalia*, 3.351.
19. Neilos the Ascetic, *The Philokalia*, 1.232.

Antony said, "He who sits alone and is quiet has escaped from three wars: hearing, speaking, seeing: but there is one thing against which he must continually fight: that is, his own heart.[20]

And again,

This story was told: There were three friends, serious men, who became monks. One of them chose to make peace between men who were at odds, as it is written: "Blessed are the peacemakers" (Matt. 5:29). The second chose to visit the sick. The third chose to go away to be quiet in solitude. Now the first, toiling among contentions, was not able to settle all quarrels and, overcome with weariness, he went to him who tended the sick and found him also failing in spirit and unable to carry out his purpose. So the two went away to see him who had withdrawn into the desert, and they told him their troubles. They asked him to tell them how he himself had fared. He was silent for a while, and then poured water into a vessel and said, "Look at the water," and it was murky. After a little while he said again, "See now, how clear the water has become." As they looked into the water, they saw their own faces, as in a mirror. Then he said to them, "So it is with anyone who lives in a crowd; because of the turbulence he does not see his sins: but when he has been quiet, above all in solitude, then he recognizes his own faults."[21]

We turn to the Desert Fathers as guides in a search for wisdom about the passions and their resolution because the monk who has left this world sees his or her sins and passions more clearly.

(I am using the words "monk" and "Desert Fathers" to refer to both men and women, both Abbas and Ammas, because women ascetics, as well as men, can plant the divine seed. "Two monks came from Pelusium to see Sarah. On the way they said to each

20. Systematic Sayings, 2.2. The sayings of the Desert Fathers were recorded in two ways, one systematic and the other alphabetic. The former organized the saying around themes, the latter by the name of the monk. The convention we will use in footnotes here is to use "2.2" when the saying comes from the systematic collection, and something like "Anthony 7" when it comes from the alphabetic collection. We are here using Benedicta Ward's translation from *The Desert Fathers: Sayings of the Early Christian Monks* (New York: Penguin Books, 2003). The systematic sayings can also be found in Owen Chadwick, ed., *Western Asceticism* (Philadelphia: Westminster Press, 1958). We will use the alphabetical sayings found in Benedicta Ward, *The Sayings of the Desert Fathers* (Kalamazoo, Mich.: Cistercian Press, 1984).

21. Systematic Sayings, 2.16.

other, 'Let us humiliate this amma.' So they said to her, 'Take care that your soul be not puffed up, and that you do not say, "Look, some hermits have come to consult me, a woman!"' Sarah said to them, 'I am a woman in sex, but not in spirit.'")[22]

We do not think the monk is an ascetic while the lay person is not; rather, the monk practices the common Christian baptismal asceticism in an exceptional way. The very purpose of calling it *liturgical asceticism* is to remember that it is the discipline incumbent upon all the people of God created by Christ. If one likes, we may say that there are desert ascetics and secular ascetics. If monks appear to live their liturgical asceticism on a larger scale, it is because they live in the desert, a land of long shadows. The monk does not do a different asceticism, he or she does it in a different way. Monks practice a specialized form of liturgical asceticism, and they can teach us because they are specialists. They are professional ascetics—they professed a vow—and it behooves us to find out what they learned. But as we do, remember that the tradition has always understood the secular Christian and the monk to be related. In fact, it is a misnomer to speak of them as two separate states, says Athanasius Pekar. "In the writings of St. Basil there is no strict distinction between the monk and the layman. For Basil, both have only one name—Christian.... Like Pachomius, Basil did not recognize the two different states, that

22. Systematic Sayings, 10.76. There are several stories of women whose ascetic virility is so strong that they disguise themselves as men, unnoticed and unbeknownst to other people until they die. Hausherr summarizes the point well. "The Fatherhood of God reaches and deifies us.... All the workers employed by Providence for this great work—from the Word Incarnate and the Holy Spirit to the most Blessed Virgin Mary and holy Church, to the last of the occasional benefactors—all those who transmit the divine life to us and who cause us to have this life more abundantly by making the Father known to us, by making us believe in his love, by trusting the fulfillment of his fatherly design, by making us love everything he loves, by making us find in this faith, this love, the peace of God and the joy of Christ. In a word, all those who contribute to creating Christ in us or reforming us according to the model of Christ, partake of divine Fatherhood and deserve analogically the name of father and mother according to the Spirit, because they make us better children of God"; see Irenee Hausherr, S.J., *Spiritual Direction in the Early Christian East* (Kalamazoo, Mich.: Cistercian Publications, 1990), 322–23.

is, the secular and the monastic state of Christian life. In their understanding, the monastic state was only the more perfect way of Christian life to which all Christians were obliged."[23] It is why Evdokimov speaks of a single asceticism, whether interiorized or exteriorized.

> Prayer, fasting, the reading of the Scriptures and ascetic discipline are imposed on all for the same reason. That is precisely why the laity develops the state of *interiorized monasticism.* Its wisdom consists essentially in assuming, while living in the world and precisely because of this vocation, the eschatological maximalism of the monastics, their joyous and impatient expectation of the coming of Christ, the *Parousia.*[24]

Evdokimov further suggests that this is symbolized by the tonsure performed in the Orthodox rite of baptism. The chrism anointing is the sacrament of universal priesthood that indicates every Christian is sealed with spiritual gifts and becomes an entirely charismatic being. Then a rite of tonsure is performed which is identical with the rite of someone entering a monastic order. "Its symbolic meaning is unmistakable—it is the total offering of one's life. . . . Thus every instant of time is directed to its eschatological dimension. Every act and word is in the service of the King. In undergoing the rite of tonsure, every lay person is a monk of *interiorized monasticism,* subject to all the requirements of the Gospel."[25]

Our fifth chapter will investigate the relationship between laity and monk more completely, but this propaedeutic was necessary in order to explain why we turn to the desert Christians for an understanding of everyone's passions. These "athletes," as tradition has called them, pushed themselves to an extreme from which the center could be seen. If the writings of the desert ascetics has served the whole Church for so many centuries, it is

23. Athanasius Pekar, O.S.B.M., *The Perfect Christian: Religious Ideal of St. Basil the Great* (Warren, Mich.: Basilian Fathers Publications, 1993), author's preface and 24.

24. Evdokimov, *Ages of the Spiritual Life,* 233.

25. Ibid., 235.

because from their extreme vantage point the central demands of liturgical asceticism can be seen more clearly. The athletes go into the desert in order to do battle with Satan, who, out of malice, seeks to instigate the passions in us. There the monks made an analysis of the passions: whence they arise, how they spread, how they are related, how they can be combated, killed, or at least weakened, and which antidotes are more effective and which less. Such information is useful to all liturgical ascetics.

The foundational taxonomy of the passions was drawn up by Evagrius of Pontus.[26] An educated and urbane man, he lived from 345 to 399, making him a contemporary with Pachomius (†346), who wrote the first eastern cenobitic rule; Paul (†348), who had fled to the desert the year before Anthony was born; Anthony (†356), "the first monk," whose life Athanasius immortalized as a primordial model; Basil (†379), who ordained him a lector; Gregory Nazianzen (†390), who ordained Evagrius a deacon; and John Cassian (†435), who was Evagrius's own pupil and carried the institutes of Egyptian monasticism to the West, where it influenced the ascetical tradition as well as future reflection on the vices and virtues. Thus Kavanagh concludes, "There can be no doubt that Evagrius stands at the fountainhead of Christian commentary on the ascetical life for both East and West, for Moscow and Constantinople as well as for Monte Cassino and Rome."[27] After an amorous affair with the wife of a nobleman in Constantinople, Evagrius fled to Jerusalem. In response to a prayer for deliverance, he had a dream in which an angel first cast him into prison, then promised him deliverance if he would depart from the city. "And when Evagrius woke up from his sleep, he thought within himself and said, 'Although the words of the oaths have been uttered in a dream, it is right that I should

26. A sketch of Evagrius's life is provided by John Etudes Bamberger, O.C.S.O., in his introduction to *The Pratikos and Chapters on Prayer* (Kalamazoo, Mich.: Cistercian Publications, 1981), xxxv–xlvii.

27. Kavanagh, "Eastern Influences on the Rule of Saint Benedict," 57.

fulfil that which I have promised'; so he put his things in a ship and departed to Jerusalem,"[28] where he first dwelled at the monastic communities of Rufinus and Melania on the Mount of Olives, but from there was directed further on to learn from monks in the deeper Egyptian deserts. Two sayings make clear that this initially required a struggle for humility by Evagrius.

Some time ago Abba Evagrius went to Scete to a certain father and said to him, "Speak some word whereby I may be able to save myself." The old man saith unto him, "If thou wishest to be saved, when thou goest unto any man speak not before he asketh thee a question." Now Evagrius was sorry about this sentence, and shewed regret because he had asked the question, saying, "Verily I have read many books and I cannot accept instruction of this kind"; and having profited greatly he went forth from him.[29]

On one occasion there was a congregation in the Cells concerning a certain matter, and Abba Evagrius spoke. And a certain elder said unto him, "We know, Abba, that hadst thou been in thine own country where thou art a bishop and the governor of many, [thou wouldst have been right in speaking]; but in this place thou sittest [as] a stranger." Now Evagrius was sorry, but he was not offended, and he shook his head, and bent his gaze downwards, and he wrote with his finger and said unto them, "Verily, it is even as thou sayest, O my fathers; I have spoken once, but I will not do it a second time."[30]

So Evagrius listened. And he learned. And he recorded what he learned in a systematized way. He was a devotee of Origen's work and borrowed from Origen the idea of stages on the way, but with a change of vocabulary. Andrew Louth explains that "[l]ike Origen, Evagrius divides the way of the soul into three stages. But instead of *ethike, physike,* and *enoptike,* he uses the terms which through his influence have become familiar: *praktike, physike,*

28. *The Paradise,* trans. E. A. Wallis Budge (London: Chatto & Windus, 1907), 1.224. Also in Palladius, *The Lausiac History* (Westminster, Md.: Newman Press, 1965), ch. 38, "Evagrius," 112.

29. *The Paradise,* 2.15.

30. Alphabetical Sayings, Evagrius 7. This translation is taken from Budge, *The Paradise,* 2.15.

and *theologia. Praktike* is the stage during which the soul develops the practice of the virtues."[31] And the practice of the virtues depends upon an examination of the heart which keeps watch upon "eight evil thoughts," or *logismoi,* which afflict the monk. Olivier Clement notes that the usual translation of *logismoi* is "thoughts," but reminds us that, more precisely, they are "the seeds of the 'passions,' those suggestions or impulses that emerge from the subconscious and soon become obsessive. In the ascetic sense, remember, the 'passions' are blockages, usurpations, deviations that destroy the human being's basic desire. They are forms of idolatry, of that 'self-idolatry' that deflects towards nothingness our capacity for transcendence."[32] The goal of the demons is to keep the monk from reaching dispassion, writes Driscoll in his massive study on Evagrius, "so they attack that part of the soul where the passions reside in such a way as to set them in motion. Evagrius describes this with a language typically precise. *Demons* inspire *thoughts,* and these, when they are allowed to linger, unleash the *passions* in us. The remedy against this system of demonic attacks is a constant vigilance over thoughts, never allowing them to linger. *Praktike* is learning this art."[33]

Here is Evagrius's list of the *logismoi,* the evil thoughts:

> There are eight general and basic categories of thoughts in which are included every thought. First is that of gluttony, then impurity, avarice, sadness, anger, *acedia,* vainglory, and last of all, pride. It is not in our power to determine whether we are disturbed by these thoughts, but it is up to us to decide if they are to linger within us or not and whether or not they are to stir up our passions.[34]

Following the Greek assessment of the soul, Evagrius sees three faculties in a human being: the concupiscible, the irascible, and the rational. If not distorted by the passions, these three facul-

31. Andrew Louth, *The Origins of the Christian Mystical Tradition: From Plato to Denys* (Oxford: Clarendon Press, 1981), 102.

32. Clement, *The Roots of Christian Mysticism,* 167.

33. Driscoll, *Evagrius Ponticus: Ad Monachos,* 13.

34. Evagrius, *Praktikos* 6.

ties could be moved properly, as Maximus the Confessor notes. "The soul is moved reasonably when its concupiscible element is qualified by self-mastery, its irascible element cleaves to love and turns away from hate, and the rational element lives with God through prayer and spiritual contemplation."[35] More on these faculties later.

Every ascetical writer will comment on the *logismoi* Evagrius has identified, because spotting them is the first step toward battling them. Lists longer than eight can be compiled, as shown by John of Damascus's example below, but they still operate within the framework of the three faculties.

The sins of the intelligent aspect are unbelief, heresy, folly, blasphemy, ingratitude and assent to sins originating in the soul's passible aspect. These vices are cured through unwavering faith in God and in true, undeviating and orthodox teachings, through the continual study of the inspired utterances of the Spirit, through pure and ceaseless prayer, and through the offering of thanks to God. The sins of the incensive aspect are heartlessness, hatred, lack of compassion, rancor, envy, murder and dwelling constantly on such things. They are cured by deep sympathy for one's fellow men, love, gentleness, brotherly affection, compassion, forbearance and kindness. The sins of the desiring aspect are gluttony, greed, drunkenness, unchastity, adultery, uncleanliness, licentiousness, love of material things, and the desire for empty glory, gold, wealth and the pleasures of the flesh. These are cured through fasting, self-control, hardship, a total shedding of possessions and their distribution to the poor, desire for the imperishable blessings held in store, longing for the kingdom of God, and aspiration for divine sonship.[36]

Tempting though it is to collate such descriptions from ascetical writers across the centuries, this is not necessary to the pur-

35. Maximus the Confessor, *The Four Hundred Chapters on Love*, 4.15.

36. John of Damascus, "On the Virtues and the Vices," in *The Philokalia* (Boston, Faber & Faber, 1981), 2.337. St. Gregory of Sinai has a similarly ordered list, though with some additional subdivisions, in *On Commandments and Doctrines*, in *The Philokalia*, 4.236; and Peter of Damaskos has an unsystematized list of 298 passions in *A Treasury of Divine Knowledge*, in *The Philokalia*, 3.205–6.

pose of this work, so here we will content ourselves with only Evagrius's own description in chapters seven to fourteen of the *Praktikos*.

The material here is intended for monks and we can see this in their categorization. The three beginning *logismoi* are ones that afflict a monk at the outset (gluttony, lust, avarice); the next three have to be confronted for the monk to persevere (sadness, anger, *acedia*); and the final two (vainglory and pride) are the most subtle because a monk could fall prey to them even after a lifetime of asceticism. We will look at what Evagrius says about each group in turn.

The first triad places gluttony at the head. Gluttony is not so much overeating as it is fixation to secure excess provisions for the future, a lack of trust in Providence. Evagrius says this temptation brings to mind concern for the stomach, worry over a long illness, anxiety over the scarcity of life's commodities, and fear in the face of illness, especially when one has seen the suffering gone through by others in the community. "The thought of gluttony suggests to the monk that he give up his efforts in short order,"[37] that is, it is a temptation to abandon the ascetical journey before one has hardly put one's foot down on the first step. Second, the demon of impurity attacks the monk as he practices continence, hoping to force him to give up this way of life. This passion "impels one to lust after bodies."[38] Third, avarice plays upon the monk's worry over the future. It "suggests to the mind a lengthy old age,"[39] a time when one will finally be unable to perform manual labor and the likelihood of famine, sickness, and poverty will be a concern. This mingles with vainglory because it produces "the great shame that comes from accepting the necessities of life from others."[40]

The second triad faces up to the difficulty of persevering.

37. Evagrius, *Praktikos*, 7.
38. Ibid., 8.
39. Ibid., 9.
40. Ibid.

The fourth passion, sadness, must be overcome in order to persist in the monastic struggle. It comes upon the monk when, at the memory of home, parents, and former life, he or she realizes "the deprivation of one's desires." These are internal temptations, when the soul "pours itself out in pleasures that are still only mental in nature,"[41] and they can seize the soul and drench it in sadness. The fifth passion, anger, is the most fierce, according to Evagrius. "In fact it is defined as a boiling and stirring up of wrath against one who has given injury—or is thought to have done so. It constantly irritates the soul and above all at the time of prayer it seizes the mind and flashes the picture of the offensive person before one's eyes."[42] The sixth passion is called *acedia,* which can be translated "sloth," but something more than simple laziness is meant.[43] *Acedia* means a lethargy about doing one's spiritual duties that is born from despondency. Evagrius notes that it afflicts the monk midday (about the fourth to the eighth hour), and came to be called the noonday demon by application of Psalm 90:6 ("The deadly disease striking at noon"). In a remarkably perceptive description of a sort of restlessness we are all familiar with, Evagrius describes how this demon works.[44]

First of all he makes it seem that the sun barely moves, if at all, and that the day is fifty hours long. Then he constrains the monk to look constantly out the windows, to walk outside the cell, to gaze carefully at the sun to determine how far it stands from the ninth hour [his meal time],

41. Ibid., 10.

42. Ibid., 11.

43. Siegfried Wenzel traces the history of this word through the Middle Ages in *The Sin of Sloth: Acedia in Medieval Thought and Literature* (Chapel Hill: University of North Carolina Press, 1967) and identifies four stages of development: (1) the monastic meaning of boredom with the cell; (2) a laicization of the concept to mean negligence in performing spiritual duties; (3) a Scholastic definition meaning "aversion of appetite from its own good because of bodily hardships that accompany its attainment"; and finally, (4) the popular image of indolence or sheer laziness. The vice consists of both a spiritual inappetence and a bodily laziness, and these streams simply parted company eventually.

44. The monk apparently knew, centuries before Pascal, that "[n]othing is so insufferable to man as to be completely at rest. . . . I have discovered that all the unhappiness of men arises from one single fact, that they cannot stay quietly in their own chamber"; see *Pensees* (New York: E. P. Dutton, 1958), nos. 131 and 139.

to look now this way and now that to see if perhaps [one of the brethren appears from his cell]. Then too he instills in the heart of the monk a hatred for the place, a hatred for his very life itself, a hatred for manual labor. He leads him to reflect that charity has departed from among the brethren, that there is no one to give encouragement. Should there be someone at this period who happens to offend him in some way or other, this too the demon uses to contribute further to his hatred.[45]

Thus *acedia* causes both memories and projections—memories of dear ones and the former way of life, and projections of an insecure future and the toil which lies ahead. The demon "drives [the monk] along to desire other sites where he can more easily procure life's necessities, more readily find work and make a real success of himself. He goes on to suggest that, after all, it is not the place that is the basis of pleasing the Lord. God is to be adored everywhere."[46]

The importance of staying in one's cell under the vow of stability was necessary to combat the passion of *acedia*. In fact, some would say this was the monastic life *in toto*. In response for a request for advice, Abba Moses says, "Go and sit in your cell, and your cell will teach you everything."[47] The Rule of Benedict disapproves of persons who "spend their entire lives drifting from region to region," and called such monks "Gyrovagues"—literally, someone who wanders (*vagari*) in circles (*gyro*).[48] The tradition compares a monk out of the cell to a fish out of water, a barren tree, or a negligent hen. "Antony said: 'Fish die if they stay on dry land, and in the same way monks who stay outside their cell or remain with secular people fall away from their vow of quiet. As a fish must return to the sea, so must we to our cell, in case by staying outside, we forget to watch inside.'"[49] An anonymous old man is recalled as having said, "A tree cannot bear fruit if it is often transplanted. So it is with the monk."[50] And Saint Syncletica

45. Evagrius, *Praktikos*, 12.
46. Ibid.
47. Systematic Sayings, 2.9.
48. Rule of Benedict, 1.
49. Systematic Sayings, 2.1.
50. Systematic Sayings, 7.36.

warned against wandering from place to place because "[j]ust as the bird who abandons the eggs she was sitting on prevents them from hatching, so the monk or the nun grows cold and their faith dies, when they go from one place to another."[51]

The final two passions are interior, spiritual battles. The seventh passion, vainglory, is particularly difficult to combat because it is a vice that "readily grows in the souls of those who practice virtue."[52] Unlike other passions, which decrease in inverse proportion to the strengthening of the virtues, this passion can increase as the virtues are strengthened because vainglory leads monks "to desire to make their struggles known publicly" and creates a desire for the trappings of a glory which is vain, like illusory healing, the ability to hear the demons, fame that would bring crowds of people to touch one's clothes or knock at one's door to seek audience, and the ever-tempting desire to attain to the priesthood. The eighth and final passion, pride, brings the soul to its most damaging fall. Although contemporary language seems to treat vainglory and pride as synonyms, in Evagrius's careful analysis vainglory is wanting honor from other human beings, and pride is snatching credit from God. "It induces the monk to deny that God is his helper and to consider that he himself is the cause of virtuous actions. Further, he gets a big head in regard to the brethren, considering them stupid because they do not all have this same opinion of him."[53]

The usefulness of Evagrius's schema is substantiated by its long life and adaptability. Evagrius has a privileged place, if not for chronological reasons,[54] then because he was the first Christian intellectual to adopt the life of the anchorites and leave be-

51. Syncletica 6; also 7.15.

52. Evagrius, *Praktike,* 13.

53. Evagrius, *Praktike,* 14.

54. Bloomfield identifies "the earliest reference to the seven chief sins in any form ... in the pseudepigraphical Testament of the Twelve Patriarchs, Testament of Reuben," which dates from about 110 B.C., five hundred years before Evagrius; see Morton W. Bloomfield, *The Seven Deadly Sins* (Ann Arbor: Michigan State University Press, 1967), 44.

hind a written integration of ascetical praxis with theological theory. He thus stands at the source of the hesychast tradition which attempts to quiet exactly the passions he names. Though posthumously condemned by the Fifth Ecumenical Council (553) for a kind of Origenist Christology, Evagrius's ascetical works on prayer were adopted in the East and corrected by a stream of theologians who isolated his ascetical theology from his less felicitous Christological teaching, and vouched for the orthodoxy of his doctrine of dispassion, including Diadochus, John Climacus, Maximus the Confessor, Symeon the New Theologian, and culminating in Gregory Palamas.[55] In the West, Evagrius's influence entered via John Cassian and Pope Gregory the Great, as Fr. Kallistos Ware summarizes.

Evagrius' disciple, St. John Cassian, transmitted this list of the eight "thoughts" to the West, but made one change in the sequence: to make more evident the connection between dejection and despondency, he moved anger up to the fourth place, after avarice. Further changes were made by St. Gregory the Great, Pope of Rome (590–604), known in the East as "Gregory the Dialogist." He set pride in a class on its own, as the source and mother of all other vices, and omitted dejection, regarding this as the same as despondency, while adding envy to the list. In this way he produced the catalogue of the "seven deadly sins," familiar to the Western Middle Ages.[56]

This identification and organization of the thoughts became the basis of Western moral theology concerning the vices and virtues, extending Evagrius's influence there.

The *logismoi* Evagrius identifies are not themselves passions, they are demonic occasions for stirring up the passions. For Evagrius, *logismos* and *demon* are virtually synonymous, says Driscoll.

It is a key feature of his theory that to each *logismos* there corresponds a demon or spirit who specializes in it. Thus, to be troubled by a thought

55. For an easy overview of these hesychastic authors, see John Meyendorff, *St. Gregory Palamas and Orthodox Spirituality* (Crestwood, N.Y.: St. Vladimir's Seminary Press, 1974).

56. Kallistos Ware, in his introduction to John Climacus, *Ladder of Divine Ascent*, 63.

is to be troubled by a demon. The true battle of the monk is with the demons themselves. Thoughts are the means used by the demons to trouble the monk. On the other hand, it is by doing battle with evil thoughts and conquering them (that is to say, battling and conquering the demons) that the monk in fact discovers true virtue in the counterpart of the evil thoughts.[57]

The *logismoi* come unbidden, and therefore no guilt is attached to having them, but there is a chain of increasing culpability if the soul acquiesces to the temptation. Although one is not responsible for having had the thought, one is definitely morally responsible for what one does with it. Abba Moses counsels Cassian that

It is, indeed, impossible for the mind not to be troubled by thoughts, but accepting them or rejecting them is possible for everyone who makes an effort. It is true that their origin does not in every respect depend on us, but it is equally true that their refusal or acceptance does depend on us.[58]

This activity of the heart is not inappropriately compared to millstones, which the swift rush of waters turns with a violent revolving motion. As long as the waters' force keeps them spinning they are utterly incapable of stopping their work, but it is in the power of the one who supervises to decide whether to grind wheat or barley or darnel. Indeed, only that will be ground which has been accepted by the person entrusted with the responsibility for the work.[59]

How can one choose something whose origin is outside oneself? John of Damascus explains.

It does not lie within our power to decide whether or not these eight thoughts are going to arise and disturb us. But to dwell on them or not to dwell on them, to excite the passions or not to excite them, does lie within our power. In this connection, we should distinguish between seven different terms: provocation, coupling, wrestling, passion, assent (which comes very close to performance), actualization and captivity.[60]

57. Driscoll, *Evagrius Ponticus: Ad Monachos,* 11–12.
58. Abba Moses, in *Conferences of Cassian,* 1.17.1
59. Ibid., 1.18.1
60. John of Damascus, "On the Virtues and the Vices," *The Philokalia,* 2.337–38.

In other words, sin is complex because any human act interweaves many motives and reasons, and none of them are simply automatic or inevitable. A truly human act, which exercises attention and alertness such as Jesus practiced, could overcome the passions by cutting them off at the stage of *logismos,* which is how Jesus can be said to be without sin. Jesus was truly tempted in the wilderness, as the Gospels record, but to be tempted is not a sin.

The culpability of each state is commented on by Philotheos of Sinai in this brief summary:

> Provocation, they say, is a thought still free from passion, or an image newly engendered in the heart and glimpsed by the intellect. Coupling is to commune with this thought or image, in either an impassioned or a dispassionate way. Assent is the pleasurable acceptance by the soul of the thing seen. Captivity is the forcible and enforced abduction of the heart, or persistent intercourse with the object, disrupting even our best state. Passion, in the strict sense, they define as that which lurks passionably in the soul over a long period. Of these stages the first is sinless; the second, not altogether free from sin; the sinfulness of the third stage depends on our inner state; and the struggle itself brings us either punishment or crowns of victory.[61]

Understanding the transition from *logismos* to sin to passion is as important to the ascetic as understanding the transition from virus to infection to death is important to a physician. Therefore we can find multiple places in the philokalic literature where the steps are treated, and any difference between them is only minor. A terse overview can be taken from Hesychios the Priest:

> The provocation comes first, then our coupling with it, or the mingling of our thoughts with those of the wicked demons. Third comes our assent to the provocation, with both sets of intermingling thoughts contriving how to commit the sin in practice. Fourth comes the concrete action—that is, the sin itself.[62]

61. Philotheos of Sinai, "Texts on Watchfulness," *The Philokalia,* 3.29.

62. Hesychios the Priest, "On Watchfulness and Holiness," *The Philokalia,* 1.1, 170.

From the city of Damascus comes a description of the steps by two spiritual masters, John and Peter, and we will interweave them to let each augment the other.

John of Damascus says the thoughts first present themselves as a *provocation,* which is "simply a suggestion coming from the enemy, like 'do this' or 'do that,' such as our Lord Himself experienced when he heard the words 'Command that these stones become bread.' As we have already said, it is not within our power to prevent provocations."[63] Peter of Damascus likewise explains that "[o]ur thoughts differ greatly one from the other. Some are altogether free from sin. Others do not initially involve sin: this is the case with what are called provocations, in other words, conceptions of either good or evil, which in themselves are neither commendable nor reprehensible."[64] What follows on provocation, Peter continues, "is known as *coupling,* that is to say, we begin to entertain a particular thought and parley with it, so to speak; and this leads us either to give assent to it or to reject it. Our reaction to the thought, if in accordance with God's will, is praiseworthy, though not highly so; but if it accords with evil, then it deserves censure."[65] John, too, is of the opinion that a person's moral accountability begins at this stage, because coupling with the thought suggested by the enemy "means dwelling on the thought and choosing deliberately to dally with it in a pleasurable manner.... Passion is the state resulting from coupling with the thought provoked by the enemy; it means letting the imagination brood on the thought continually."[66] Now, therefore, because the thought has been embraced by the intellect, it must be *wrestled* with, says John. "Wrestling is the resistance offered to the impassioned thought. It may result either in our destroying the passion in the thought—that is to say, the impassioned thought—

63. John of Damascus, "On the Virtues and the Vices," *The Philokalia,* 2.338.
64. Peter of Damascus, "A Treasury of Divine Knowledge," *The Philokalia,* 3.207.
65. Ibid.
66. John of Damascus, "On the Virtues and the Vices," *The Philokalia,* 2.338.

or in our assenting to it."[67] The intellect either "conquers it or is conquered by it," notes Peter, "and this brings the intellect either credit or punishment when the thought is put into action."[68] One should destroy the passion in the thought, either preemptively, by noticing the thought at its inception and resisting it, or by wrestling with it once one has coupled with it. If one repeatedly neglects to do so, then occurs "the forcible and compulsive abduction of the heart already dominated by prepossession and long habit,"[69] which John calls *captivity,* and after it, *assent,* which is "giving approval to the passion inherent in the thought."[70] Peter reverses the sequence of these last two steps, calling assent "a pleasurable inclination of the soul towards what it sees," and saying assent leads to the "state of seduction, or captivity, in which the heart is induced forcibly and unwillingly to put the thought into effect."[71] The final result, for John, is *actualization* which puts "the impassioned thought into effect once it has received our assent."[72] Peter observes not only the commission of sin, but the finalization of the passion. "When the soul dallies for a long time with an impassioned thought there arises what we call a *passion.* This in turn, through its intercourse with the soul, becomes a settled *disposition* within us, compelling the soul to move of its own accord towards the corresponding action."[73]

The final, succinct summary we will recount is made by John Climacus in *The Ladder of Divine Ascent.* As is the case throughout his work, his genius is to sum up the tradition in succinct clarity. His summary of the components out of which a passion is created is as follows:

67. Ibid.

68. Peter of Damascus, "A Treasury of Divine Knowledge," *The Philokalia,* 3.207.

69. John of Damascus, "On the Virtues and the Vices," *The Philokalia,* 2.338.

70. Ibid.

71. Peter of Damascus, "A Treasury of Divine Knowledge," *The Philokalia,* 3.207.

72. John of Damascus, "On the Virtues and the Vices," *The Philokalia,* 2.338.

73. Peter of Damascus, "A Treasury of Divine Knowledge," *The Philokalia,* 3.207. The volumes of the *Philokalia* contain a glossary at the back of each volume that gives a helpful summary description of these terms.

Among the discerning Fathers, distinctions are recognized between provocation, coupling, assent, captivity, struggle, and the disease called passion, which is in the soul. These blessed Fathers say that provocation is a simple word or image encountered for the first time, which has entered into the heart. Coupling is conversation with what has been encountered, whether this be passionately or otherwise. Assent is the delighted yielding of the soul to what it has encountered. Captivity is a forcible and unwilling abduction of the heart, a permanent lingering with what we have encountered and which totally undermines the necessary order of our souls. By struggle they mean force equal to that which is leading the attack, and this force wins or loses according to the desires of the spirit. Passion, in their view, is properly something that lies hidden for a long time in the soul and by its very presence it takes on the character of a habit, until the soul of its own accord clings to it with affection.[74]

This view of temptation, then, is far more nuanced and complex than is the case in more superficial doctrines of sin. Although someone might see a person as less culpable because he or she cannot prevent the thoughts, someone else might see a person as all the more culpable because his or her will was free to do battle at numerous points along the process before the passion became habit.

All of these analyses make it clear that it is easier to initiate the struggle at the first thought than to wait and have to wrestle with the final passion. Passions grow stronger the longer they develop and the longer they are permitted to persist. Credit is nevertheless given a person for putting up a struggle at any point. Once a brother went to ask his elders about this. Some said that evil thoughts defile a man; others said they do not because one might think of vile actions but not do them. The brother was discontented with these diverse answers, so sought an experienced hermit who told him that everyone is required to act according to his capacity. When pressed, he explained further:

74. John Climacus, Step 15, "On Chastity," *The Ladder of Divine Ascent*, 182.

So he said, "Look here, suppose there was a valuable jug and two monks came in, one of whom had a great capacity for a disciplined life, and the other a small capacity. Suppose that the mind of the more disciplined man is moved at the sight of the jug and he says inwardly, 'I'd like to have that jug,' but the idea leaves him at once, and he puts away any thought of it, then he would not be defiled. But if the less disciplined man covets the jug and is strongly moved by an impulse to take it, and yet after a struggle he does not take it, he would not be defiled either."[75]

Still, even if both struggles are honored, it is nevertheless easier to wrestle with a baby than a grown man, so most of the time the Fathers recommend opposing the passion in its smaller form, while still a *logismos,* which was the interpretation consistently given to Psalm 137:9 which recommends dashing the infant's head against a stone. To accomplish this requires constant attentiveness, spiritual sobriety, and watchfulness (*nepsis*). "If we can confront the first of these things, the provocation, in a dispassionate way, or firmly rebut it at the outset, we thereby cut off at once everything that comes after,"[76] like cutting off the head of a snake before the whole body enters the house. The goal of a true ascetic would be the capacity to look on things without passion, but that requires an attentiveness difficult to achieve. Maximus says, "First the memory brings up a simple thought to the mind, and when it lingers about it arouses passion. When it is not removed it sways the mind to consent, and when this happens the actual sinning finally takes place. Thus the all-wise Apostle, in writing to Gentile converts, bids them to remove first of all the effect of the sin, then to backtrack in order to end up at the cause."[77]

Two facts should be clear by now. The first is that we do not suffer the passions because we have physical bodies; the second is that physical experiences (and even memories of physical expe-

75. Systematic Sayings, 10.81.
76. John of Damascus, "On the Virtues and the Vices," *The Philokalia,* 2.338.
77. Maximus the Confessor, *The Four Hundred Chapters on Love,* 1.84.

riences) may be occasions for the passions.[78] John Climacus wonders whether it is the thought which introduces a passion into the body (such that if the mind does not take the lead the body will not follow), or do *logismoi* have their origin in the capacity of the body to experience things sensual? In the face of this enigma of how body and soul intertwine, John confesses ignorance. "If anyone can do so in the Lord, let him explain what really happens. It would greatly benefit those living actively to understand this.... Some passions seem to enter the body by way of the soul, and some work in the opposite way."[79] It seems, then, that passions of the soul can afflict the body, and passions of the body can afflict the soul, but this is no surprise given biblical anthropology which sees a human being as either an embodied spirit or a spirited body. Mark the Ascetic finds body and soul so intertwined that he says, "[i]n our ascetic warfare we can neither rid ourselves of evil thoughts apart from their causes, nor of their causes without ridding ourselves of the thoughts. For if we reject the one without the other, before long the other will involve us in them both at once."[80] But the ascetics make it clear that even if it is the body's sensibility which occasions the *logismoi,* the passions would not have resulted except for our spiritual fall, and so the body itself is innocent; the corruption of our heart cannot be accredited to it dwelling in a material body.

Symeon the New Theologian forcefully expresses this teach-

78. A saying of the Desert Fathers tells of a monk on a journey with his elderly mother who "took off his cloak, and wrapped it round his hands, so as not to touch his mother's body" when he carried her across a river. "His mother said to him: 'Why did you wrap your hands like that, my son?' He said: 'Because a woman's body is fire. Simply because I was touching you, the memory of other women might come into my mind" (4.68). But no matter what the source of thoughts, memories or present perceptions, the thoughts are to be dealt with the same way. "A hermit asked a brother, 'Do you often talk with women?' The brother said, 'No.' He went on, 'My temptations come from paintings old and new, memories of mine which trouble me through pictures of women.' But the hermit said to him: 'Do not fear the dead, but flee the living; flee from consenting to sin or committing sin, and take a longer time over your prayers'" (5.6).

79. John Climacus, *The Ladder of Divine Ascent,* 183.

80. Mark the Ascetic, "No Righteousness by Works," *The Philokalia,* 1.140.

ing when he says "that which follows its nature does not fall under condemnation."[81] He applies this to the human person by a rather complex syllogism. The body itself has neither liberty nor will, he says, but rather it is moved by the soul. Therefore whatever movement the body could make on its own could only take place after soul and body have been separated (death), and at such a time, in such a state, the natural movement made by the body is a movement toward corruption. Movement toward corruption would never be directed by the soul's intellectual faculty, and therefore it cannot be called rational. So if the body's own movement is irrational, "it is clear that it is also nonsinful and without condemnation before God. Rightly so, for that which follows its nature does not fall under condemnation."[82] Therefore, Symeon concludes, it is not the body that seeks lust, voluptuousness, gluttony, greed in eating, excessive sleep, idleness, and pretentiousness in dress, and "Let nobody therefore think that he is being driven to these things and compelled by his own body! It is not true."[83]

Adam and Eve suffered no such discord in paradise, and their sensuality could have been used in other than passionate ways. Theodoros the Great Ascetic confirms this anthropology, which is not about a conflict between soul and body, but is about the problem of not letting sensory things lead us to God.

> I do not say that Adam ought not to have used the senses, for it was not for nothing that he was invested with a body. But he should not have indulged in sensory things. When perceiving the beauty of creatures, he should have referred it to the source and as a consequence have found his enjoyment and his wonder fulfilled in that, thus giving himself a twofold reason for marveling at the Creator. He should not have attached himself, as he did, to sensory things and have lost himself in wonder at them, neglecting the Creator of intelligible beauty.[84]

81. Symeon the New Theologian, *The Discourses* (New York: Paulist Press, 1980), 269.

82. Ibid.

83. Ibid.

84. Theodoros the Great Ascetic, "Theoretikon," *The Philokalia*, 2.44.

In the homilies, Isaac the Syrian also insists that the vitality of the powers of both the body and the soul were given by God for the benefit of man and woman. In his homilies he says these "passions" (to use the modern sense of the word) become passions (to use the ascetical sense of the word) by being directed to the wrong end.

Every passion that exists for our benefit has been given by God. The passions of the body have been implanted in it for its benefit and growth, and the same is true with respect to the passions of the soul. But whenever the body is forced by a privation of what is proper to it to be outside of its own well-being and to follow after the soul, it is enfeebled and harmed. And whenever the soul, abandoning what belongs to her, follows after the body, she is immediately harmed.[85]

In the discourses, Isaac is even more blunt.

For by nature the soul is not subject to passion.... We believe that God has not made his image subject to passion.... Therefore we believe that the passions of the soul are not natural as the philosophers maintain.... [When the nature of the soul] is moved by passions, all the members of the church acknowledge that it has gone outside its nature. Therefore the passions [must have] entered the nature of the soul afterward; it is not right at all to consider passions to be natural to the soul. Even though the soul is moved by them, it is evident that it is moved by something outside of itself and not on its own.[86]

An interesting phrase—a passion is the result of a "nature gone outside its nature." The natural faculty cannot be deleted by Satan, but it can be misdirected. The faculties of soul and body should be exercised rightly and toward the right end, and when they are not then they are wounded and nature goes outside its nature. That which follows its own nature is not condemned; our problem is that we don't do nature naturally any more.

We don't will naturally any more, either. To make this point, the Greek Fathers distinguished our natural will from what they

85. Isaac the Syrian, Homily 3, *The Ascetical Homilies,* 19.

86. Isaac the Syrian, *On Ascetical Life* (Crestwood, N.Y.: St. Vladimir's Seminary Press, 1988), (3.3, 5), 44.

called gnomic will (from *gnome,* which means willing in accordance with an opinion, or intention, or inclination). Fr. Andrew Louth explains the use of these two terms in Maximus.

Willing is, for Maximus, something that is rooted in the nature of rationality, something underlined in several definitions he cites from Clement of Alexandria: "Willing is a natural power, that desires what is natural. Willing is a natural desire that corresponds to the nature of the rational. . . ." But with fallen creatures, their own nature has become opaque to them, they no longer know what they want, and experience coercion in trying to love what cannot give fulfillment. For in their fallen state, rational creatures are no longer aware of their true good, which is God. Various apparent goods attract them: they are confused, they need to deliberate and consider, and their way of willing shares in all this.[87]

The sixth ecumenical council said there was no gnomic will in Christ, but fallen human beings deliberate (*gnome*) with difficulty about whether to do the good. Had our appetites remained true, they would not have become passionate appetites but remained natural appetites, a truth Maximus finds in Scripture. "Scripture takes away none of the things given by God for our use but it restrains immoderation and corrects unreasonableness. For example, it does not forbid eating or begetting children or having money or managing it, but it does forbid gluttony, fornication, and so forth. Nor does it even forbid us to think of these things, for they were made to be thought of; what it forbids is thinking of them with passion."[88]

The precise definition given by Maximus the Confessor of a blameworthy passion is "a movement of the soul contrary to nature."[89] It is a mistake (indeed, the fundamental lie) to say sin is natural. It is not natural to sin. "No wickedness, no heresy, not even the devil himself can deceive anyone unless he counterfeits

87. Andrew Louth, *Maximus the Confessor* (New York: Routledge Press, 1997), 60–61.
88. Maximus the Confessor, *Four Hundred Chapters on Love,* 3.66.
89. Maximus the Confessor, *Four Centuries on Love,* 1.35.

virtue,"[90] comments Dorotheos of Gaza. Sin is a thoroughly unnatural, inhuman act, contrary to and incompatible with human nature. It thwarts humanity, subverting and distorting our beginning and end. Sin is subhuman—sainthood is full humanity. In this respect, passion names an illogical character.[91] John Climacus identifies the true and counterfeit versions.

God neither caused nor created evil and, therefore, those who assert that certain passions come naturally to the soul are quite wrong. What they fail to realize is that we have taken natural attributes of our own and turned them into passions. For instance, the seed which we have for the sake of procreating children is abused by us for the sake of fornication. Nature has provided us with anger as something to be turned against the serpent, but we have used it against our neighbor. We have a natural urge to excel in virtue, but instead we compete in evil. Nature stirs within us the desire for glory, but that glory is of a heavenly kind. It is natural for us to be arrogant—against the demons. Joy is ours by nature, but it should be joy on account of the Lord and for the sake of doing good to our neighbor. Nature has given us resentment, but that ought to be used against the enemies of our souls. We have a natural desire for food, but not surely for profligacy.[92]

When sin made havoc in our soul, our passions turned the world (God's creation) into the "world" (a state of rebellion), and turned the body (our corporeality) into "flesh" (*sarx*—"an obscure but invincible complicity that the power of darkness finds in us").[93]

In the background stands the tripartite anthropology, mentioned above, that derives from a Greek anthropology that sees the soul as having three faculties. Human beings can reason, they can desire, and they can be stirred to vehement feeling, so

90. Dorotheos of Gaza, *Discourses and Sayings* (Kalamazoo, Mich.: Cistercian Publications, 1977), 162.

91. George Berthold writes, "Thus passion in this sense is not a mere emotion but rather has an illogical character (cf. Evagrius, *Praktikos* 6). Maximus himself tells us that he learnt his teaching from Gregory of Nyssa, that passions were not originally included in man's nature but were introduced after the fall into that part of nature inferior to reason"; see Berthold, *Maximus the Confessor: Selected Writings,* note 74, p. 91.

92. John Climacus, Step 26, *The Ladder of Divine Ascent.*

93. Louis Bouyer, "The Two Economies," *God and His Creation,* edited by A. M. Henry, O.P. (Chicago: Fides), 471–72.

the three faculties are called the intellective, the concupiscible, and the irascible. Maximus describes a healthy state by saying, "The soul is moved reasonably when its concupiscible element is qualified by self-mastery, its irascible element cleaves to love and turns away from hate, and the rational element lives with God through prayer and spiritual contemplation,"[94] and he describes an unhealthy state by saying "[a]ll passionate thoughts either excite the concupiscible, disturb the irascible, or darken the rational element of the soul."[95] Combating the vices will have to be done on all three fronts. "Almsgiving heals the irascible part of the soul; fasting extinguishes the concupiscible part, and prayer purifies the mind and prepares it for the contemplation of reality."[96]

These three faculties are symbiotic: they live together and operate together in a person. Therefore the ascetical discipline is practiced upon each of the three, and all of the three. The ascetical tradition finds a connection between purity of heart and clarity of mind. This accounts for the fact that the most intelligent person is not always the most virtuous person, and the person who owns the most books is not always the freest from the vices. Only when the concupiscible and irascible faculties are healthy will the intellective faculty function as it should: the purifying activity of *askesis* will have an effect upon our capacity to see the truth. We will know more truth the less we sin. The light by which Mrs. Murphy sees the world after a lifetime of liturgical asceticism may be clearer because her eye is not cloudy. The concupiscible element, rightly exercised, is no more sinful than the exercise of the intellective or irascible faculties. Our appetites have been given us by God, and what will fulfill those appetites has also been given us by God. This is a clear repudiation of dualism. It is also a repudiation of a base and popular misunder-

94. Maximus the Confessor, *Four Hundred Chapters on Love,* 4.15.
95. Ibid., 3.20.
96. Ibid., 1.79.

standing that believes a concupiscible faculty turned astray is worse than an irascible faculty turned unjust, or an intellectual faculty turned dark. The hierarchy of moral evils is backward in this puritanical corruption. The ascetical tradition in fact thinks that distortions of the intellectual capacity (e.g., pride, vainglory) and of the irascible capacity (e.g., anger, envy) are more damnable than those of the concupiscible capacity (e.g., lust, drunkenness). This is probably why, speculates Maximus, Jesus gave the more potent cure to sins of irascibility. "It happens that the passions of the irascible part of the soul are harder to combat than those of the concupiscible. Thus it is that a better remedy for it was given by the Lord: the commandment of love."[97] The passions are equal opportunity corrupters. They do not only work upon our corporeality, but also pervert our reasoning and our capacity to be moved in feeling.

How the passions are to be battled on all three of these fronts will be the subject of the next chapter, so let us conclude by considering the effect of the passions on man and woman's liturgical vocation.

Anthropos is a microcosm. Microcosm means a "small world," but not in the sense of a fractionated part of the whole (a kitchen is not the microcosm of a house), rather in the sense that everything found in the larger order can be found in the smaller order (a dollhouse is a microcosm of a house). In men and women, all that makes up the cosmos on its largest scale, namely, matter and spirit, can be found on a smaller scale. The reason why *anthropos*—of all beings in the universe—is called microcosm is because the human being is equipped for both sense perception and intellectual vision. Theodoros writes that Adam could have apprehended and enjoyed both sensory things and intelligible things without harm, since "the first man … was as able to commune with intelligible things through the intellect, as he was

97. Ibid., 1.66.

with sensory things through the senses."[98] No other creature is enrolled as citizen in both realms, and it is this dual citizenship that is humanity's ontological potential for priesthood. Men and women possess full corporeality and full spirituality by their very ontological makeup, participating in both the visible and invisible realms of the cosmos. There is a material world to be celebrated: the angels know it, but cannot experience it; the animals experience it, but cannot know its *logoi* (signs of the *Logos* in created things). Only man and woman can praise God for a world that they take in through the senses and wonder at by their intellect. "Within the visible world, man is as it were a second world" says Ilias the Presbyter, and "without man and thought both the sensible and the intelligible worlds would be inarticulate."[99] By two different potentials, *anthropos* is in communion with the angel and the angleworm.

Being created in the image of the *Logos,* human beings are capable of knowing the *logoi* in material things (which is why Adam could name things—he could call things as they really are). Symeon the New Theologian pictures human beings as created to see by two suns, two lights, two eyes, and only when they are both in operation are we fully human.

> Know then that you are double
> And that you possess two eyes,
> The sensible and the spiritual.
> Since there are also two suns
> There is also a double light,
> Sensible and spiritual,
> And if you see them, you will be the man
> As you were created in the beginning to be.[100]

98. Theodoros the Great Ascetic, "Theoretikon," *The Philokalia,* 2.44.

99. Ilias the Presbyter, "Gnomic Anthology IV," *The Philokalia,* 3.61. For a treatment involving Scholastic epistemology, see Fagerberg, "Cosmological Liturgy and a Sensible Priesthood," *The New Blackfriars* 82, no. 960 (February 2001): 76–87.

100. Symeon the New Theologian, *Hymns of Divine Love* (Denville, N.J.: Dimension Books, 1976), 123.

Had *anthropos* remained liturgical priest, man and woman would have mediated God's blessings to matter, and mediated the glory of material creation into the celestial song of praise. This world would have been paradise, and the starting place for *anthropos* to ascend to heaven, body and soul. Symeon continues:

> And what kind of life they would have lived, being immortal and incorrupt, strangers to sin, sorrows, cares, and difficult necessities! And how, prospering in the keeping of the commandments and the good ordering of the dispositions of the heart, in time they would have ascended into the most perfect glory, and being changed, would have drawn near to God; and the soul of each one would have become light-bearing by reason of the illuminations which would have been poured out upon it from the Divinity! And this sensuous and crudely material body would have become as it were immaterial and spiritual, above all senses; and the joy and rejoicing with which we then would have been filled by fellowship one with the other, in truth would have been unutterable and beyond human thought.[101]

Bodies are good. Senses are good. Matter is good. Asceticism has nothing to do with dualism. But we are blind in one eye and we don't see the world so well any more, and we don't look so good ourselves, either. Failing to offer the holy oblation to God, *anthropos* doesn't act naturally, that is, according to his created nature. It is not unnatural for an animal to see only by the sensible sun; it is not unnatural for an angel to see only by the spiritual sun; but for *anthropos* to forfeit sight under either sun is to be corrupted. In its corrupted state, our structure as microcosm makes us homesick for our original destiny (our pre-destination).

The intelligibility of the concept of liturgical asceticism depends upon the assumption that man and woman were created to be liturgists who would delight God by delighting in God's works, seeing the cosmos by two suns. God's joy would be increased by the delight that *anthropos* feels for the world, feels from the world. But, alas, the passions have disrupted our dox-

101. Symeon the New Theologian, *The First Created Man* (Platina, Calif.: St. Herman of Alaska Brotherhood, 1994), 88.

ology, our innocence is gone, and to be restored to our anthropological potential requires asceticism. From the beginning, man and woman were called to be *homo adorans,* which is how Schmemann defines the human person:

> The unique position of man in the universe is that he alone is to bless God for the food and life he receives from Him. He alone is to respond to God's blessing with his blessing.... All rational, spiritual and other qualities of man, distinguishing him from other creatures, have their focus and ultimate fulfillment in this capacity to bless God, to know, so to speak, the meaning of the thirst and hunger that constitutes his life. "*Homo sapiens,*" "*homo faber*" ... yes, but, first of all, "*homo adorans.*" The first, the basic definition of man is that he is the priest.[102]

As microcosm, indeed, *because* microcosm, man and woman should have ordered their knowledge of a genuine uni-verse of matter and spirit together. Upon perceiving the beauty of creatures, *anthropos* should have referred that beauty to its source, having what Theodoros called "a twofold reason for marveling at the Creator. They should not have attached themselves to sensory things and lost themselves in wonder at them alone neglecting the Creator of intelligible beauty."[103] Failing to refer finite goods (truth, beauty, and goodness) to the Eternal One (who is True, Beautiful, and Good) is to live in a nonsacramental state. It is to treat the world as an end in itself, instead of as a means to our ultimate end in God. Augustine said our perversion leads us to use what we should enjoy, and enjoy what we should use. The Fall darkened the spiritual light of our eyes so we no longer see the world sacramentally and we have forfeited our liturgical responsibility as royal priest. To seek to live independently of God is death, and Symeon the New Theologian observes that since *anthropos* is both spirit and body, death has affected both spirit and body, and *anthropos* is in need of both spiritual and bodily resurrection.

102. Schmemann, *For the Life of the World,* 15.

103. Theodoros the Great Ascetic, "Theoretikon," *The Philokalia,* 2.44.

> One should know that since a man has a body and a soul, therefore he has two deaths also: one, the death of the soul, and the other, the death of the body. Likewise, there are also two immortalities, one of the soul and one of the body, even though both of them are in one man, for the soul and the body are one man. Thus, in soul Adam died immediately, as soon as he had tasted; and later, after nine hundred and thirty years, he died also in body. For, as the death of the body is the separation from it of the soul, so the death of the soul is the separation from it of the Holy Spirit.... Later, for this reason, the whole human race also became such as our forefather Adam became through the fall—mortal, that is, both in soul and body. Man such as God had created him no longer existed in the world.[104]

Sin has a triple consequence that affects the relationship of *anthropos* to what lies below, within, and above: sovereignty over creation below was forfeited by man and woman losing dominion within themselves for having rebelled against God above. The repair of this disordered love therefore requires a discipline (an *askesis*) which leads to dispassion (*apatheia*) which can be considered a first resurrection. The second resurrection, of the body, will have to wait for the general judgment, but if asceticism is possible it is because baptism has already initiated a believer into the paschal mystery of Christ to share in his Resurrection. When this happens, a Christian can progress from the image of God to the likeness of God, and *anthropos* can again stand aright, stand with fear and attend, and so offer the holy oblation in peace.

104. Symeon the New Theologian, *The First Created Man,* 45.

3 THE CURE
Askesis

We have been at pains to distinguish liturgical asceticism from dualism, and this will become all the more important in this chapter as we seek to understand the purpose of the ascetical exercises. Some of the more muscular and heroic exploits of the early monastics could easily be misunderstood as a loathing of the material body by the modern secularist who is all too eager to indulge the body and is all too unacquainted with asceticism in general and liturgical asceticism in particular. Stoicism, or Manichaeism, or other philosophical systems can produce a behavior similar in appearance to liturgical asceticism, but radically different in fact. Christianity transformed ancient ascetical practices in a way analogous to the transformation Christianity effected upon ancient philosophical teachings. Driscoll observes that Christ himself remains Christianity's distinctive core, which distinguishes Christianity from all other wisdoms. "Philosophy's contribution has become a virtually inextricable part of the Christian monastic heritage. Evagrius himself is witness, however, to how at base this monastic heritage has a distinctive Christian face which distinguishes it from all other traditions of spiritual exercises, from all other cultural manifestations of monasticism."[1] Our purpose in this chapter will not be to give a complete record of actual and recommended ascetical practices; the reader can find that elsewhere. We have not set out to describe what the ascetics do, or how, but rather *why* they do it. Our purpose is apologetic, an attempt to understand the purpose of asceticism itself, and to argue that such a purpose must be observed from within the framework of life in Christ's Church, that is, liturgical life. In Louth's words, "Ascetical theology is about how we come to know God, it is not about some kind of spiritual technique; to come to know God is a matter of experience, not speculation; for a Christian to come to know God is to respond to a God who has made himself known."[2]

When the ascetical masters spoke of hating the world, they were speaking a different language game than the dualist. The dualist meant he was disgusted with the world; the Christian ascetic meant he hated any obstacle that enslaved the spirit, including an excessive attachment to the world or to himself. Pekar claims the phrase "hate the world" is a Semitic expression that means "to love less,"[3] which means an attitude to adopt when the world is ranked above God. Paul Evdokimov summarizes: "Thus, to hate means to oppose an obstacle, an excessive attachment to life here below or a fear of death—all of which makes the spirit captive."[4] The passions are disordered love, love that lacks appropriate hierarchy. This disorder is not only disastrous, it is idolatrous for loving something with the love that should be reserved for God alone. To be righteous, the lover must come to love the right object with the right measure. That means, for all of us, loving some things less than we love them now, and loving God more than we love him now. The ascetical discipline is train-

1. Driscoll, *Evagrius Ponticus: Ad Monachos*, 212.
2. Louth, *Maximus the Confessor*, 33.
3. Pekar, *The Perfect Christian*, 96.
4. Evdokimov, *Ages of the Spiritual Life*, 204

ing for love, correctly oriented and properly intense. This means that the negative act of hating the world is but the flip side of the positive act of loving God more. To choose A is to not choose B; turning away is constitutive of turning toward; "you cannot look to heaven and to earth at the same time,"[5] says John Climacus. If the word *hate* expresses a note of opposition, it is in the sense of contrasting two opposites: to look upward is the simultaneous opposite of looking downward, and to look Godward is to simultaneously turn away from the passions. One cannot look passionately at the world and lovingly at God at the same time because, John Kronstadt explains, "As the soul is single, it cannot love two opposite objects."[6] We have spoken of the liturgical paradox which affirms that although the world is good, it is not man and woman's final good. Creation does not contain its own end, and to treat creation as if it does changes the world into the "world" about which Scripture warns us. When this happens, nothing in the world has changed, but everything about the world is different for us. Things are not wrong, but we have wronged things by loving them in the wrong measure.

The remedy for this state of affairs is not more information, the remedy is therapeutic asceticism. This implies that the task of liturgical renewal is not primarily gnostic, done with study, but ascetic, done in the heart. It is reparative of our original state, as Evdokimov notes: "Asceticism undoes the act by which Adam ceased to be fully himself, in wishing to belong only to himself and in refusing to go beyond himself in God. It takes up again the vocation of Adam and pursues a conformity to the *obedient Christ*.... The goal aimed at by the ascetics was a state anterior to fallen nature.... They sought to reach the unsullied structure of the self 'made in the image of God.'"[7] The world's sacramentality will not be restored simply by an act of cognition, it will require a

5. John Climacus, Step 3, "On Exile," *The Ladder of Divine Ascent*, 88.
6. John of Kronstadt, *My Life in Christ*, 306.
7. Evdokimov, *Ages of the Spiritual Life*, 121.

liturgical asceticism, because our capacity to receive matter sacramentally requires a pure heart. The monk left the world to attend to the *logismoi* and thus reconnoiter the spiritual landscape in which the demons tempt him, but it was not freedom from matter the monk sought, it was freedom to pray in the full communion made possible now by Christ's Incarnation. The kenosis of God is the basis of liturgical asceticism. Christian liturgical asceticism could not have existed before the Incarnation any more than iconography—and for the same reason. In the words of Evagrius, "If Moses, when he attempted to draw near the burning bush, was prohibited until he should remove the shoes from his feet, how should you not free yourself of every thought that is colored by passion seeing that you wish to see One who is beyond every thought and perception?"[8] And again, "A man in chains cannot run. Nor can the mind that is enslaved to passion see the place of spiritual prayer. It is dragged along and tossed by these passion-filled thoughts and cannot stand firm and tranquil."[9]

Liturgical asceticism is being unshackled from the passions so one can be made swift at prayer, and this reveals the true, positive character of *askesis*. Since it is the property of an appetite to desire an object, a human being's concupiscible faculty must attach itself to something; therefore progress toward God cannot be accomplished by simply trying to obstruct the faculty of desire. It must be fastened onto a higher object. Maximus is crystalline on the matter. "Unless the mind finds something better than [the passions] to which it can transfer its desire, it will not be completely persuaded to disdain them."[10] John of the Cross casts this in terms of appetites.

We have a figure of this in Exodus where we read that God did not give the children of Israel the heavenly manna until they exhausted the flour brought from Egypt. The meaning here is that first a total renunciation

8. Evagrius, *Chapters On Prayer,* no. 4.
9. Ibid., no. 71.
10. Maximus the Confessor, *The Four Hundred Chapters on Love,* 3.64.

is needed, for this bread of angels is disagreeable to the palate of anyone who wants to taste human food.... Oh, if spiritual persons knew how much spiritual good and abundance they lose by not attempting to raise their appetites above childish things, and if they knew to what extent, by not desiring the taste of these trifles, they would discover in this simple spiritual food the savor of all things.[11]

Emptying the plate of sand may appear to be negative, but it is for the positive purpose of filling the plate with bread. Olivier Clement defines *askesis* as "learning to transform our vital energy into love,"[12] and says its purpose is "to divest oneself of surplus weight, of spiritual fat. It is to dissolve in the waters of baptism, in the water of tears, all the hardness of the heart, so that it may become an antenna of infinite sensitivity, infinitely vulnerable to the beauty of the world and to the sufferings of human beings, and to God who is Love, who has conquered by the wood of the cross."[13] In fact, if this positive asceticism does not accompany negative, disciplinary asceticism, the latter is of no use. The reason for the athlete's drills on the field is readiness to run the race; the reason for the ascetic's drills is to be prepared for God's approach. God initiates, God knocks, God approaches, and the believer keeps himself in readiness for it, so the masters claimed the prodigal son was the model of asceticism when he came to himself and said, "I will get up and go to my father." Such is precisely the life-giving result of asceticism. Getting up from the mud of the pigpen is hardly an act of self-loathing, it is an act of coming to one's senses. Whatever "negative" aspect there is to asceticism is only because "[a]sceticism is an apophatic aspect of presence, witnessing to the sufficiency of God and to the fullness of the Center."[14]

11. John of the Cross, *The Ascent of Mt. Carmel,* 1.5.3 (Mahwah, N.J.: Paulist Press, 1987), 70.

12. Clement, *The Roots of Christian Mysticism,* 126.

13. Ibid., 131.

14. Bruno Barnhart, "A Monastic Compass," in *Following the Star from the East: Essays in Honour of Archimandrite Boniface Luykx,* edited by Andriy Chirovsky (Ottawa,

Ascetical practices can be treated in many contexts, and as a means to many ends, as we have already acknowledged. For example, because self-discipline is prerequisite to any human development and maturity, there is a sort of *natural asceticism* which children must learn in order to grow up with self-control and integrity, and achieve a kind of *moral asceticism,* which is the courage to do the right thing. Theophan the Recluse does not overlook this fact in his manual on spiritual transformation, and his opening chapters include practical comments on ordinary developmental stages in children concerning food and sleep and fidgetiness. But this self-control is only preliminary to *spiritual asceticism,* which has the goal of raising up our spiritual consciousness and activity of life. "That is, we must show: the essential pull of the ascetically laboring spirit towards God."[15] Such self-control is required to enter into the heart and discover what had previously been hidden by a multitude of frantic distractions, namely, how to submit to God. When grace perfects human nature, then the natural, moral, and spiritual asceticism can be raised to the *liturgical ascetical* act of longing for God. "Yearning for God is the goal. But at first, it is only in intention, sought for. It should be made real, alive, like a natural pull that is sweet, earnest, and uncontrollable. Only this kind of pull can show that we are in our place, that God accepts us, that we are going to Him."[16] All the ascetical fathers indicate that the initial steps may be forced, and may at first seem bitter, but they soon become natural and sweet.

Since human beings were created as *homo viator*—beings in process, beings on the way, created to grow from image of God to likeness of God—it is possible to speculate that even our prelapsarian hunger for God would have required a kind of *aske-*

Ontario, Canada: St. Paul University and Sheptytsky Institute of Eastern Christian Studies, 1992), 95.

15. Theophan the Recluse, *The Path to Salvation: A Manual of Spiritual Transformation* (Forestville, Calif.: St. Herman of Alaska Brotherhood, 1996), 310.

16. Ibid., 13.

sis to bring it to final fruition. We now experience asceticism primarily as a therapeutic struggle against sin, so we are ignorant of what humanity's asceticism would have looked had Adam and Eve not sinned, just like we are ignorant of what biological death would have looked like had there been no sin. God's economy of salvation had to take sin into account when mankind was barely out of the starting gate, but had Adam and Eve's journey from the Garden of Eden to the eternal Jerusalem remained on track, it seems possible to construe it as an ascetical labor. Ephrem of Syria considers them to have still been living on the lower mountain slopes of Paradise when they were expelled, and sees the Tree of Knowledge "as a boundary to the inner region of Paradise," serving "as a sanctuary curtain, veiling the Holy of Holies from sight."[17] The Tree of Life was hidden from their sight for two reasons, explains Sebastian Brock in his introduction to Ephrem's *Hymns on Paradise*. First, God hid the Tree of Life behind the Tree of Knowledge so that the former's beauty might be reserved as a reward for keeping the commandment of obedience; and second, so its surpassing beauty might not make the temptation to eat the forbidden fruit irresistible. But will humankind, then, ever see this Tree of Life? Ephrem's *Hymn on Virginity* describes the Tree's reaction and resourcefulness.

> Greatly saddened was the Tree of Life
> When it beheld Adam stolen away from it;
> It sank down into the virgin ground and was hidden
> —to burst forth and reappear on Golgotha;
> Humanity, like birds that are chased,
> Took refuge in it
> So that it might return them to their proper home.
> The chaser was chased way, while the doves
> That had been chased
> Now hop with joy in Paradise.[18]

17. Ephrem the Syrian, *Hymns on Paradise* (Crestwood, N.Y.: St. Vladimir's Seminary Press, 1990), 60.

18. Ephrem the Syrian, *The Hymns on Virginity and On the Symbols of the Lord*, 16.10

Man and woman had an invitation to journey further up the mountain to more complete union with God, and this invitation has not been retracted by God even when humankind forsook it. However, its accomplishment required a new economy.

Liturgical asceticism is traversing the path of our destruction in reverse. The first Adam and Eve sinned by disobedience; therefore the trait required of the second Adam will be radical, free obedience, done for the sake of love of God. Humanity abandoned its designated path to life in an act of deadly disobedience; therefore the recapitulation of creation will require an act of obedience even to the point of death. The cross stands between our present state and our resurrected glory, and liturgical asceticism corroborates the death of Christ in our own bodies by taming those passions that accompany life-in-the-body so that we may notarize with our hope that death has not been victorious. Instead, death has been made a portal to the new age, if grasped in a radical act of faith.

By suggesting here that even Adam and Eve knew ascetical obligations, we are seeking to present asceticism as fundamentally positive, even though our asceticism no longer looks like theirs because ours is done by a sinner, and carries with it an element of suffering that comes from the self-opposition found in a nature divided against itself. Although the image of God was obscured, it was not obliterated, therefore even in exile from the Garden of Eden we still thirst for holiness. Evdokimov notes that "[a]s every copy is attracted to its original, man as an image aspires to go beyond himself in order to cast himself into God and to find there the appeasement of his longing. Holiness is nothing else but an unquenchable thirst, an intensity of desire for God. By its light the asceticism of spiritual attention learns the inestimable art of seeing everything as an image of God."[19] This thirst

(New York: Paulist Press, 1989), 332. This translation is taken from Sebastian Brock's introduction to *Hymns on Paradise* (Crestwood, N.Y.: St. Vladimir's Seminary Press, 1990), 60–61.

19. Evdokimov, *Ages of the Spiritual Life*, 157.

for God is still present in fallen man and woman, if confused and lessened, and this thirst is the birth of asceticism. In the case of a fallen nature—in contrast to the nature we were created with—adhering to God additionally requires opposing the world, and this begins with opposing ourselves. Symeon the New Theologian bids us remember "that 'the kingdom of heaven is entered forcibly, and those who force themselves take possession of it' (Mt 11:12); ... apply force to yourself."[20] Force must be used to overcome something that stands as an obstacle between oneself and a goal. If salvation and beatitude are our goal, what stands in our way? What obstacle prevents us from attaining happiness? What gates must be forced with ascetical leverage, what locks smashed by fasting, what chains broken by prayer? What must be violently overcome? Certainly not God, who is all love. Rather, ourselves. "[I]t is by doing violence to yourself that you shall enter the kingdom of heaven."[21] "It is good that a man discipline his whole self for God's sake. As it is written, 'The kingdom of heaven suffereth violence, and the violent take it by storm' (Matt. 11:12)."[22]

Some radical thing must be done to bring us back to our senses and cause us to realize that the sensible world is not our final good. Then we can enjoy this material world with the liberty that kings and queens should have when they rule their kingdom, and their kingdom does not rule them. Theophan concludes:

> The spirit hates sin, but the flesh and the soul are sympathetic to it and cling to it because they are clothed in passions. Goodness or the will of God are beloved by the spirit, but the body and soul are not sympathetic to it, are repulsed by it, or if not that, do not know how to do it. Therefore one who has resolved according to his zeal to be faithful to his promise, now that he has realized the necessity, has also resolved to endure in doing good and to attach himself to some good work.... He

20. Symeon the New Theologian, "Practical and Theological Texts," *The Philokalia*, 4.55.

21. Pachomius, *The Pachomian Koinonia: Vol. 1, The Life of Saint Pachomius and His Disciples* (Kalamazoo, Mich.: Cistercian Publications, 1980), 32.

22. Systematic Sayings, 7.43.

should oppose the demands of his body and soul and, denying them, force himself to do the opposite. Because the body and soul do not leave his personality but rather comprise it, this is the same as opposing oneself in the bad and forcing oneself to the good. *Self-opposition and self-forcing*—these are the two aspects of zeal born in the soul, forming as it were the beginning of asceticism.[23]

This involves a risk of misperception. Since the ascetical enterprise involves opposing oneself there is a risk at the beginning of confusing which voice one is hearing: is it that of the original man who hates sin, or the fallen man who is sympathetic to the passions? Is the self being forced too far (which will result in discouragement and abandonment of the ascetical life), or is the self not being forced far enough (which will produce no progress and result in a smug self-satisfaction)? The difficulty of maintaining the right ascetical tension was always a concern.

A hunter happened to come by and saw Antony talking in a relaxed way with the brothers, and he was shocked. The hermit wanted to show him how we should sometimes be less austere for the sake of the brothers, and said to him, "Put an arrow in your bow, and draw it." He did so, and Antony said, "Draw it further" and he drew it further. He said again, "Draw it yet further," and he drew it some more. Then the hunter said to him, "If I draw it too far, the bow will snap." Antony answered, "So it is with God's work. If we always go to excess, the brothers quickly become exhausted. It is sometimes best not to be rigid."[24]

The *askesis* is rendered useless if we do not hit the right note, and the ascetic is worse off than when he began. "Abba Antony said: 'Some wear out their bodies by fasting; but because they have no discretion, it puts them further away from God.'"[25] A young ascetic should be apprenticed to a spiritual father who can distinguish the end from the means, the tactics from the strategic goal, the *scopos* from the *telos*. This was Abba Moses' message to John Cassian.

Cassian was a monk in Bethlehem, but around 385 he trav-

23. Theophan the Recluse, *The Path to Salvation*, 209.

24. Systematic Sayings, 10.2.

25. Systematic Sayings, 10.1.

eled to Egypt, where he remained almost fifteen years, eventually becoming a disciple of Evagrius. From there, Cassian brought the wisdom of the Egyptian desert back to Europe. He had seen the lives of the Desert Fathers and wrote a record of their discipline in the *Institutes;* he had interviewed the Desert Fathers, and recorded these interviews in the *Conferences*. One is a conference with Abba Moses, who explains the monk's proximate and distal goals to Cassian. "All the arts and disciplines have a certain scopos or goal, and a telos, which is the end that is proper to them, on which the lover of any art sets his gaze and for which he calmly and gladly endures every labor and danger and expense."[26] Abba Moses gives three examples: first, farmers who suffer heat and frost when plowing, and who pull brambles and weeds from their land; second, merchants who brave storms when they transport their goods across the sea; third, soldiers who think nothing of far journeys, hardships, and risking their lives in battle. The farmer has the immediate goal of fertile crops, the merchant of making a good sale, and the soldier of power and place. But in addition to the immediate scopos, each of them has an ultimate *telos,* as well. The farmer wishes to live well, the merchant to become rich, and the soldier to attain glory. The two goals are tightly interrelated because the ultimate goal is the reason for undergoing the labor, and the labor is a necessary means to attain the ultimate goal. Then Abba Moses applies this to the monastic life:

> Our profession also has a scopos proper to itself and its own end, on behalf of which we tirelessly and even gladly expend all our efforts. For its sake the hunger of fasting does not weary us, the exhaustion of keeping vigil delights us, and the continual reading of and meditating on Scripture does not sate us. Even the unceasing labor, the being stripped and deprived of everything and, too, the horror of this vast solitude do not deter us.... The end of our profession, as we have said, is the kingdom of God or the kingdom of heaven; but the goal or scopos is purity of heart, without which it is impossible for anyone to reach that end.

26. John Cassian, *Conferences,* 1.2.1.

Fixing our gaze on this goal, then, as on a definite mark, we shall take the most direct route.[27]

Abba Moses says that he and his companions are only following the teaching of St. Paul when the apostle told believers "[h]aving your reward, indeed, in holiness, but your end in eternal life" (Romans 6:22). The monks understand purity of heart to be the scopos. "It is as if [Paul] had said in other words: Having your scopos, indeed, in purity of heart, but your end in eternal life.... Whatever therefore can direct us to this scopos, which is purity of heart, is to be pursued with all our strength, but whatever deters us from this is to be avoided as dangerous and harmful."[28]

It would be counterproductive if one's asceticism produced a rigid discipline that made one too stiff to bend in charitable hospitality. That is true. But it may require an ascetical discipline to make a stiff neck flexible enough to bow in humility. *Agape* and *askesis* work hand in hand, as Cassian learned when he inquired why a certain old man in Egypt broke his fast when he received guests. "Fasting is always possible," the monk replied, "but I cannot keep you here for ever. Fasting is useful and necessary, but we can choose to fast or not fast. God's law demands from us perfect love. I receive Christ when I receive you, so I must do all I can to show you love. When I have said goodbye to you, I can take up my rule of fasting again."[29]

The ascetic's immediate goal of overcoming the passions is but a means to the ultimate end, which is eternal life or beatitude. Or, we might say, the immediate goal of overcoming the passions is so that one can be gripped by the attraction of beatitude. So long as one is ruled by the passions, the good and true and beautiful things of God have no attraction. A magnet attracts steel, and it is as if the ascetic strives to become steelier in order that Christ would exert a greater attraction upon him. It is not Christ's love that asceticism tries to alter, it is our own capacity

27. Ibid., 1.2.3.

28. Ibid., 1.5.2.

29. Systematic Sayings, 13.2.

to find Christ's love attractive that asceticism tries to improve. Liturgical asceticism is the synergistic response to grace's presence, and the response is necessary for God's love to get a grip on us. The final purpose of liturgical asceticism, then, is not to improve our personality, or contribute to social harmony, or attain personal goals by strategic sacrifice. Grace is the engine of liturgical asceticism, and "[g]race aims above all at the reconstruction in us of the image of God (*imago Dei*), of our initial form, tending toward God, as a copy of the Original."[30] Asceticism is the process of making the icon more accurate to the prototype. Asceticism recreates our appetite for God by disciplining our appetites for the world. As a carpenter has plans in his mind before he raises his hammer, so God has an Idea of all things before the universe began, and *anthropos* must oppose the corruption of his nature in order to become the liturgical being as thought by God. If, as Christian theology insists, evil is not real but the negation of being, then the passions do not make up the real person, they are the negation of a person's full and final being. To live subject to the passions is to be unnatural and less real; it is asceticism that builds up reality. The purpose of asceticism is not to produce a vacuum—for there is no life in a vacuum—it is to foster the gift of eternal life by preparing purified hearts for it.

This is why the passions cannot be overcome by only throttling the vices; the virtues must be nourished. A positive force of life must crack through packed earth. Olivier Clement says,

> Asceticism requires discernment. To move from the blessings of this life, which are fundamentally good, to a radical demand to go beyond them, we must first have become aware of a higher perfection, and have received a pledge of God's "sweetness" (even if later he has to withdraw it and ask us to go through the desert places). Lacking the discernment, ascesis is apt to be self-interested or Pharisaical, in danger of withering purposelessly between earth and heaven.[31]

30. Evdokimov, *Ages of the Spiritual Life*, 192.
31. Clement, *The Roots of Christian Mysticism*, 140.

Asceticism ultimately raises our minds and our appetites to higher things. Ascetical theology is usually described negatively as "cutting off the passions," but this is only in service to something more. "Maximus does not play down this negative side," says Louth, "but he supplements it with a positive emphasis on the importance of deeper and purer love. 'A pure soul is one freed from the passions'—there is the negative emphasis, but there follows—'and constantly delighted by divine love.'"[32] If a glass was filled with oil and one wished to remove that oil, one way to do it would be to pour in water, which, being heavier, would sink to the bottom and raise the oil until it spilled over the sides and ran off. Asceticism is the weight of love undermining the passions so that they run off.

Gregory of Nyssa asks us to imagine the power of asceticism by a different liquid illustration. Consider how unserviceable water is when it is dispersed into separate channels. "So long as it flows this way it will be entirely useless for the cultivation of the soil. Its waters are spread out too much; each single channel is small and meagre, and the water, because of this, hardly moves."[33] But if those diffused channels could be collected into a single stream we could have "a full and compact waterflow" which would be useful for the needs of life. This is what it is like with the human mind.

> If it spreads itself out in all directions, constantly flowing out and dispersing to whatever pleases the senses, it will never have any notable force in its progress towards the true Good. But now recall the mind from all sides, and make it collect itself, so that it may begin to operate in that function which is preferably connatural to it, without scattering and wasting itself: then the mind will find no obstacle in its rise to heaven and in its grasp of the true meaning of reality.
>
> Often water contained in a pipe bursts upwards because of the force of the pressure, and it does this against its natural downward motion because it has nowhere else to flow. So too is it with the mind of man.

32. Louth, *Maximus the Confessor*, 40.
33. Gregory of Nyssa, *From Glory to Glory*, 103.

If it is confined on all sides by the water-tight pipe of chastity, if it has no other outlet, it will be raised up by the very tendency of its motion towards a love of higher things.[34]

That this is not dualism is proven by the fact that this asceticism uses the body; the dualist has no use for the body. Progress in liturgical asceticism depends upon the *unity* between soul and body, and supposes that constraints imposed upon the body can raise the mind to God.

The final stage replaces the passions with new, weightier, higher desires. "To avert passions by memories of virtues is easier and also more beautiful than to conquer them in battle."[35] As anyone who has fallen in love knows, love makes sacrifice not only easier, but a joy. And asceticism is an act of love. Only this premise will crack our old prejudices about Christian asceticism being masochism, or hatred of the world, or disgust with one's body, or just for monks, or only expressed by celibacy, or beating one's head against the wall during Lent because it feels good to stop at Easter. Asceticism is what is required in order to love better.

Fr. Karl Rahner, S.J., wrote an insightful essay entitled "Reflections on the Theology of Renunciation." Granted, he is here commenting on a particular form of renunciation—that commended by the Evangelical Counsels and expressed as a permanent form of life—but he thinks this vowed state of life is simply the perfection of a love incumbent on all the baptized: "Christian perfection consists simply and solely in the perfection of the love which is given us in Christ by the Spirit of God who is communicated to us in justification and sanctification."[36] All asceticism in general, and evangelical renunciation in particular, is based upon God's supernatural love that takes hold of human persons and their world "and bursts them wide open, opening them out

34. Ibid.

35. Isaac of Nineveh, *On Ascetical Life* (6.17), 109.

36. Karl Rahner, S.J., "Reflections on the Theology of Renunciation," *Theological Investigations* (New York: Crossroad, 1982), 3.47.

into the life of God himself, a life which has already arrived even though it is still hidden in faith."[37] Therefore this renunciation is of a supernatural order, and cannot be fitted into natural categories.

> Renunciation in the "supernatural order" ... cannot be adequately explained (and in its properly Christian nature cannot be explained at all) from the standpoint of a purely natural ethics. It is not in its profoundest nature a datum or demand of the "*lex naturalis*." In other words, it cannot in its proper essence be derived as an exigency of or a training in the harmony of human nature. It cannot be explained as a "tactical offensive measure" against concupiscence.... It may even be doubted whether in *this* respect—as measured by the "normal" person—renunciation is the "better" means for attaining the harmony of the natural desires under the command of the spirit. Hence it is no accident ... that renunciation (e.g. in celibacy) did not exist before Christ, but is clearly deduced in the New Testament from the saving situation present only once Christ had appeared, and that, as imitation of Christ, it presupposes that the Lord whom we are to follow has appeared.[38]

It may seem tautological to say that Christian asceticism is not possible without Christ, but that tautology is precisely the key to our definition of liturgical asceticism. Deification was offered to *anthropos* when the paschal mystery was accomplished and extended to the Church. Liturgical asceticism depends upon the mysteries of Christ becoming the mysteries of the Church; liturgical asceticism is sacramental in nature. The cross was the price of God's kenotic movement, and bearing the cross in ourselves is the cost of our ascensional response.

Liturgy begins with the dawning of the eighth day, and in this age certain laws of the old order have been altered. For example, the law of Moses was right in prohibiting the writing of icons, but after the Incarnation this changed: the uncircumscribable one became circumscribed and iconography was possible. Similarly, the Incarnation has changed the case of celibacy. The law of

37. Ibid., 48.
38. Ibid., 49–50.

Moses was right in discouraging celibacy based upon the orders of creation, but after the eighth day this changed. (Liturgical celibacy is different from other unmarried states, whether personal, social, or spiritual.) Although the term *monachos,* from which "monk" derives, does not appear in the Septuagint, its meaning is parallel to the word *lebaddo,* which occurs in Genesis 2:18: "It is not good for man to be alone." (Some later manuscripts do, in fact, use *monachos* to translate *lebaddo.*) They both convey the idea of one, alone, single, being the only one. Genesis tells us how the situation of "the man" as *lebaddo* is remedied.

> [B]y the subsequent creation of woman. He is alone, single in the sense of not yet married, and this is perceived by God to be an unfortunate condition. This principle, that "it is not good for man to be alone," reflects the common view of the Old Testament and Judaism that denies positive meaning to celibacy, voluntary or otherwise. It is a view that, in fact, is contradicted by Paul in 1 Cor 7:1, one of the two principal New Testament texts used to defend or inspire Christian celibacy.[39]

The only way to understand Christian celibacy is in an eschatological light. If the eighth day has not dawned, then Christian celibacy is false; if Christian celibacy is true, it is because the eighth day has truly dawned. This is the way to understand Athanasius's argument that Christianity is the true religion because the Church has more virgins than the pagan religions have.

To make this point, Rahner applies a distinction commonly made in Western Scholasticism. Goods that are ordered to an end were called *bonum utile,* and goods that contain their own justification were called *bonum honestum.* The latter type are not "good for" something; they are simply good. Counted among the goods classified as *bonum honestum* are "the marital union, and the freedom of development of human existence by being able to decide for oneself about the material presuppositions and auton-

39. *RB 1980: The Rule of St. Benedict in Latin and English with Notes,* edited by Timothy Fry, O.S.B., Appendix I, "Monastic Terminology: Monk, Cenobite, Nun" (Collegeville, Md.: Liturgical Press, 1981), 305–6.

omy of one's existence (i.e. riches and independence)."[40] It would miss the point altogether to treat marriage as a *bonum utile* and inquire, "What is it good for?" Such a question would confuse a true good with a utilitarian good. Now, one ought never renounce a higher good for a lower one. It would be "senseless" and "ethically perverse" to give up these values since "a positive value can be sacrificed only for the sake of a higher value."[41] Freedom, marriage, autonomy are good, they are good in themselves, they are the highest natural goods, they are *bonum honestum,* and "in a purely natural order there would therefore be no other values for the sake of which they could be sacrificed."[42] Yet freedom, marriage, and autonomy are exactly the goods the monk renounces! The good of freedom is renounced by vowing stability and conversion of life, the good of marriage by vowing celibacy, and the good of autonomy by vowing obedience.[43] If Christian renunciation is not a blatant case of Manichaeism, or if it is not an ethically perverse act of exchanging higher goods for lower ones, or if it is not a denial of the natural and human goods of creation, then a new state of affairs must have come to pass which presents to *anthropos* a good higher than the highest natural good.

To reiterate: Christ makes liturgical asceticism possible because liturgical asceticism is an eschatological act of hope in the Resurrection, and that hope is accompanied by faith and love. In the case of natural and finite renunciations, a lower value may be surrendered for a higher value that one can experience, but in the case of liturgical asceticism, a *bonum honestum* is surrendered for something that cannot be experienced in the same sense. This supernatural and infinite eschatological good can be experienced, but it is experienced by faith, in hope, and as love,

40. K. Rahner, "Reflections on the Theology of Renunciation," 50.

41. Ibid., 52.

42. Ibid., 50.

43. I am aware of the difference between a monk (who vowed stability, obedience, and conversion of life) and a member of a religious order (who according to medieval Western formula vowed poverty, chastity, and obedience).

which are the theological virtues bestowed in baptism. Monasticism can only be practiced by a baptized person; monasticism assumes baptism. Asceticism springs from baptism as the sacramental act of death and resurrection, which asceticism substantiates by personal act. The asceticism of which we speak is liturgical in origin, form, and purpose. The death and rising which baptism sacramentally bestows must be made real and actual and embodied in one's life, for "[t]he new birth into Christ is a voluntary one and is in need of constant ratification through observance of the commandments."[44] Baptism, therefore, is not being pickled in holy water until Judgment Day (a font of ecclesiastical formaldehyde); baptism is initiation into eschatological battle, and it is only then, says Rahner, that "this renunciation of one value in favour of the other takes on a characteristic proper to Christian renunciation and to it alone: the giving up of a value which can be experienced in favour of a value possessed only by faith and hope, and this as a realizing expression of the love of God, in so far as this love is eschatological and not so much in so far as it is also cosmic."[45]

It is a phenomenological fact that celibacy, fasting, solitude, physical labor, and other forms of ascetical renunciation existed before Christianity, and continue to exist outside of Christianity. They are directed to various ends, be these ends personal, religious, moral, or self-disciplinary. Our thesis, simply stated, is that to the degree that liturgical asceticism is directed toward substantiating shared life with Jesus, and to the degree that its source is sacramental immersion into Jesus' life, and to the degree that this discipline frees the baptized for participation in the Mystical Body of Christ, to that degree, we say, liturgical asceticism is distinct. Liturgical asceticism is the life of Christ lived in us. "He let himself be pierced with nails since He wished to

44. George Berthold, note 17 on Maximus's "Commentary on the Our Father," in *Maximus: Selected Writings*, 120.

45. K. Rahner, "Reflections on the Theology of Renunciation," 52.

uproot the passions which had been nailed to the heart of Adam. For this reason we sing: All creation bless the Lord and exalt Him forever!"[46] Liturgical asceticism is the response made by the People of God to the irruption of the eternal into history, the eighth day into our secular week, the Son of God into flesh. This liturgical asceticism initiates us into something higher than mere morality, so Evdokimov says something higher than morality is required to deal with the passions. "The moral principle alone can never oppose and resist the passions; it gives in every time."[47]

The good that is higher than the highest natural goods is one that is as yet transcendent, but one in which we can already partake. This is an antinomy, as true of asceticism as it is of liturgy. The Church-at-liturgy encounters her Lord sacramentally and eschatologically while she still experiences his absence. Because the Kingdom of God has been inaugurated and is lived in supernatural charity, known in revealed faith, and believed with inspired spiritual hope, therefore Christians make ascetical renunciation—whether as a permanent state of life, in the case of a monk, or as a regular manner of life, in the case of the Christian still in the world. Those who live the Evangelical Counsels represent this transcendent good in their bodies, and they do this as part of the Church's evangelical witness to the world. They are walking icons of hope. Rahner thus concludes by saying the Church displays the inner life of her eschatological transcendence of love in two ways: both sacramentally and existentially.

> [This] happens *sacramentally* (above all) in the sacraments of baptism and the Eucharist, in which man baptized into the death of Christ proclaims this death until He comes again; and happens *existentially* in Christian renunciation.... The Evangelical Counsels are therefore an inalienable and essential element of the appearance of the Church, in so far as she must represent tangibly and cause to appear what she lives

46. *The Office of Matins* (Uniontown, Pa.: Sisters of the Order of St. Basil, 1989), 170.
47. Evdokimov, *The Art of the Icon*, 39.

interiorly: the divine love which transcends the world eschatologically. And conversely, attachment to the Church is essential to the Evangelical Counsels, since they exist precisely as the appearance of that principle which is proper to the Church and *thus* is shared by the individual.[48]

Liturgical asceticism is the art of patience when confronted by the eschaton. To the inquirer who puzzles over Lenten fasts and asks, "Can't you eat meat?" the Christian response is "We can; but not yet." (This is also the very answer Adam and Eve should have given to the serpent's question in the garden of Eden.) No Christian gives up meat or wine out of a vegetarian or teetotaler impulse. Rather, by choosing not to avail himself even of things that he reckons good, the liturgical ascetic performs an act of submission, prioritizes the goods of this world in light of an eternal Good, and trains the muscles of patience. Paul Claudel writes, "It seems as if the acorn knows its destiny and carries within itself an active idea of the oak required of it. And in the same way it seems as if memory and foresight join together in the hearts of Adam's sons to deny the immediate the right to prevail."[49] Liturgical asceticism denies the immediate the right to prevail in a soul that is created for eternal things. In a normal week, the number of days when meat is allowed outnumber the day of fasting six to one, but there is definitely time set aside in the Christian week and in the Christian year to appreciate the gift by refraining from it; to remember that man does not live by bread alone; to realize by means of one day's renunciation that all the food received the other six days is by grace; to deny the right of the body to prevail over the spirit, and to deny the temporal the right to prevail over the eternal. All the baptized are called to these seasonal workouts; some of the baptized are called to train harder and more constantly at it; but both of their ascetical disciplines are a direct response to the eighth day, applicable to all of the Church some of

48. K. Rahner, "Reflections on the Theology of Renunciation," 55.
49. Paul Claudel, *The Essence of the Bible* (New York: Philosophical Library, 1957), 64.

the time (laity), and to some of the Church all of the time (monks).

Liturgical asceticism is an act of sacrifice, and sacrifice is an act of love, never disgust. When one sacrifices, one offers what one considers precious, not despicable. Who presents a gift to his beloved made out of some inferior thing? Who constructs a gift out of something he believes is bad? So how could monks offer their celibacy to God unless they believed marriage was good? Remember that the same Church that praised celibacy recognized marriage as a sacrament. "Esteem of virginity for the sake of the kingdom and the Christian understanding of marriage are inseparable, and they reinforce each other."[50] To be an ascetic first requires being a healthy and well-grounded person; it requires a solid ego strength, not an underdeveloped sense of self-worth. Ascetical discipline exceeds the norm, it is not the result of failing the norm. But this makes it impossible to judge Christian ascetical behavior by ordinary religious, moral, psychological, or social norms. At its heart, the liturgical fast must be an act of self-discipline, but it can never be an act of self-loathing. A Christian may not be celibate because he is a misogynist any more than he may fast because he is an anorexic.

Human beings possess a common nature, but as a person (hypostasis) each human being is individual. Therefore, asceticism treats each person in a radically individual way. Each monastic followed a rule that was his or her own *politeia* ("a rule of life" or "a special resolution"), and not everyone followed the same *politeia* because there was an idiosyncratic quality to each person's *askesis*. That is why the Christian witness to asceticism could do no better than to offer the "Lives of the Desert Fathers," because the book presents ruled lives, not general rules. One asceticism does not fit all; there are as many ascetical disciplines as there

50. Catechism of the Catholic Church, para. 1620. Pope John Paul II said, "Perfect conjugal love must be marked by that fidelity and that donation to the only Spouse ... on which religious profession and priestly celibacy are founded"; see *Theology of the Body* (Boston: Pauline Books & Media, 1997), 277.

are consciences that seek God, and therefore the best way to explain ascetical practice is to introduce us to individual ascetics. The reason why a single, general behavior pattern cannot be prescribed is because each *politeia* is an antidote prepared in exact proportion to the mix of passions it is designed to cure. The *politeia* must be an exact counterpoise to the imbalances suffered by the heart. There is only one *telos,* of course, and all share the common scopos of purity of heart, but the battles fought along the way to that purity will differ according to what healing a particular heart requires. That is why beginners sought out masters and "asked for a word," and it also explains how one monk might discover, in humility, the more excellent discipline of another. Fr. Irenee Hausherr observes,

> Each ascetic was permitted to follow a program of his own, which he could keep all his life or else change if he discovered something better. St. Hilarion had a meal with Bishop Epiphanius but refused to eat the fowl which was served because, as he explained, "From the time I took the habit I have never eaten meat." To this St. Epiphanius replied, "For my part, since taking the habit I have never let anyone go to sleep while he still held something against me, nor have I ever gone to sleep myself with bitterness towards any man." Hilarion's response was, "Your *politeia* is better than mine."[51]

Symeon the New Theologian explains how simply his master initially guided his *politeia.* His master, Symeon the Pious, gave him a spiritual book by Mark the Hermit that contained the command, "When you seek healing, take heed to your conscience. Do what it says, and you will find profit." Speaking about himself in the third person, the younger Symeon describes himself as a struggling monk who

> did no more than carry out the simple command that old man had given him, every evening before he laid himself to sleep on his bed. So when

51. Irenee Hausherr, *The Name of Jesus* (Kalamazoo, Mich.: Cistercian Publications, 1978), 166. See also his study of the spiritual father, *Spiritual Direction in the Early Christian East* (Kalamazoo, Mich.: Cistercian Publications, 1990).

his conscience told him, "You must perform additional reverences and say more psalms, and repeat 'Lord, have mercy,' for you can do it, he obeyed with eagerness and without hesitation. He did all these things as if God Himself had told him so. From that time on he never went to bed with his conscience reproaching him and asking him, "Why have you not done this?"[52]

His evening prayers became longer; tears flowed from his eyes; he prostrated himself more frequently and as if the Lord were physically present; he stood motionless, with feet together; he recited prayers to the Mother of God, accompanied with groans and tears. So his prayer grew longer every evening and continued till midnight, and one night a flood of divine radiance appeared from above and filled all the room.

John Chrysostom refers to the catechumenate as a "wrestling school," where catechumens make preparation for the upcoming contest. He encourages them to learn

to get the better of that evil demon. For it is to contend with him that we have to strip ourselves, with him after baptism are we to box and fight. Let us learn from thence already his grip, on what side he is aggressive, on what side he can easily threaten us, in order that, when the contest comes on, we may not feel strange, nor become confused, as seeing new forms of wrestling; but having already practiced them amongst ourselves, and having learnt all his methods, may engage in these forms of wrestling against him with courage.[53]

The faithful on earth are called the "Church militant" and at baptism the pattern of Jesus' life is imprinted on them. What did Jesus do after his baptism in the Jordan? He went into the wilderness to do battle with the evil one. So also the Christian will find himself in the wilderness by divine will, once having passed through the mystical Jordan of the font. "The Spirit Himself now in us will make us encounter Satan, just as the Spirit led Jesus away into the desert, after His baptism in the Jordan, to

52. Symeon the New Theologian, *The Discourses*, 244–45.
53. John Chrysostom, *First Instruction to Catechumens*, ch. 4.

be tempted by the devil,"[54] says Louis Bouyer in summary, and the ascetics knew that "the more the spiritual life progresses the more it enters into conflict with Satan. The monks' withdrawal into solitude appeared to earlier spiritual masters as a decision to attack the demon openly, in imitation of Jesus, whom the Holy Spirit Himself had led into the desert for this purpose."[55] This is also how Maximus conceives the desert scene.

> When the devil, who deceived man from the beginning, and thereby had power of death, had seen [Jesus] receive at baptism the Father's testimony and, as man, the Holy Spirit from heaven, consubstantial to Himself, and also when he then saw him come into the desert to be tempted by himself: then he mustered all his battle force against Him, thinking that in some way he might make even Him prefer the substance of this world to love for God. Now then, as the devil knew that there are three things by which every human is moved—I mean food, money, and reputation, and it is by these too that he leads men down to the depths of destruction—with these same three he tempted Him in the desert.[56]

We are not guaranteed success in every encounter with the demons but that does not excuse us from the match. "Wrestlers are not the only ones whose occupation is to throw others down and to be thrown in turn. The demons too wrestle—with us. Sometimes they throw us and at other times it is we who throw them."[57] But no athlete will gain any victory unless he has set aside everything that can give the adversary a hold on him. This was a prevalent typology applied to the bodily anointings in the rites of initiation: like a wrestler, the catechumen is anointed from head to foot in preparation for the match.[58] Returning to

54. Louis Bouyer, *The Paschal Mystery: Meditations on the Last Three Days of Holy Week* (Chicago: Henry Regnery, 1950), 158.

55. Ibid., 159.

56. Maximus, *The Ascetic Life* (New York: Newman Press), 109.

57. Evagrius, *The Praktikos*, 35.

58. For baptismal typologies, see Hugh M. Riley, *Christian Initiation: A Comparative Study of the Interpretation of the Baptismal Liturgy in the Mystagogical Writings of Cyril of Jerusalem, John Chrysostom, Theodore of Mopsuestia, and Ambrose of Milan* (Washington,

the vices will only enable the enemy to get a better grip upon the Christian, the way a wrestler might throw sand upon the oiled body of his opponent.

Gregory of Nyssa uses the Egyptian army in the Exodus story to work out this typology of Christian baptism in his work *The Life of Moses.* The horses, the chariots and their drivers, the archers and armed soldiers are all "the various passions of the soul by which man is enslaved. For the undisciplined intellectual drives and the sensual impulses to pleasure, sorrow, and covetousness are indistinguishable from the aforementioned army.... The passion for pleasures is to be seen in the horses who themselves with irresistible drive pull the chariot." [59] As Pharaoh's soldiers were all drowned in the Red Sea, so all the demons and passions are drowned in the baptismal sea, and in neither case should we allow anything of the opposing army to come along to the other shore. "If anyone wishes to clarify the figure, this lays it bare: Those who pass through the mystical water in baptism must put to death in the water the whole phalanx of evil—such as covetousness, unbridled desire, rapacious thinking, the passion of conceit and arrogance, wild impulse, wrath, anger, malice, envy, and all such things."[60] Gregory is adamant that "no remnant of evil should mix with the subsequent life. Rather we should make a totally new beginning in life after these things, breaking the continuity with evil by a radical change for the better."[61] But what if it should happen that someone does bring along something of the old, does still serve the old tyrant, does couple with the old passions and dallies with them after baptism? "If someone should still serve them, even if he should happen to have passed through the water, according to my thinking

D.C.: The Catholic University of America Press, 1974), and Jean Danielou, *The Bible and the Liturgy* (Notre Dame, Ind.: University of Notre Dame Press, 1956).

59. Gregory of Nyssa, *The Life of Moses* (New York: Paulist Press, 1978), 83.

60. Ibid., 84.

61. Ibid.

he has not at all touched the mystical water whose function is to destroy evil tyrants."[62]

Baptism is the return to Paradise from which our journey to fullness in God was to have begun, and liturgical asceticism is the resumption of that journey to God. Salvation is the possibility for the shipwrecked to resume a journey whose sole goal is union with God. It is the same journey that Adam and Eve should have made, but now we, their children, resume it with this difference: now we are in Christ, and Christ accompanies us as brother on our journey to union with the Father. (*O Felix Culpa!* "O Happy Fall," the Latin Easter Exultet proclaims.) Liturgical asceticism witnesses to the possibility of efficacious death. Remember that the monks considered themselves dead in the desert;[63] remember, too, that the monks were the heirs of the martyrs;[64] remember, finally, that the word *martyria* means "witness." The monks are the new martyrs: new witnesses. Evdokimov recounts what the Holy Spirit immediately did after peace with the Roman Empire was declared in the Edict of Constantine.

> The Holy Spirit immediately "invented" the "equivalent of martyrdom." In fact, the witness of the martyrs to "the one thing needful" is passed on to monasticism. "The baptism of blood" of the martyrs gave way to "the baptism of asceticism" of the monks. The celebrated *Life of St. Anthony,* written by St. Athanasius, describes this father of monasticism as the first who had attained holiness without tasting martyrdom. When humanity had sunk below itself, monastic asceticism raised it above its own nature. Monasticism's *metanoia,* or transformation, deepened Baptism's second birth which brought to life already the "little res-

62. Ibid., 85.

63. When Abba Poemen confessed envy, Abba Ammonas said to him, "Poemen, are you still alive? Go, sit down in your cell; engrave it on your heart that you have been in the tomb for a year already"; see Alphabetical Sayings, Poemen 2.

64. "In times past, when heresies prevailed, many chose such death through martyrdom and various tortures. Now, when we through the grace of Christ live in a time of profound and perfect peace, we learn for sure that cross and death consist in nothing else than the complete mortification of self-will"; see Symeon the New Theologian, *The Discourses,* 232.

urrection." While the body awaits this glorification, the soul is already immortal.[65]

Both the martyr who has died and the monk who has died to the world witness to the new fact that an eschatological day has dawned that is worth dying for. They witness to the new creation, the Church, being formed under the Divine Artist's hand. Theirs is a witness to sanctity. "Martyrdom means witness. But to bear witness to Christ to the point of death is to become one who has risen again. Christian martyrdom is a mystical experience.... Martyrdom was the first form of sanctity to be venerated in the Church. And when there were no longer any martyrs in blood, martyrs in ascesis, monks, came instead."[66] In this case, *askesis* means a training of oneself in the mystical life, or exercise in the mysteries, which is participation in the Mystery of Christ.

A person is both body and soul; sacraments affect the whole person, body and soul; and so also liturgical asceticism concerns both body and soul. This is sometimes a stumbling block for the modern Cartesian, who wants to know what disciplining the body has to do with redeeming the soul? Doesn't religion have to do with the mind, emotion, spiritual piety, and not exterior acts of the body? On the one hand, the Desert Fathers, such as Mother Theodora, are certain that the more important *askesis* is training of the spirit. Physical heroics do not especially impress the demons. Amma Theodora taught that only humility could save, not asceticism or vigils or suffering.

> There was an anchorite who was able to banish the demons; and he asked them, "What makes you go away? Is it fasting?" They replied, "We do not eat or drink." "Is it vigils?" They replied, "We do not sleep." "Is it separation from the world?" "We live in the deserts." "What power sends you away then?" They said, "Nothing can overcome us, but only humility." Do you see how humility is victorious over the demons?[67]

65. Evdokimov, *Ages of the Spiritual Life,* 134.
66. Clement, *The Roots of Christian Mysticism,* 257 and 258.
67. Alphabetical Sayings, Theodora 6. A similar story is in the Sayings of the Desert

On the other hand, the argument that spiritual humility is more important than physical discipline is a little too easily and quickly ceded by a world that has difficulty denying itself anything. In closing, then, we would like to consider this riddle of the body-soul relationship in more detail. Clarity on this point would confirm that Christian ascetics are not dualists.

The physical *askesis* was a ladder by which the ascetic climbed toward spiritual heights. Abba Moses says bodily disciplines such as solitude, night vigils, manual labor, nakedness, and reading are undertaken "so that by them we may be able to acquire and keep a heart untouched by any harmful passion, and so that by taking these steps we may be able to ascend to the perfection of love."[68] The steps of this ladder are those bodily disciplines that empower the heart, the spirit, the mind for its climb. But how? Perhaps no one expresses the mystery of the intricate connection of soul to body, and body to soul, with as much poignancy as the master of the ladder, John Climacus.

By what rule or manner can I bind this body of mine? By what precedent can I judge him? Before I can bind him he is let loose, before I can condemn him I am reconciled to him, before I can punish him I bow down to him and feel sorry for him. How can I hate him when my nature disposes me to love him? How can I break away from him when I am bound to him forever? How can I escape from him when he is going to rise with me? How can I make him incorrupt when he has received a corruptible nature? How can I argue with him when all the arguments of nature are on his side? . . .

He is my helper and my enemy, my assistant and my opponent, a protector and a traitor. I am kind to him and he assaults me. If I wear

Fathers. "Abba Macarius was once returning to his cell from the marsh carrying palm-leaves. And the devil met him by the way, with a sickle, and wanted to run him through with the sickle, but could not. The devil said: 'Macarius, I suffer much violence from you, for I cannot overcome you. For whatever you do, I do also. If you fast, I eat nothing: if you keep watch, I get no sleep. But it is only one quality in you which overcomes me.' And Abba Macarius said to him: 'What is that?' The devil answered: 'Your humility—that is why I cannot prevail against you'" (Systematic Sayings, 15.26).

68. John Cassian, *Conferences*, 1.7.1.

him out he gets weak. If he has a rest he becomes unruly. If I upset him he cannot stand it. If I mortify him I endanger myself. If I strike him down I have nothing left by which to acquire virtues. I embrace him. And I turn away from him.

What is this mystery in me? What is the principle of this mixture of body and soul?[69]

We are concerned with the mystery of a being (*anthropos*) whose principle of unity has been damaged, with the result that spirit and body are in tumultuous discord.[70] Christian asceticism has never found it necessary to condemn the body as an obstacle to spiritual life; in fact, Christian spiritual life has made the soul's progress dependent on the soul's union with the body. Fasting, to take but one example, seems only to concern the stomach, but in fact fasting is done for the sake of the whole person.

Fasting ends lust, roots out bad thoughts, frees one from evil dreams. Fasting makes for purity of prayer, an enlightened soul, a watchful mind, a deliverance from blindness. Fasting is the door of compunction, humble sighing, joyful contrition, and end to chatter, an occasion for silence, a custodian of obedience, a lightening of sleep, health of the body, an agent of dispassion, a remission of sins, the gate, indeed, the delight of Paradise.[71]

69. John Climacus, Step 15, "On Chastity," *The Ladder of Divine Ascent*, 185–86.

70. In what follows I will use the term *soul* and *spirit* interchangeably, though they are not strictly synonymous. From the Greek tradition Christianity inherited the concept of soul as the animating force of a body (animals have souls), and from the Hebrew tradition it inherited the concept of spirit as the immortal intellectual principle that knows God. "The soul vivifies the body and makes it a living flesh. The spirit spiritualizes and makes of both a spiritual being" (Evdokimov, *Ages of the Spiritual Life*, 155). The reason for the confusion between terms is that in man the spirit also functions as the material organism's form, which is the function of soul. Anscar Vonier explains this in Western Scholastic language this way: "By soul, Catholic philosophy understands a principle of life and sensation for the body," and in the case of men and women "that spiritual substance which we call the human soul, has both spirit-functions and soul-functions.... [Therefore] two definitions are possible. We might call the human soul a soul that has spirit-functions; or we might call it a spirit that has soul-functions. The second definition is truer ... but in order of time, the soul-functions precede the spirit-functions"; see Anscar Vonier, *The Human Soul* (St. Louis: B. Herder, 1913), 17–20.

71. John Climacus, Step 14, "On Gluttony," *Ladder of Divine Ascent*, 169.

John Climacus concludes, "The soul indeed is molded by the doings of the body, conforming to and taking shape from what it does."[72]

The practice of liturgical asceticism rests upon two fundamental Christian doctrines that inform its theological anthropology: incarnation and bodily resurrection. Any ascetical discipline resting on principles other than these—say, for example, that the soul waits to be emancipated from the body, or that the body acts independently of the soul, or that matter and spirit cannot unite, or that body and soul are together annihilated at death—would result in an entirely different kind of asceticism. Even if two systems of ascetical discipline shared surface similarities due to the fact that there are only a finite number of ways to practice physical self-renunciation (e.g., if both systems recommended celibacy and fasting), liturgical asceticism would be entirely different by motive and teleology from dualistic asceticism.

Liturgical asceticism's paradoxical tension between body and spirit assumes that spirit and body are united to such a degree that the fall of the former has affected the latter, and sensations of the latter can be the occasion for *logismoi* in the former. As we are now, things in the world can stir up our passions and threaten us. The act of taking from the Tree of Knowledge issued not only from the spirit's pride at the prospect of knowing good from evil, but also from the eye's delight at the fruit. In the biblical account, the forbidden fruit aroused a spiritual desire that was at the same time sensual.

> It arouses desires by its sensual and aesthetic appeal. "The tree was good for food, pleasing to the eyes, and desirable." The arrow of temptation that wounded human freedom and perverted its choice went beyond the formal disobedience. We can see the essential of the fall: the desirable fruit sensually coveted, immerses us in the life of senses chosen in preference to a spiritual deepening of our communion with God.

72. John Climacus, Step 25, "On Humility," *Ladder of Divine Ascent*, 227.

We appear guilty not so much negatively by disobedience, but positively by not enriching ourselves by nearness to God."[73]

As Schmemann pointedly says, "In our perspective, the 'original' sin is not primarily that man has 'disobeyed' God; the sin is that he ceased to be hungry for God and God alone.... The only real fall of man is his noneucharistic life in a noneucharistic world."[74] But liturgical asceticism restores our appetite for God. Being an indivisible body and spirit, *anthropos* sins in an indivisible way, and spirit and body are therefore affected simultaneously. So Maximus concludes, "Every passion always consists of a combination of some perceived object, a sense faculty and a natural power—the incensive power, desire or the intelligence, as the case may be—whose natural function has been distorted."[75]

It was not meant to be so. According to Maximus, the sensible world should have provided the five senses with information when the senses activated the faculties of the soul through their apprehension of the inward essences (*logoi*), and through this the *Logos* would have been revealed. Then it would have been like the whole cosmos was theophanous, revealing God. The ascetic nears precisely such a state again. Had the soul used the senses to aid its faculties, the soul would have discerned the *logoi* in all the visible things where God was hidden and proclaimed in silence. But once the passions corrupted our faculties, and disrupted the union that should have adhered between sense and intellect, then nature was no longer directed toward supernature. Theologians explored the riddle of this mystery by capitalizing on the account of Adam and Eve being stripped of the glory with which God had covered them, becoming naked. Symeon the New Theologian affirms the goodness of creation, as well as

73. Evdokimov, *Ages of the Spiritual Life,* 171.

74. Fr. Alexander Schmemann, *For the Life of the World* (Crestwood, N.Y.: St. Vladimir's Seminary Press, 1963), 18.

75. Maximus the Confessor, "Various Texts on Theology, the Divine Economy, and Virtue and Vice," *The Philokalia,* 2.177.

the fact that all things were brought into being precisely for man and woman, by observing, "[w]hen [Adam] was king of all these visible objects, did they harm him with regard to virtue? In no way whatever. On the contrary, had he continued to give thanks to God who had made him and given him all things, he would have fared well. Had he not transgressed the commandment of his Master he would not have lost this kingship, he would not have deprived himself of the glory of God."[76] But when the man and woman sinned, they were stripped, or peeled, or naked[77] of the glory in which they had been clothed. So when God called out, Symeon continues, it was not because the Omniscient One did not know where the man and woman were; rather, God called out in order to make them conscious of their guilt and call them to repentance.

He says, "Adam, where are you?" "Understand yourself, realize your nakedness. See of what a garment, of how great glory, you have deprived yourself. Adam, where are you?" It is as though He spoke to encourage him, "Yes, come to your senses, poor fellow, come out of your hiding place. Do you think you are hidden from Me? Just say, 'I have sinned.'" ... But [Adam] does not say this. He does not humble himself, he does not bend. The neck of his heart is like a sinew of iron.... Obviously this is the death of the soul, and this is what took place the same hour. By this Adam was stripped of the robe of immortality.[78]

In the anthropology of asceticism, then, a distinction can be discerned between nudity and nakedness; between being naked and being in an unclothed state, as Erik Peterson observes:

Prior to [the Fall] there was indeed unclothedness, but this lack of clothing was still not nakedness. Nakedness certainly presupposes lack of clothing, but it is not identical with it. The realization of nakedness is

76. Symeon the New Theologian, *The Discourses*, 94.

77. C. S. Lewis, a student of words, points out that "[t]he word naked was originally a past participle; the naked man was the man who had undergone a process of naking, that is, of stripping or peeling (you used the verb of nuts and fruits)"; see *The Four Loves* (New York: Harcourt, Brace and Co., 1960), 147.

78. Symeon the New Theologian, *The Discourses*, 94.

connected with the spiritual act which Scripture calls the "opening of the eyes." In other words, a metaphysical change affecting man's mode of being could be perceived with the spiritual eye.... [A]fter sin, Adam and Eve "had" the human body differently from the way they had it before.... *The body was man's in a different way before the Fall, because man was God's in a different way*.... Certainly, *man was created by God unclothed*—that is, he had his own nature distinct form that of God—*but he was created in this unclothed nature so that he might be clothed with the supernatural garment of glory*.[79]

Having their body in a different way after the Fall, man and woman experience the world in a different way, as well. The earth that should yield to their hand now rebels; the world that should be sacrament now tempts; the food that should nourish is now hollow and decayed; we eat dead food that cannot ultimately keep us alive. Because *anthropos* did not pay attention to God with the eye of the soul, Maximus says, he neglected the light of spiritual contemplation, and then

willingly, in the manner of a blind man, felt the rubbish of matter with both his hands in the darkness of ignorance, and inclined and surrendered the whole of himself to the senses alone. [When he] took the first-fruits of food from the forbidden tree, in which he had been taught beforehand that fruit and death went together, he changed the life that is proper to fruit, and fashioned for himself a living death for the whole of the time of this present age. For if death exists as the corruption of coming to be, the body that is preserved in being by the flux of nourishment is always naturally suffering corruption as it is dissolved by flux itself.[80]

As a result, we have been clothed with a garment of skin. This is not, as some Greek philosophers thought, the body, as such. Since man and woman were created both body and soul it is not compatible with Christian liturgical asceticism to say that *anthropos* is supposed to be spirit alone (like an angel), and that possession of a body was the result of sin. The garment of skin refers to

79. Erik Peterson, "A Theology of Dress," *Communio* 20, no. 3 (1993): 560–61; emphasis in original.

80. Maximus the Confessor, "Difficulty 10," in *Maximus the Confessor*, trans. Andrew Louth (New York: Routledge, 1996), 126.

the abnormal human traits of mortality and corruptibility (now so familiar to us as to fool us into thinking they are normal). Jean Danielou explains this in Gregory of Nyssa's writings. "Human nature, as it is now, cannot be as God intended it in the beginning, and as it will surely be in the end. What has been added to human nature, to this image of God in man, according to Gregory, is the *garment of skin* (Gen 3:21). This *garment of skin* in us is made up of all those things which we have in common with animals; it is: 'sexual union, conception, childbirth, dirt, nursing, food, excrement, the gradual growth of the body towards maturity, adulthood, old age, sickness and death.'"[81]

For the ascetic, capable of spiritual combat, there is a promise of possessing the world, including the body, in a different way. The human capacity to create and transform is a condition for the capacity to transform this creation into the Kingdom of God, a capacity restored when the Christian is baptized and receives the anointing of the Holy Spirit. Olivier Clement pinpoints this transfigurative capacity. "As free human beings with a capacity to 'create positively,' we are challenged to keep faith with the great transformation in Christ, such that we transform likewise, in the Holy Spirit, the relationship that in this world we necessarily have with material things—our genetic inheritance, psychological and social background—so that finally we transform the materials themselves."[82] Unlike forms of moral or ethical asceticism, liturgical asceticism does not mainly concern the improvement of the human being in his or her present state; it concerns coming into a transformed state. The practice of liturgical asceticism is a matter of clothing the human being in incorruptibility, clothing naked *anthropos* in the glory of God. What liturgical asceticism wishes to accomplish requires sacramental grace, which is why liturgical asceticism has nothing to do with Pelagianism,

81. Jean Danielou, introduction to *From Glory to Glory*, 11.
82. Clement, *The Roots of Christian Mysticism*, 130.

no matter how emphasis is given to the necessity of a human responsive act.

According to Sebastian Brock, Ephrem summarizes the whole salvation economy as a story of four robes found at creation, the Incarnation, baptism, and the resurrection of the dead.

> Basically there are four main episodes which go to make up this cosmic drama: at the Fall, Adam and Eve lose the "Robe of Glory" with which they had originally been clothed in Paradise; in order to re-clothe the naked Adam and Eve (in other words, humanity), God himself "puts on the body" from Mary, and at the Baptism Christ laid the Robe of Glory in the river Jordan, making it available once again for humanity to put on at baptism; then, at his or her baptism, the individual Christian, in "putting on Christ," puts on the Robe of Glory, thus re-entering the terrestrial anticipation of the eschatological Paradise, in other words, the Church; finally, at the Resurrection of the Dead, the just will in all reality reenter the celestial Paradise, clothed in their Robes of Glory.[83]

There is peace within the liturgical ascetic, and all around the liturgical ascetic. There is peace within, because bodily impulses finally obey the spirit, which, in turn, obeys God. There is peace all around—peace with nature, so two lions bury the hermit Paul, and crocodiles line up in the river to make a crossing for the monk; peace between man and woman in the sacrament of marriage, at the cost of each dying to their own ego; peace between the human race and the angels; and peace between God and man. The objective of liturgical life is nothing short of deification, but the price for donning the garment of immortality is doffing the garment of skin.

As liturgy is participation in the eschaton even before its historical arrival, so asceticism is the art of practicing death and resurrection ahead of the final judgment—liturgical asceticism is

83. Ephrem, *Hymns on Paradise,* introduction by Sebastian Brock (Crestwood, N.Y.: St. Vladimir's Seminary Press, 1990), 67. The Office of Matins sings, "You took upon yourself the condemnation of those who were rejected and condemned, O Christ. And after being stripped, you were placed on the tree of the cross for those who had been stripped by sin"; see *The Office of Matins,* 187.

preemptive mortification. Liturgical asceticism both flows from and is prerequisite for the liturgy, because liturgy is fed from the wellsprings of resurrection. Our *asceticism* is liturgical because it owed to participation in the mysteries of Christ celebrated in the Church, and our *liturgy* is ascetical because for fallen people to have the mind of Jesus is a disciplined struggle. Jesus went into the desert after his baptism not to spare us the struggle, but to do battle with the tempter, defeat Satan, and give us hope. Whether our intellective, irascible, and concupiscible faculties prefer the substance of this world over love of God is the fundamental ascetical question. Liturgical asceticism is our imitation of Christ, and we begin by imitating Christ's death, as Louis Bouyer has said. "Christ died for us, not in order to dispense us from dying, but rather to make us capable of dying efficaciously."[84] The second Adam shows the path to the children of the first Adam who had been misled and wandered far off track; Christ uncovered the ascetical path leading from Eden to heaven that lay hidden and overgrown from lack of use.

84. Bouyer, *The Paschal Mystery*, xiv.

4 THE JOY

Apatheia

If it has been made adequately clear that in the ascetical tradition the word *pathos* ("passion") usually means a disordered desire, then it should be equally clear that we cannot translate its opposite, *apatheia,* by the English word *apathy*. "Apathy" has come to mean inertness or indifference deriving from a general lack of interest, and the liturgical ascetic is certainly not apathetic about the redemption of creation and mankind and himself. This is as true for the secular ascetic who remains in the world as for the desert ascetic who leaves it. In the ascetical tradition, the passions are whatever distort the image of God in *anthropos,* therefore the true opposite to *pathos* is an undistorted, proper, ordered relationship between God, spirit, body, and cosmos. "The word itself [*apatheia*] is indeed taken from the Stoic philosophers, where it had a long and venerable history.... It was taken over by the Christians early, long before Evagrius. Indeed, it was used by the most orthodox of Fathers and was applied to Christ himself. Ignatius of Antioch is the first to employ it in this way."[1] *Apatheia*

1. John Bamberger, introduction to *The Praktikos,* lxxxiii.

places man and woman again in the world with a restored dignity that receives all creation as sacramental gift from God, and offers all creation as eucharistic offering back to God.

By mixing vocabularies, Paul Evdokimov can even say we should be passionate about overcoming the passions:

> The ideal state has the most paradoxical name of *apatheia* which means "impassible passion," and designates a most *impassioned* state, for it is a question of awakening the spirit from its sluggishness and making man wide awake, *neptikos*. It takes a whole life to live what faith affirms once for all, and it is for this reason that the spirit is watchful....
>
> Ascetic impassibility then is not insensibility. Neither does it seek to resemble those whom Bernanos called "the stoics with dry eyes," nor to cultivate delight in bloody mortifications and in the groanings of the flesh. By lack or by excess, the two destroy the balance, and manifest an asceticism that is illusory and "without fruit." For ascetics, the capacity to become impassioned indicates their inward dynamism, which must be oriented, not suppressed.[2]

To indicate this difference between *apatheia* and apathy, the preferred translation has been "dispassion" or "passionlessness." In this way, says Ware, the ardor, fervor, and zeal of *apatheia* can be indicated. "It is a denial of the passions, regarded as the contranatural expression of fallen sinfulness; but it is a reaffirmation of the pure and natural impulses of our soul and body. It connotes not repression but reorientation, not inhibition but freedom; having overcome the passions, we are free to be our true selves, free to love others, free to love God. Dispassion, then, is no mere mortification of the passions but their replacement by a new and better energy."[3] At stake here is discovering what is normal for human beings, and what is abnormal. The concept not only reaches back, protologically, to what man and woman should be, but it reaches forward, eschatologically, to what man and woman should become. And what man and woman should become is love. Andrew Louth finds this point in Maximus, and

2. Evdokimov, *Ages of the Spiritual Life*, 194–95.
3. Kallistos Ware, introduction to John Climacus, 32.

finds it repeatedly. *Apatheia* is prerequisite to doing nature naturally, at last.

> [Maximus] is aware of the danger of an *apatheia* that is merely disinterestedness: *apatheia* must be a purified love. He seeks to prevent misunderstanding here with his very definition of passion: "passion is an impulse of the soul contrary to nature" (Centuries on Love II.16). The passions to be expelled are those that are contrary to nature: there are natural passions that are perfectly proper. *Apatheia,* then, is the restoration of what is natural (that is, what is in accordance with unfallen nature). But Maximus goes further than this. For him, detachment from the irrational parts of the soul is the aim of ascetic struggle, but only so that, in their purified state, they can be reincorporated in the whole human being, itself consumed by a passionate love for God. It is not so much detachment, as sublimation: "When the human intellect is constantly with God, the desire grows beyond all measure into an intense longing for God and the incensiveness is completely transformed into divine love" (Centuries on Love II.48).[4]

There was debate among the ascetical masters whether *apatheia* can be attained fully in this life. On the one hand, they are inclined to say so. "What more has to be said?" asks the great synthetic summarizer John Climacus. "The dispassionate man no longer lives himself, but it is Christ who lives in him (cf Gal 2:20)."[5] If the state of dispassion is the fact of Christ living within us, then in that sense one may say a saint has reached *apatheia*. On the other hand, one always feels a note of caution in the tradition, since the passions remain an abiding temptation. To assume they have been vanquished can be an act of pride that throws open the gate for them all to return, this being the reason why pride is dealt with so sternly. Whatever external acts are controlled, it is at least clear that "one thing that dispassion certainly does *not* mean for John [Climacus] is immunity from temptation, impeccability, a condition in which we are no longer capable of sinning. John is entirely clear that no such state is possible 'this

4. Louth, *Maximus the Confessor,* 41.
5. John Climacus, Step 29, "On Dispassion," 284.

side of the grave.'"[6] Therefore, when Abba Abraham heard of an old man who had kept the discipline for fifty years and one day said, "I have destroyed lust and greed and vanity," he came to him with three hypotheses to correct the old man's mistake.

Abraham said to him, "Supposing you go into your cell and find a woman on your mat, could you think she was not a woman?" He said, "No. But I fight against my thoughts, so as not to touch her." Abraham said, "Then you have not killed lust, the passion is still alive; you have imprisoned it. Suppose you were walking along a road and saw stones on one side and gold in jars on the other, could you think the gold and the stones were of the same value?" He answered, "No, but I would resist my desire and not let myself pick it up." Abraham said to him, "Then the passion still lives, you have only imprisoned it." He went on, "If you heard that one brother loved you and spoke well of you, and another brother hated you and slandered you, and they both came to visit you, would they both be equally welcome to you?" He said, "No, but I would force myself to treat him who hates me just as well as him who loves me." So Abraham said to him, "Then your passions are alive, only in some measure holy men have got them chained."[7]

Although some heroic ascetics are hyperbolically said to have vanquished the passions, the Fathers seem to concur that their elimination cannot be assured since the *logismoi* will remain with us until the end. The ascetic's life therefore depends on watchfulness, or *nipsis,* which the translators of the *Philokalia* describe in their glossary as "[l]iterally, the opposite to a state of drunken stupor; hence spiritual sobriety, alertness, vigilance. It signifies an attitude of attentiveness, whereby one keeps watch over one's inward thoughts and fantasies, maintaining guard over the heart and intellect."[8] Isaac the Syrian says, "We are not so bold as to say that anyone has achieved this [purity of the mind] without experience of evil thoughts, but in such a case he would not be clad with a body. For until death we cannot dare to say that our

6. Ware, introduction to John Climacus, 33.
7. Systematic Sayings, 10.15.
8. Glossary in *The Philokalia,* 367.

nature is not warred upon or harmed. And by experience of evil thoughts I mean not to submit to them but to make a beginning to struggle with them."[9]

Nevertheless, the Christian does live under an eschatological light, and the ascetic's life is not conflict without respite. So Golitzin does say, encouragingly, "*Apatheia* does not, perhaps, mean the cessation of passionate thoughts here below, but it clearly does insist that the intellect ceases to be ruled by these forces. It is thus the pre-condition for all further spiritual development, the requisite ordering and directing of the soul's movement toward further knowledge."[10] Even if the light of the eschaton is not yet full in the sky, it has dawned. John Climacus uses the language of inaugurated eschatology to define dispassion, not as a form of death, but as "resurrection of the soul prior to that of the body."[11] And Isaac the Syrian says that to be pure in mind is neither to be like a brute beast who has no knowledge of evil, nor to remain on the level of an infant, nor to remain aloof from all human affairs, rather, "purity of the mind is this: to be rapt in things divine, and this comes about after a man has practiced the virtues."[12] *Apatheia* does not produce an apathetic and cautious morality within us; it initiates us into Pentecostal sanctity. Such a prospect makes everything else look inconsequential by comparison, and accounts for why the greater asceticism is performed by the greater lover. Without an experience of this great love, the more extreme ascetical exercises will escape our understanding. *Apatheia* is a precondition for the direct and intimate knowledge of God for which the ascetic is seeking, and such a knowledge

is not the automatic or the guaranteed conclusion of a process. It is not like the logical outcome of a faultlessly constructed argument. There is

9. Isaac the Syrian, Homily 3, *The Ascetical Homilies*, 20.

10. Alexander Golitzin, *Et Introibo Ad Altare Dei: The Mystagogy of Dionysius Areopagita, with Special Reference to Its Predecessors in the Eastern Christian Tradition* (Thessaloniki, Greece: 1994), 331.

11. John Climacus, Step 29, "On Dispassion," 282.

12. Isaac the Syrian, Homily 3, *The Ascetical Homilies*, 20.

no assurance that a man will come to it at the end of a long journey. But to many it was a prize and a prospect so glittering that all else looked puny by comparison; and, besides, there were tales told of some who, so it seemed, had actually been granted that supreme gift of a rendezvous.[13]

Asceticism is a price that love gladly pays.

Purity of heart consists of quieting the noise of flesh and mind, and such quiet is a condition for true *theologia*. Augustine describes the unimaginable event in this way (it is literally unimaginable, since it is communion with the Creator who transcends all created images, and can only be experienced):

Imagine a man in whom the tumult of the flesh goes silent, in whom the images of earth, of water, of air and of the skies cease to resound. His soul turns quiet and, self-reflecting no longer, it transcends itself. Dreams and visions end. So too does all speech and every gesture, everything in fact which comes to be only to pass away. All these things cry out: "We did not make ourselves. It is the Eternal One who made us." And after they have said this, think of them falling silent, turning to listen to the One Who created them. And imagine Him speaking. Himself, and not through the medium of all those things. Speaking Himself. So that we could hear His word, not in the language of the flesh, not through the speech of an angel, not by way of a rattling cloud or a mysterious parable. But Himself. The One Whom we love in everything.... Eternal life would be of a kind with this moment of understanding.[14]

This is the quiet—the *hesychasm*—that permits the ascetic to hear creation's hierophonic declaration, the theological Word of God himself drawing near and presenting himself to the liturgical theologian.

Since we are struggling with the liturgical dimensions of asceticism, and the ascetical dimensions of liturgy, we have not made it our task to detail particular steps along the path of the ascetical life. But the path itself does concern us. The reader should seek

13. Colm Luibheid, preface to John Climacus, *Ladder of Divine Ascent*, xvii.

14. *The Confessions*, 9.10.25. This translation is Colm Luibheid's in the preface to John Climacus.

out other descriptions of the discipline (fasting, temperance, poverty, joyful hope, meekness, ready obedience, humility, and charity, etc.); our goal here is to look at the three stages in Evagrius's systematization as a whole, and see what they contribute to an understanding of liturgical asceticism.[15] It will be helpful to review once again the three stages because it enlarges the context for talking about *apatheia*.

Evagrius's doctrine of the ascetical life is set forth in his book *Praktikos,* and its first entry identifies the three stages he envisions: praxis, plus two kinds of contemplation. "Christianity is the dogma of Christ our Savior. It is composed of *praktike,* of the contemplation of the physical world and of the contemplation of God."[16] Think of it as 1, 2a, and 2b.[17] Three stages stand under two major divisions: "*praktike,* where the concern is purifying the passionate part of the soul; and knowledge [*theoria*], where the rational part of the soul devotes itself to contemplation and knowledge."[18] The word "stage" must not be interpreted in such a way that we are led to believe an antecedent period is left behind when the person reaches a subsequent period; all three stages will occupy a person until he or she dies. These are not like grades in school that we leave behind after we have passed them; to the contrary, it is more like after some success in the first stage, the work of the second is added, and then the third. Or, think of the theater and imagine that these are ways that an ascetic stages his or her life's work.

Evagrius calls the first stage *praktike.* As its name indicates, it is highly practical, concerning methods for dealing with the passions. *Praktike* seeks a state of freedom—*apatheia*—which

15. They have had lasting influence upon other spiritual authors. What Evagrius calls *praktike, physike, theologia* is treated by Western spirituality as *purification, illumination, union.*

16. Evagrius, *Praktikos,* 2.

17. See also David Fagerberg, "Prayer as Theology," in *A History of Prayer: The First to the Fifteenth Century,* edited by Roy Hammerling (Leiden: Brill, 2008), 117–36.

18. Driscoll, *Evagrius Ponticus: Ad Monachos,* 9.

Bamberger says "marks a decisive turning point in the spiritual itinerary of the Christian. It is the door to contemplation, or more exactly, its vestibule. For charity, the finest fruit of *apatheia,* is the door to contemplation."[19] Louth points out the philosophical background of the term, and how Evagrius gave it monastic focus.

> *Praktike* is the stage during which the soul develops the practice of the virtues. This use of the word *praktikos* is a new departure. It usually means "concerned with business, with activity"; Aristotle had spoken of the *bios praktikos,* the active life, in contradistinction to the contemplative life, *bios theoretikos.* This is what *praktikos* means for Evagrius's friend, Gregory Nazianzen, who contrasts the active life, *bios praktikos,* with that of the monk. For Evagrius, however, far from *praktike* having anything to do with the active life, it presupposes *hesychia,* the life of quiet of the monk (or contemplative, we would say). *Praktike* is the life of struggle with the demons, a struggle to overcome temptation and subdue the passions.[20]

Or, again:

> [*Praktike* was] the term that classical philosophers had coined for the active life of engagement in the world in contrast to *theoretike,* used to designate a life of intellectual activity (contemplation). *Praktike,* however, for Evagrius, does not mean life in the world, rather it refers to the initial stage of the spiritual life which is characterized by effort or activity, the effort of striving to follow the commandments and cultivate virtues, and of struggling against temptation.[21]

Though the monks train in this spiritual life in a different way than secular Christians do, there is only one Christian spiritual life. Like the monk, the liturgical ascetic must also begin at the point of struggle with the passions. Driscoll sees a chain of efforts. "*Demons* inspire *thoughts,* and these, when they are allowed to linger, unleash the *passions* in us. The remedy against this system of demonic attacks is a constant vigilance over thoughts, never

19. Bamberger, introduction to *The Praktikos,* lxxxvii.
20. Louth, *The Origins of the Christian Mystical Tradition,* 102.
21. Louth, *Maximus the Confessor,* 35–36.

allowing them to linger. *Praktike* is learning this art."[22] Kavanagh describes it as a "practical discipline of oneself by which a certain initial ordering of basic passions is brought about."[23] He points to the final chapter of The Rule of Benedict, where the founder of Western monasticism describes his book as a "little Rule for beginners," and says that if someone has had some success with this beginning, then whoever aspires to the perfect life should turn to the teachings of the holy fathers. Kavanagh concludes, "Benedict clearly expects all of this not as the consummation of spiritual endeavor but as the first 'rudiments of the monastic life.'… In other words, a *Praktikos*. What lies beyond all this he does not go into."[24] But Evagrius will. Evagrius will identify two stages beyond *praktike*. The fundamental division for him is between discipline and contemplation (*praktike* and *theoria*), but contemplation is of two types according to their objects. They differ according to whether one is contemplating created natures or God.

Evagrius calls the second stage *physike* because, Louth says, the first stage "is followed by that of natural contemplation (*physike*, the Greek for 'natural'): this is the beginning of contemplation, in which the purified mind is able to contemplate the natural order and understand its inner structure."[25] The ascetical exercises are required to set one's mind free for such understanding. "*Praktike* leads to *apatheia*. That the soul is on the verge of reaching *apatheia* becomes manifest when the soul can pray without distraction, when it is unconcerned about the things of the world in the time of prayer.… So, as the soul attains *apatheia*, the *nous* becomes aware of itself, its own light, its own powers: it enters into *theoria*."[26] Each stage has its own appropriate affect upon the soul, and together they produce the freedom that the ascetic desires. Clement writes,

22. Driscoll, *Evagrius Ponticus: Ad Monachos*, 13.
23. Kavanagh, "Eastern Influences on the Rule of Saint Benedict," 57–58.
24. Ibid., 60.
25. Louth, *Maximus the Confessor*, 35–36.
26. Louth, *The Origins of the Christian Mystical Tradition*, 106–7.

> Contemplation begins only after the completion of ascetical exercises (*praxis*), the aim of which is the achievement of interior freedom (*apatheia*), that is to say, the possibility of loving. Contemplation consists of two stages: direct communion with God is the aim, of course, but first we must come to "knowledge of creatures" or "contemplation of nature" (*physike theoria*), that is, the contemplation "of the secrets of the glory of God hidden in his creatures."[27]

This is more than a nature walk in the woods. It is seeing nature as God's creation, and the laws of providence at work in it, and that requires a light shed upon nature by Scripture. Bamberger says this stage "includes penetration into the meaning of Scripture. Also included is the structured order of the universe, the varieties of natural phenomena and the natural symbols that fill our world—all these provide material for the pure of heart to grow in understanding of the ways of God with men, and so reveal something further about the nature of God himself."[28] This natural contemplation is spiritual insofar as one sees beyond the appearances to know the Creator in the signs of his creatures. It sounds like a training in sacramental vision, or a capacitation for hierophany. Kavanagh says the upshot of *physike* is not information, but a manner of life.

> Here one struggles to know the world as it truly is by studying and reflecting on holy scripture, the structured order of the universe, natural phenomena, and the symbols by which all creation is expressed by language and one's culture. *Theoria physike* does not stop, however, with natural knowledge and poetic insight. It must result in a morality, a manner of life commensurate with such knowledge and insight. Here the practical discipline that was preparatory for asceticism is recapitulated on a higher level.[29]

It would seem, then, that in the stage between being an ascetic and being a theologian, one must become a physician. Not the medical kind. Not the scientific kind, either. Evagrius's phys-

27. Clement, *The Roots of Christian Mysticism,* 213.
28. Bamberger, introduction to *The Praktikos,* lxxxix.
29. Kavanagh, "Eastern Influences on the Rule of Saint Benedict," 57–58.

ics transcends our splintered definition because his is the kind of physics that heals (like the former) by means of knowing (like the latter). A true physician knows the world to be a temple. He knows what matter is for, and therefore knows the cure for what is the matter with the world. Evagrius writes in chapter 82 of the *Praktikos,* "Just as the soul perceives its sick members as it operates by means of the body, so also the spirit recognizes its own powers as it puts its own faculties into operation and it is able to discover the healing commandment through experiencing the impediments to its free movement."[30] Only a healed eye that sees by the light of Mt. Tabor can view the cosmos in this way. It is a vision available to everyone who washes their eyes with the waters of baptism, and bathes them in tears. "Contemplation in this view, then, is not a mere luxury for a few specially favored souls. It is the indispensable activity of every Christian who would become perfect."[31] *Theoria physike* is a contemplation of nature, of beings, of the created. "That God can be known from his works was proclaimed by all the Fathers.... For the friends of God the universe therefore becomes an open book, a school for souls."[32]

Evagrius calls the third stage *theologia*. Kavanagh summarizes how the stages are each involved with *apatheia*:

> *Apatheia* for Evagrius is a dynamic and abiding equilibrium of lucid clarity that comes about, in its initial degree, as we said, as the ordering of basic passions associated with the first stage of the discipline. It then appears in a heightened manner when the ascetic's "contemplation of nature" progresses into a morality, a manner of life at peace with creation. *Apatheia* finally consummates itself in the contemplation of God in and for his own sake.[33]

Though it is a marvel to see God mediated in the thousand mirrors of a thousand creatures, the contemplation of the physical world is penultimate to the third and final stage, that of *theolo-*

30. Evagrius, *Praktikos,* 82.
31. Bamberger, introduction to *The Praktikos,* lxxxvii.
32. Spidlik, *The Spirituality of the Christian East,* 336–37.
33. Kavanagh, "Eastern Influences on the Rule of Saint Benedict," 58.

gia, which Louth says is "understood in the usual patristic sense, not as some kind of academic study, but as knowledge or contemplation of God, a knowledge which is transforming, so that the mind becomes God, or is deified."[34] Here one contemplates God himself—but not as a rational exercise, rather as noetic experience. "It amounts to the experiential knowledge of God through the highest form of prayer."[35] Now we begin to get the first glimpse of what Evagrius meant when he said "[i]f you are a theologian you truly pray. If you truly pray you are a theologian."[36] Participation in the life of the Trinity is the ultimate goal of ascetical prayer, which is more than rational knowledge about God: it is experiential knowledge of the Trinity made possible by the Son's revelation of the Father and made available by the Holy Spirit's indwelling in us as God's temple. John Cassian translates *apatheia* into Latin as *puritas cordis*—blessed are the pure in heart, for they shall see God; theology is vision. The whole aim of asceticism is to capacitate a person for prayer, and the highest experience of prayer is *theologia*. Kavanagh summarizes.

> The third stage Evagrius called *theoria tes hagias triados* or "contemplation of the Holy Trinity." For him this is synonymous with *theologia*—not "theology" as an academic discipline but as the supreme calm, steady regarding of the Godhead as it is in itself. The knowledge of this sort of prayer and contemplation is effortless because it is simple: it circles peacefully, quietly, closer to God than God's own external attributes. Its quality is the "apathy" of possession: its source is in God himself, its end is total union (*henosis*) in God, what in the West would come to be termed the "beatific vision."[37]

A lifetime of liturgy in all its dimensions—the liturgical year, the liturgy of the hours, the Divine Liturgy, the fasts and feasts, the sacraments and sacramental—is required to give a person this calm, steady, ascetical regard of the Godhead. Liturgy is the

34. Louth, *Maximus the Confessor,* 36.
35. Bamberger, introduction to *The Praktikos,* lxxxiin231.
36. Evagrius, *Chapters on Prayer,* 60.
37. Kavanagh, "Eastern Influences on the Rule of Saint Benedict," 57–58.

perichoresis of the Trinity kenotically extended to invite our synergistic ascent into deification. By her ascetical formation in the liturgical life, Mrs. Murphy becomes a theologian.

This theology is a gift, but synergistically received. "This kind of penetration into the Divinity is an exalted state and as such is beyond the mere capacity of man. Man can only pray for it and humbly and gratefully receive it as a gift.... In this mysticism at its highest point it is the Blessed Trinity that is the object of vision.... Pure prayer brings the soul to a glorious experience of interior light."[38] In the introductory letter to Anatolius accompanying *The Praktikos,* Evagrius gives his succinct summary of the spiritual life by quoting what he claims was said when the monastic habit was conferred.

> The Fathers speak the following words to the young monks: "The fear of God strengthens faith, my son, and continence in turn strengthens this fear. Patience and hope make this latter virtue solid beyond all shaking, and they also give birth to *apatheia.* Now this *apatheia* has a child called *agape* who keeps the door to deep knowledge of the created universe. Finally, to this knowledge succeed theology and the supreme beatitude."[39]

The necessary role of asceticism becomes clearer. The ascetical tradition finds a connection between purity of heart and clarity of mind, and that connection is *agape,* child of *apatheia* who opens the door to contemplation. This fact is especially taken up by Maximus the Confessor as he unfolds the consequences of love. George Berthold summarizes Maximus's view of theology by describing it as "direct communion with God in pure prayer, and 'to theologize [*theologein*] 'is to pray in spirit and in truth."[40] In Maximus's own words:

> The mind that has succeeded in the active life advances in prudence; the [mind] in the contemplative life, in knowledge. For to the former it

38. Bamberger, introduction to *The Praktikos,* xc–xci.

39. Evagrius, "Introductory Letter to Anatolius," which accompanies the *The Praktikos,* edited by Bamberger, 14.

40. George Berthold's note 82 in *Maximus Confessor: Selected Writings,* 92.

pertains to bring the one who struggles to a discernment of virtue and vice, while to the latter, to lead the sharer to the principles of incorporeal and corporeal things. Then at length it is deemed worthy of the grace of theology when on the wings of love it has passed beyond all the preceding realities, and being in God it will consider the essence of himself through the Spirit, insofar as it is possible to the human mind.[41]

All this is summarized in Evagrius's terse remark "The goal of the ascetic life is charity; the goal of contemplative knowledge is theology."[42]

Theologia is not just knowing; it is better understood as a kind of participation, and there is no true knowledge of God without love, because the God whom we are understanding by experiential participation is a love-filled perichoresis bowing the heavens to come near to us. Training in theology is training in love, which involves an ascetical defeat of all distortions of love. This capacitates us for life in the Kingdom of God, as Evdokimov describes it. "It is in the offering of the heart to God that the Spirit manifests itself and introduces the human being into the eternal circulation of love between the Father and the Son, and this is the 'Kingdom.'"[43] The fact that prayer is a gift, resulting from the Trinity having reached out to invite our ascension, can be sensed in the various definitions Evagrius gives in *Chapters on Prayer.*

3. Prayer is a continual intercourse of the spirit with God.
35. Prayer is an ascent to the spirit of God.
52. The state of prayer can be aptly described as a habitual state of imperturbable calm [*apatheia*]. It snatches to the heights of intelligible reality the spirit which loves wisdom and which is truly spiritualized by the most intense love.
58. If you wish to pray then it is God whom you need. He it is who gives prayer to the man who prays.
60. If you are a theologian you truly pray. If you truly pray you are a theologian.

41. Maximus, *Four Hundred Chapters on Love,* 2.26.
42. Evagrius, *Praktikos,* 84.
43. Paul Evdokimov, "Saint Seraphim of Sarov," *Ecumenical Review* 15 (April 1963): 273.

62. The Holy Spirit takes compassion on our weakness, and though we are impure he often comes to visit us. If he should find our spirit praying to him out of love for the truth he then descends upon it and dispels the whole army of thoughts and reasonings that beset it. And too he urges it on the works of spiritual prayer.

69. Stand guard over your spirit, keeping it free of concepts at the time of prayer so that it may remain in its own deep calm. Thus he who has compassion on the ignorant will come to visit even such an insignificant person as yourself. That is when you will receive the most glorious gift of prayer.[44]

Tomas Spidlik urges us to find the splendor of the word "theology," now shopworn from long use. "The ancient Christian East understood the practice of theology only as a personal communion with *Theos,* the Father, through the *Logos,* Christ, in the Holy Spirit—an experience lived in a state of prayer."[45] Theology is seeing all things by the light of Mt. Tabor, and this light still shines from the altar of the Lord.[46] That is why liturgy is a *locus theologicus.* Doing liturgical theology will require a conversion of mind (*nous*), because theological *episteme* stands upon liturgical *askesis.* The capacity for theology will depend upon a renewed mind, a *meta-nous,* that is, *metanoia,* or repentance. Does Mrs. Murphy have the capacity for this wisdom? Then she can theologize. A liturgical ascetic becomes a theologian. In the words of Archimandrite Vasileios, "True theology is always living, a form of hierurgy, something that changes our life and 'assumes' us into itself: we are to become theology. Understood in this way, theology is not a matter for specialists but a universal vocation; each is called to become a 'theologian soul.'"[47] There is an ascetical cost to liturgical theology.

The difference between *praktike* and *theoria,* therefore, is not

44. Evagrius, *Chapters on Prayer.*

45. Spidlik, *The Spirituality of the Christian East,* 1.

46. See David Fagerberg, "The Cost of Understanding Schmemann in the West," *St. Vladimir's Theological Quarterly* 53, nos. 2–3 (2009): 179–207.

47. Archimandrite Vasileios, *Hymn of Entry: Liturgy and Life in the Orthodox Church* (Crestwood, N.Y.: St. Vladimir's Seminary Press, 1984), 27.

a division that separates, it is a distinction within a unity. Praxis and theory; doing and knowing; discipline and spiritual knowledge—these both together make up one ascetical complex. A person cannot contemplate spiritual things so long as his or her soul is distracted in its appetites (concupiscible passions) and distorted in its incensive power (irascible passions). The rational part of the soul cannot turn to contemplation unless the concupiscible and irascible faculties are apathetic. A person has unified faculties, therefore concupiscible or irascible passions will affect the workings of memory, imagination, intellect, understanding, insight, reason, speculation, and wisdom. "For Evagrius, passions in the concupiscible and irascible parts have to be defeated for virtue to be established in the rational part."[48] Thus, virtue and contemplation are codependent. They are as unified as body and soul. Isaac the Syrian says, "Now, just as it is impossible for the soul to come into existence and birth without the complete formation of the body, so it is impossible that contemplation which is the second soul, the spirit of revelations, be formed in the womb of the intellect ... without the bodily practice of virtue."[49] One cannot know God (liturgical theology) without first being established as an ordered person (liturgical asceticism), because spiritual knowledge is a fruit for which the initial ascetical discipline is the necessary precondition. *Theologia* is the flower on the bush of *apatheia* when it is rooted deeply in *praktike*. Viewed from the bottom up, from root to flower, we may say asceticism leads to *apatheia,* which begets *agape,* and this opens the door to *theoria.* Or, viewed in a downward direction, from flower to root, Evagrius can write, "*Agape* is the progeny of *apatheia. Apatheia* is the very flower of *ascesis. Ascesis* consists in keeping the commandments. The custodian of these commandments is the fear of God which is in turn the offspring of true faith."[50] In the healthy person the

48. Driscoll, *Evagrius Ponticus: Ad Monachos,* 126.
49. Isaac of Nineveh, *On Ascetical Life* (2.25), 39.
50. Evagrius, *Praktikos,* 81.

concupiscible and irascible faculties will aid *theoria,* according to Driscoll.

Perfect passionlessness means that health is established in the two passionate parts of the soul, the concupiscible and the irascible. Then these two parts work together to maintain the soul in this state and to leave it free for its higher parts, the rational, to function for knowledge. The concupiscible part *desires* virtue and knowledge. The irascible part *fights* the evil thoughts which attack all three parts of the soul. In the passionless soul, thoughts from the passionate part no longer mount up to darken the mind, and thereby is the rational part ready to pass into knowledge.[51]

Apatheia exists when all the parts of the soul are healed and act according to their proper nature. Maximus says "the soul is moved reasonably when its concupiscible element is qualified by self-mastery, its irascible element cleaves to love and turns away from hate, and the rational element lives with God through prayer and spiritual contemplation."[52] Christ is our model for such dispassion, and as the new Adam he reveals what human nature should have been, then elevates our fallen nature through the Holy Spirit's application to us of the fruits of the paschal mystery so we may share his filial relationship with the Father. "Prayer, contemplation, knowledge—these are the mind's true activity. The mind can enter these when it is rid of evil thoughts, when the irascible is healthy, when it is filled with love."[53] We cannot love properly so long as we are afflicted by self-love, Maximus says, because apart from the call of God, we are in a state of *philautia* (self-love) and from this condition all the passions flow.[54] But when healed, the liturgical ascetic has a mind returned to its paradisiacal condition. "What characterizes such a mind? A gentle soul! Once again, gentleness summarizes the whole life of *praktike* and prepares the way for *praktike*'s goal: the

51. Driscoll, *Evagrius Ponticus: Ad Monachos,* 10–11.
52. Maximus the Confessor, *Four Hundred Chapters on Love,* 4.15.
53. Driscoll, *Evagrius Ponticus: Ad Monachos,* 234.
54. Louth, *Maximus the Confessor,* 38.

mind able to fix itself on that for which it longs. Such a mind is a pure mind."[55]

How the soul can remain gentle is another opportunity for us to make an apologetic for calling this asceticism liturgical. The capacity for *apatheia* comes from the Christian liturgical mysteries, and not from philosophical secret knowledge or psychological coping mechanisms. The patience of the liturgical ascetic is not the same as the patience of the stoical ascetic, because the latter derives from indifference toward the temporal face of death, while the former derives from faith in a victory over death that has entered time. It is precisely this hopeful patience that Olivier Clement calls "a form of interiorized monasticism. It is the opposite of despondency.... Patience puts its trust in time. Not merely in ordinary time, where death has the last word and where time erodes, separates and destroys everything, but time mingled with eternity, as it is offered to us by the Resurrection."[56] Stoicism, and all similar types of philosophical gritting of teeth, teaches us how to put up with time, while liturgical asceticism teaches Christ, the wisdom of God, who redeemed time and made time a tool of our redemption. The patience and gentleness of soul that we are talking about comes from faith in the Resurrection, celebrated every eighth day when the liturgical ascetic stands in the eschatological light beaming from the mysteries of Christ (the sacraments of the Church).

Gregory of Nyssa speaks at length about a different perception of time afforded us by eschatology. He contrasts cyclical time with time that contains the eternal. He likens life in cyclical time to the condition of the Hebrew slaves in the mud pits of Egypt, observing that our "receptacles for pleasure" can be filled, but they're always emptied again before the next pouring. "As soon as a person satisfies his desire by obtaining what he wants, he starts to desire something else and finds himself empty again;

55. Driscoll, *Evagrius Ponticus: Ad Monachos*, 318.

56. Clement, *Three Prayers* (Crestwood, N.Y.: St. Vladimir's Seminary Press, 2000), 79.

and if he satisfies his desire with this, he becomes empty once again and ready for another."[57] We may enjoy finite pleasures repetitively, but every finite pleasure is subject to the power of death. Cyclical experiences flow into the soul like rivers empty into the sea, Gregory says, only the sea grows no larger. "What is the purpose of this passage of water constantly filling what is already filled? Why does the sea continue to receive this stream of water without being increased by the addition?"[58] The Russian Orthodox philosopher Vladimir Solovyof also points out that a pleasure lasts only for the moment it is being experienced, and after that it is no longer a pleasure but a memory. Just as one cannot remember pain, only having been in pain, so one cannot remember pleasure, only having had a pleasure. "All pleasures when they are over cease to be pleasures, and we know this beforehand. Hence the idea of a sum of pleasures is meaningless: the sum of zeros is not any larger than a simple zero."[59]

True peace is not achieved by stacking up a collection of pleasurable moments because our mortal receptacles, bound to death, will be empty before the next pouring. But God will increase our capacity for immortal things, by ascetical dilation, until we can contain all the beatitude for which God created us. We are made for Immortal happiness—which does not mean how long the happiness will last, but from whom it must come. Already, one can participate in this eternal dimension through an entity called the Church, which God has brought into existence and is bringing to completion: its charter is the Incarnation of Jesus, in whom the divine and human were united, and who is the firstborn of many brothers and sisters with whom he shares his life. Liturgical life is therefore participation in Christ's life in the Father, accomplished in us by the Holy Spirit. Resurrection is affirmed and death is overcome at every moment. Chris-

57. Gregory of Nyssa, *From Glory to Glory*, 87–88.
58. Ibid., 85.
59. Vladimir Solovyof, *The Justification of the Good* (London: Constable, 1918), 123.

tian liturgists are formed by baptism, which was called "a return to Paradise" where death has no dominion (so baptisteries were decorated like the Garden of Eden); they are fed at the Eucharist, whose antidote to death was called the "medicine of immortality"; and they are disciplined in spiritual asceticism as a sort of preemptive mortification. Asceticism pries our allegiance away from the fading goods of the flesh to eternal goods of the spirit, not because temporal things are not good, but because they are only temporary. They were meant to be pointers, stepping stones. Liturgical asceticism consists of overcoming death by death, and being capacitated to contain the glory of God. Though space, time, and matter will evanesce, they are capable of being made into a three-sided liturgical loom on which eternal life is woven, one day to be gently lifted off by the master weaver, without dropping a stitch, and fitted into his own radiant garment. The sepulcher has become a birth canal.

To realize that we were made for eternity radically reorientates priorities, as the saints have always witnessed. Gregory of Nyssa counsels, "If you realize this you will not allow your eye to rest on anything of this world. Indeed, you will no longer marvel even at the heavens. For how can you admire the heavens, my [son], when you see that you are more permanent than they? For the heavens pass away, but you will abide for all eternity with Him who is forever."[60]

The *apatheia* which asceticism affords comes not from disregard of the world, then, but from a proper hierarchy of values. The spell-binding power of such peace was an objective for the Western Middle Ages, too, according to Etienne Gilson. "*Pax*: a magical word for medieval souls, sweetly and tranquilly announcing the most precious and yet most elusive of goods. For lack of this man wanders restlessly on from object to object."[61]

60. Gregory Nyssa, in Danielou, *From Glory to Glory*, 162.

61. Etienne Gilson, *The Spirit of Medieval Philosophy* (New York: Charles Scriber's Sons, 1940), 271–72.

But the Christian ascetic proposes a solution to this restlessness that is different from that of the Greek philosophers.

> The whole ascesis of Epicurean and Stoic ethics is, in this sense, purely negative; it demands renunciation of all and offers no compensation. Christian ascesis on the other hand is positive; instead of frustrating desire by denying its object, it fulfils it by revealing its meaning, for if it can be satisfied with nothing in this world, that is perhaps because it is made for something greater than all the world. Man, then, must either make up his mind to be content with goods that cannot content him—and that would be to recommend a resignation that is first cousin to despair—or else he must renounce desire itself; for it is mere folly to wear oneself out in trying to appease a hunger reborn with every sop that is flung to it. But if he does this what shall he receive in return? No less than all.[62]

Liturgical asceticism is an attitude toward the world that comes from seeing the world in a different light. But this light cannot be self-generated, as the philosopher might think; it is an eschatological light, and it comes from God, as the liturgical theologian experiences.

The connection between *physike* and *theoria* is not just serial; they are connected by the hinge of love, as we have seen. "This *apatheia* has a child called *agape,* who keeps the door to deep knowledge of the created universe. Finally, to this knowledge succeed theology and the supreme beatitude."[63] Evagrius says at the very beginning of the *Ad Monachos,*

> Faith: the beginning of love.
> The end of love: knowledge of God.[64]

Faith, love, knowledge; *pistis, agape, gnosis.* Love is the thread that connects faith with *theologia*; love is the trunk between root and flower; faith and knowledge are love's *terminus ad quo* and *terminus ad quem.* However, it would be a grave mistake to think Evagrius has mere cognition in mind when he speaks of this knowledge of God (*gnosis Theou*). Bouyer makes clear at several

62. Ibid.

63. Evagrius, *Letter to Anatolius,* 14.

64. Evagrius, *Ad Monachos,* para. 3 (Driscoll, *Evagrius Ponticus: Ad Monachos,* 41).

places in his study of the term that *gnosis* becomes "a divine vision that makes immortal."[65]

Knowledge flowers from union.... Gregory, in his *Sixth Homily on the Beatitudes,* explains that, for the Bible, "to know means the same thing as to possess," and, a little further on, that "he who knows God possesses through this knowledge all the good things that actually exist." Gnosis itself is defined, in the opusculum to Hieron ... as "participation (*metaousia*) in God." This is what the *Sixth Homily on the Canticle* expresses in a similar way by saying that there is produced between the soul and God "a mutual compenetration, God coming into the soul and the soul being transported in God," or again that the soul becomes "susceptible of the divine indwelling."[66]

Gnosis is an apprehension of the secrets of God concerning the world and man, and uniquely the great secret: the "mystery" of Christ and His Cross, which recapitulates all history, reconciles all creation with its creator.[67]

Mystery is not something to know, it is something to be and do. If this would finally dawn on us, we would recognize the liturgical and ascetical dimensions of theology. Louth traces a valuable distinction here to a comment made by Aristotle about the Eleusinians: the initiates "do not learn (*mathein*) anything, rather they experience (*pathein,* or suffer) something."[68] This is repeated by that great theologian of the mysteries, Dionysius, who distinguishes two types of theological language. One is manifest, knowable, philosophical, capable of proof; the other is ineffable, mystical, symbolic, and presupposes initiation. And that latter kind of theology is explicitly said not to teach anything. Dionysius here follows his master, Hierotheus, whose wisdom comes from experiencing (*pathon*) the divine things he learned about. "For he had a 'sympathy' with such matters, if I may express it

65. Louis Bouyer, *The Spirituality of the New Testament and the Fathers,* vol. 1 of *A History of Christian Spirituality* (New York: Seabury Press, 1982), 249. It was an ancient understanding that the eye seized the object it looked upon and took it into itself. So take care what you see. You begin to look like what you look at. If we are to become like God, he must let himself be seen; deification depends upon incarnation.

66. Ibid., 367.

67. Ibid., 239.

68. Andrew Louth, *Denys the Areopagite* (Wilton, Conn: Morehouse-Barlow, 1989), 25.

this way, and he was perfected in a mysterious union with them and in a faith in them which was independent of any teaching."[69] It seems appropriate to describe liturgical asceticism as the cultivation of a "sympathy" with divine things offered by the liturgical mysteries, and to describe liturgical theology as knowing those mysteries by "suffering" them.

It is wrong, then, to place love in opposition to knowledge, Driscoll says, because "love is not merely a passageway; it must remain a permanent part of the life of one who has entered into knowledge.... Love remains a permanent part of knowledge for a necessary reason: because knowledge means knowledge of a God who is love."[70] The liturgical life requires knowing God through exercising (*askesis*) our capacity for love. In order to know and love God, the Christian must begin by purification so that he or she can approach God with the highest power of the human soul. Such *theoria* is a natural longing of the soul, anyway. In the words of Isaac the Syrian, *praktike* "purifies the passionate part of the soul through the power of zeal; contemplation refines that part capable of knowing by means of the energy of the love of the soul, which is its natural longing."[71] To know God (to be a theologian), one must become love, and this is liturgical asceticism's very purpose.

> In the theological tradition of which Evagrius was a part, there was a widely diffused tenet, stemming directly from Platonism, that only like could know like, that knowledge could be had on its deepest level only by a participation in the object to be known. Thus, to know God one must be like God; it must be a knowledge by participation.... This is why *love* is the door to *knowledge*. Ultimately it is God whom one *knows*, and God is *love*.[72]

In the first stage of contemplation identified by Evagrius, *physike* arrives at knowledge of the *Logos* through his *logoi* lying hid-

69. Dionysius, *The Divine Names*, 2.9
70. Driscoll, *Evagrius Ponticus: Ad Monachos*, 222.
71. Isaac of Nineveh, *On Ascetical Life* (2.21), 37.
72. Driscoll, *Evagrius Ponticus: Ad Monachos*, 297–98.

den within each creature, like a fossil lies hidden within shale until the stone is broken open. This knowing is an accomplishment of the whole person. Because the person is a complex of intellective, concupiscible, and irascible faculties, the knowledge begins with a conversion that straightens out our bent faculties. Because the fall has darkened the *nous,* we now look at our neighbor with lust, we look at the goods of the earth avariciously or gluttonously, we look at God as a threat to our freedom. The *nous,* or "eye of the heart," cannot see without opaqueness and distortion. Without dispassion, contemplative knowledge can know neither the physical world nor God accurately. The stages of contemplation are connected because the liberated mind journeys from contemplation of God in nature to contemplating God in himself. Maximus explains: "when the mind is completely freed from the passions it journeys straight ahead to the contemplation of created things and makes its way to the knowledge of the Holy Trinity."[73] In the dispassionate soul, the world bears lucid testimony to its Creator and beckons the seer to come up higher and contemplate its maker. Failure to do so, and remaining fixated on the creature, wounds the creature. When man and woman do not fulfill their cosmic priesthood, nature is wounded, because by our failure matter cannot fulfill its end any more. Thus, Ephrem describes the reaction of the sun to human idolatry.

> The sun bellowed out in silence to the Lord against his worshippers.
> It was a suffering for him, the servant, that instead of his Lord he was
> worshipped.
> Behold the creation is joyful that the Creator is worshipped....
> Since fools honored the sun, they diminished him in his honor.
> Now that they know he is a servant, by his course he worships his Lord.
> All the servants are glad to be counted servants.
> Blessed is he who set the natures in order!
> We have done perverse things that we should be servants to servants.[74]

73. Maximus the Confessor, *The Four Hundred Chapters on Love,* 1.86.

74. Ephrem, *Hymns on the Nativity,* in *Ephrem the Syrian: Hymns* (New York: Paulist Press, 1989), 180–81.

Had Adam and Eve not forfeited their liturgical vocation as cosmic priests, then sun and earth and air and elements would have rejoiced for being used in a cosmic liturgy of praise. And the nearer the saint comes to *apatheia,* the more he or she is at peace with creation.

There is much talk these days about the sacramentality of creation, which is fine enough, but recovery of the world's sacramentality cannot be thought to rely on cognition alone, without *askesis.* It will require a liturgical asceticism. The restoration of sacramentality will not come from education, it will have to come from uprooting the passions, since creation did not cease to be sacramental to Adam and Eve because they became stupider, but because they became passionate. Louth writes,

> Natural contemplation is so called because at this stage the mind is able to contemplate the *logoi* that lie behind the natural order. In Christian usage, this notion of the *logoi* can be traced back to Origen: they are the principles in accordance with which everything in the cosmos was created through the Word of God, the *Logos.* In the fallen world they are no longer clear to us; we tend not to see *God's* meaning in the world and all its parts, rather we tend to see the world in relation to ourselves and read into it *our* meaning.... To see the *logoi* of the natural order is to see it as it is and to be freed from our private prejudices, which are rooted in the disorder created in our hearts by the passions. It is also to understand the providence and judgment of God.... From this point on, the soul can progress to the final stage of contemplation of God, of *theologia.*[75]

Intensifying the world's sacramentality will be a matter of conversion: it does not come about by our deduction, but by our death. Adam and Eve's concupiscible appetites did not see the Tree of Knowledge as it was meant to be seen, and the sons of Adam and daughters of Eve inherited these cataracts and no longer see the world as gift. Eyes blinded by the passions are unable to see through creation, to God, because they look at creation,

75. Louth, *Maximus the Confessor,* 37.

beguiled. That is why, although liturgical asceticism is a spiritual exercise, it involves the discipline of our bodily appetites. The world is both our means of worship and God's means of communion with us. When the liturgy does the world the way it was meant to be done, it is an ascetical accomplishment and a theological vision. This sight is purified seeing, and this knowledge is dispassionate knowing. All things will then direct the attention of a liturgical ascetic to God. Fr. Godfrey Diekmann says "Water, all water, can be called holy because it is a sacrament, a sign of God's power and beauty and love. Blessing water, or using it in liturgy, simply reveals more convincingly the fulfillment of water's intrinsic sacramentality. Liturgical word and sacrament are, so to speak, the intensification, the visible concentration of what is already incipiently present."[76] Until we discipline our proclivity to twist all things egocentrically, we cannot raise our hands in true *orans*. This liturgical ascetical theology applies both inside the sacred temple and outside in the profane world. Paul Evdokimov explores this relationship in *The Art of the Icon: A Theology of Beauty*.

> The final destiny of water is to participate in the mystery of the Epiphany; of wood, to become a cross; of the earth, to receive the body of the Lord during his rest on the Sabbath.... Olive oil and water attain their fullness as conductor elements for grace on regenerated man. Wheat and wine achieve their ultimate *raison d'etre* in the eucharistic chalice.... A piece of being becomes a hierophany, an epiphany of the sacred....
>
> Nothing in the world remains foreign to [Christ's] humanity, everything has received the seal of the Holy Spirit. This is why the Church in turn blesses and sanctifies all of creation: green branches and flowers fill the churches on the day of Pentecost; the feast of Epiphany has its "Great Blessing of the Waters and all Cosmic Matter"; at the *litya* during vespers, the church blesses wheat, oil, bread and wine ... ; at the feast of

76. Godfrey Diekmann, "Celebrating the Word," in *Celebrating the Word: The Third Symposium of the Canadian Liturgical Society*, edited by James Schmeiser (Toronto: Anglican Book Centre, 1977), 19.

the Exaltation of the Cross, the Church blesses the four corners of the earth.... Cosmic matter thus becomes a conductor of grace, a vehicle of the divine energies."[77]

The highest *theoria* is a state of prayer; it is *theologia,* and the one who truly prays is a theologian. "This is the realm of prayer, which Evagrius regards as a state rather than an activity, not so much something you do as something you are. In this state the soul recovers its true nature: 'the state of prayer is an impassible habit which snatches up the soul that loves wisdom to the intellectual heights by a most sublime love.'"[78] Every liturgist is called to such a theological vocation, to become a theologian soul, but there is an ascetical price to be paid for it. *Apatheia* calms the passions so that the mind can seek its natural longing, and under the weight of grace the mind is sunk into the heart where the beginning of the way to the Kingdom of God can be found. "The ladder of the Kingdom is within you, hidden in your soul. Plunge deeply within yourself, away from sin, and there you will find steps by which you will be able to ascend."[79] Blessed are the pure in heart, for they shall not simply think about God, or talk about God, or write about God, they shall see God. "Gain God for yourself," said Symeon the Elder to his pupil, Symeon the New Theologian, "and you will not need a book."[80]

What liturgical asceticism seeks to attain in *apatheia,* through charity, is bliss. Fr. Pavel Florensky describes bliss as preserving our self from our self. "Bliss as rest from ceaseless, greedy, insatiable desire; as the self-confinement and self-concentration of the soul for eternal life in God. In other words, the fully authoritative and therefore eternally realized command to oneself: *ma-kar,* 'do not devour yourself'—that is the task of asceticism."[81]

77. Evdokimov, *The Art of the Icon,* 117–18.

78. Louth, *Maximus the Confessor,* 37. The quote is from Evagrius, *On Prayer,* 53.

79. Isaac the Syrian, Homily 2, *The Ascetical Homilies,* 11.

80. Symeon the New Theologian, *Discourses,* 124.

81. Pavel Florensky, *The Pillar and Ground of the Truth* (Princeton, N.J.: Princeton University Press, 1997), 140.

Such bliss is elusive, but even the faintest suspicion that it could be real is enough to stir us to begin to climb. The first rung of the ladder to this Kingdom of God is deep within a person. The goal of liturgical asceticism is this state of quiet, which Maximus describes in the contemplative person:

in quietness he holds converse with himself, and by industrious study of divine providence that divinely cares for the universe he is ineffably taught the wise economy through a contemplative knowledge of beings; from there, through hidden [mystical] theology, which in ineffable ecstasy is entrusted to the pure mind alone through prayer, he becomes unutterably conversant with God, as in a cloud and unknowing, and is inscribed by the finger of the God, the Holy Spirit, within himself, in his mind, with the dogmas of piety, and outside, like Moses and the tablets, with the graces of virtue.[82]

Hesychasm is the Greek term for this silence of heart. It is not the quiet of an empty vacuum, it is the quiet of a full presence, professes Isaac the Syrian.

The man of many concerns can never be meek and quiet, because the necessary demands of his affairs (on which he expends his efforts) compel him to be involuntarily and unwillingly disturbed, and completely disperse his calm and stillness.... Without freedom from concerns do not seek for light within your soul, nor for calm and stillness when your senses are lax, nor for collected senses amid engaging affairs. Do not multiply your occupations, and you will not find turmoil in your intellect, or in your prayer. Without unceasing prayer you cannot draw near to God; and to introduce some other concern into your mind during the toil of prayer is to cause dispersion in your heart.[83]

The rungs on the ladder of divine ascent described by John Climacus seem to crowd closer together at the top. After an ascent of twenty-six steps (describing the break with the world, the fundamental virtues, and the struggle against the passion), he pauses briefly to summarize everything that has gone before, and then he treats, in quick succession, Stillness, Prayer, Dispassion, and

82. Maximus, "Difficulty 10," in Louth, *Maximus the Confessor*, 122.
83. Isaac the Syrian, Homily 19, *The Ascetical Homilies*, 98.

then the thirtieth step, "On Faith, Hope and Love." From that last rung he proclaims that "[l]ove, dispassion, and adoption are distinguished by name, and name only. Light, fire, and flame join to fashion one activity. So too with love, dispassion, and adoption."[84] Charity, *apatheia,* and deification are distinguished only by name. Neither charity nor deification are only for monks; so also *apatheia* is as much for the secular Christian as the monastic Christian.

The passions had turned us away from God, and we had become disoriented; *apatheia* consists of being reoriented: turned back to the East, to the eschatological skyline that lies just on the other side of the Eucharistic altar. Liturgical asceticism is liturgical realignment. Hence, liturgy is the locus for *askesis,* just as liturgy is the locus for theology. The goal of liturgical asceticism is nothing else than deification, which is the purpose and consequence of the Incarnation. "For Maximus, the themes of dogmatic theology provide an outline that is filled in by his ascetical theology, that is, his theology of the Christian life: the manifestation of God's glory prefigures our glorification, the Son's self-emptying foreshadows our self-emptying—in short, God the Word's becoming human opens up the possibility of human beings becoming God."[85] But as the Incarnation involved the Son's self-emptying (*kenosis*), so our deification will require us to empty ourselves of the passions. "The way up is the way down: the *kenosis* of the Son demands the *kenosis* of the adopted sons."[86]

This Taboric light has been known to illuminate not only creation, but to also shine forth from the saints of Christ themselves. God became human so that *anthropos* might be made divine. "He does not change their nature, but causes only that they, as long as they are in such union with the fire, are themselves fire."[87] It happened in the fifth century Egyptian desert:

84. John Climacus, *The Ladder of Divine Ascent* (New York: Paulist Press, 1982), 287.
85. Louth, *Maximus the Confessor,* 34. 86. Ibid.
87. Symeon the New Theologian, *The First Created Man,* 73.

Lot went to Joseph and said, "Abba, as far as I can, I keep a moderate rule, with a little fasting, and prayer, and meditation, and quiet: and as far as I can I try to cleanse my heart of evil thoughts. What else should I do?" Then the hermit stood up and spread out his hands to heaven, and his fingers shone like ten flames of fire, and he said, "If you will, you can become all flame."[88]

It happened in an eleventh-century Byzantine monastery:

One day, as he stood and recited, "God, have mercy upon me, a sinner," uttering it with his mind rather than his mouth, suddenly a flood of divine radiance appeared from above and filled all the room. As this happened the young man lost all awareness [of his surroundings] and forgot that he was in a house or that he was under a roof. He saw nothing but light all around him and did not know if he was standing on the ground. He was not afraid of falling; he was not concerned with the word, nor did anything pertaining to men and corporeal beings enter into his mind. Instead, he was wholly in the presence of immaterial light and seemed to himself to have turned into light.[89]

And it happened in a nineteenth-century Russian forest:

Then Father Seraphim took me very firmly by the shoulders and said: "We are both in the Spirit of God now, my son. Why don't you look at me?"

I replied: "I cannot look, Father, because your eyes are flashing like lightning. Your face has become brighter than the sun, and my eyes ache with pain."

Father Seraphim said: "Don't be alarmed, your Godliness! Now you yourself have become as bright as I am. You are now in the fullness of the Spirit of God yourself; otherwise you would not be able to see me as I am."[90]

Liturgical asceticism is the cost of becoming combustible.

88. Systematic Sayings, 12.8.

89. Symeon the New Theologian is speaking about himself in the third person, *The Discourses*, 245–46.

90. The account of Motovilov's experience with St. Seraphim is found in Archimandrite Lazarus Moore, *St. Seraphim of Sarov: A Spiritual Biography* (Blanco, Texas: New Sarov Press, 1994), 196.

5 MONK AND LAIC

We have been presenting asceticism as something that is an obligation upon all baptized Christians as an exercise of their vocation to holiness, and whereas the fulfillment of that vocation depends upon sacramental participation in the mystical body of Christ, and is celebrated in the corporate liturgical life of that body, we are inclined to call it liturgical asceticism. Kavanagh compares the monks to trailblazers of a path that others will also walk. "While the demands of the discipline are so staggering that only full-time ascetics can truly master its requirements (this due to the fallenness of human nature and its consequent disorder), it is a discipline open to all, required of all, and made accessible to all by the example, wisdom, and passion of full-time ascetics, whose lives are thus spent in service of all. Ascetics blaze the trail all must follow, but they do not walk it alone."[1] The trail they blaze is one that leads up to the city of God described in the book of Revelations, says Bouyer. We are all strangers and pilgrims on earth, with heaven as our true home.

1. Kavanagh, "Eastern Influences on the Rule of Saint Benedict," 57.

> The redeemed, once they have crossed the river of baptism, move upward to the city in a white throng. This company, ecstatically echoing the timeless adoration of the hypercosmic powers in hymns to their newly-won salvation, mounts up towards Christ, the cornerstone.... For, it cannot be said too often, monastic life is simply the perfect flowering of the Christian life. The monastery is simply the apex of the pilgrim Church. Or, if you prefer, it is the anticipated realization of its eternal destiny. And it is so because, like the heavenly city, it is essentially a choir of adoration, a liturgical society.[2]

In this chapter, then, we wish to make a point about the relationship between the Christian who has left the world (the monk) and the Christian who remains in the world (the ordinary Christian), even as both of them strive to overcome the world (as a fallen and rebellious state) and mount up to the city of God. Grasping this requires a series of clarifying affirmations. All Christians are called to be ascetics, though not all are called to be monks. But that a secular Christian is not called to be a monk does not mean that secular Christian lacks a call to holiness through asceticism. Liturgical asceticism is incumbent on all, and monasticism is a special type that has been called forth by the Holy Spirit in service to the whole Church. Monasticism is not an alternative form of Christianity, it is a special form of Christian communion, one that exists in order to witness to the world and minister to the Church. It is true that most of the ascetical literature came from monks, and was written as instruction for their monastic life, but the literature has application to every Christian if we properly understand the relationship between the monk and the laic.

We are borrowing term "laic" from Nicholas Afanasiev. A Christian is not "lay" by default of not being something else, that is, not being ordained a priest or professed a monk; a Christian becomes "a lay person" by virtue of being baptized and becoming one of the people of God. It seemed beneficial to Afanasiev, therefore, to have a term that can identify the layman and laywoman by

2. Bouyer, *The Meaning of the Monastic Life,* 36–37.

a positive definition of what they are, not by contrast with what they are not. Afanasiev therefore creates the neologism *laic* in his work, *The Church of the Holy Spirit*. Translator Vitaly Permiakov explains this term in a footnote. "Strictly speaking, there is no such word in Russian, at least there was not until Afanasiev. It seems that he coined the word on the basis of the Greek to create an analogy to the term 'cleric.' He uses this term so as to connote the 'sacred rank' which the 'laic' is—the 'laic' is not a non-cleric in a modern sense of a 'lay person,' i.e. one not initiated into a sacred order."[3] All the baptized are initiated into a sacred order as liturgists to celebrate the divine liturgy. So alongside the Russian *mir'anin* (Greek *biotikos*), which would mean "lay" in the sense of nonprofessional, nonexpert, nonspecialist, Afanasiev uses the Russian *laik* (Greek *laikos*) in order to assert that the baptized person is "initiated into a sacred clerical order, the royal priesthood of God in Christ."[4] The traditional use of "laity" would have to include monks, too, as persons not ordained, and we wish to distinguish the monastic ascetic from the secular ascetic—the Christian still in the world. So Afanasiev's neologism "laic" seems helpful.

Two meanings of the word "world" are in operation. In a first sense, it means creation, which is good since it comes from the hand of God. In a second sense, it means the rebellious realm, which is distorted since Satan has had his hand in it. So when the monk flees the "world," it is sin he is fleeing, not matter, not cosmos, not his own body-spirit humanity. The monk longs as much for the resurrection of the body, and the transfiguration of creatures, and the spiritualization of matter, as do the rest of us, and the monk is not running from the world that God created. He leaves the world (of sin) but remains in the world (of creation). The laic, in a mirror way, remains in the world (of creation) but cannot be of the world (of sin). Both are fleeing the one world,

3. Vitaly Permiakov, translator of Nicholas Afanasiev, *The Church of the Holy Spirit* (Notre Dame, Ind.: University of Notre Dame Press, 2007), 277n4.

4. Ibid., 278.

and neither are disparaging the other world. Both the monk and the laic have left the world for the Kingdom of God!

As we shall see below, there are numerous stories indicating that being in the desert is no guarantee that one is out of the world (as sin), and being in the world is no sign that one is not pursuing holiness (and freedom from sin). Abba Poemen makes the point by contrasting outward and inward behavior. "One man seems silent of speech, but is condemning other people within his heart—he is really talking incessantly. Another man seems to talk all day, yet keeps his silence: for he always speaks in a way that is useful to his hearers."[5] Nikitas Stithatos makes the point by warning that the environment does not a monk make:

> I have heard people say that one cannot achieve a persistent state of virtue without retreating far into the desert, and I was amazed that they should think that the unconfinable could be confined to a particular locality. For the state of virtue is the restitution of the soul's powers to their former nobility and the convergence of the principal virtues in an activity that accords with nature. Such a state is not achieved adventitiously, by external influences; it is implanted within us at our creation, by virtue of our endemic divine and spiritual consciousness; and when we are impelled by this inner consciousness in accordance with our true nature we are led into the kingdom of heaven which, in our Lord's words, is "within us" (cf Luke 17:21). Thus the desert is in fact superfluous, since we can enter the kingdom simply through repentance and the strict keeping of God's commandments. Entry into the kingdom can occur, as David states, "in all places of His dominion"; for he says, "In all places of His dominion bless the Lord, O my soul" (Ps 103:22).[6]

If asceticism is the work of controlling the passions, then don't ask *where* asceticism is done, ask *who* is an ascetic.

The laics have a vocation to holiness, but it is one that involves the world (creation). The laic pleases God by bringing the reign of God upon matter, cultures, families, art, philosophy, the domestic Church, and so forth. That is how the laic exercises Christ's

5. Alphabetical Sayings, Poemen 10.51.

6. Nikitas Stithatos, "On the Practice of the Virtues," *The Philokalia*, 4.97–98.

offices of prophet, priest, and king in the world. Their baptismal priesthood derives from Christ, in whom they were immersed at baptism and whose pattern they now follow in discipleship. Maximus suggest that this pattern of holy life is presented in the saints of the Scripture, and invite our mimicry. "For God provides equally to all the power that naturally leads to salvation, so that each one who wishes can be transformed by divine grace. And nothing prevents anyone from willing to become Melchisedec, and Abraham, and Moses, and simply transferring all these Saints to himself, not by changing names and places, but by imitating their forms and way of life."[7]

The laic can learn lessons of liturgical asceticism from monastic asceticism if those lessons are transposed from the key in which they were heard in the desert to a key in which they can be sung in the city. The monk doesn't do something the laic shouldn't do, but he does it in a different way, and the laic benefits from seeing this *askesis* concentrated to such potency. We conclude that there is therefore no competition or antagonism between monk and laic; indeed, the two bring each other to fulfillment in some way. The laic's final end is not monasticism, it is heaven. But the monk gives the laic a sighting of his destiny by living the angelic life on earth. Metropolitan John Zizioulas reminds us, "Without the ascetic dimension, the person is inconceivable. But in the end the context of the manifestation of the person is not the monastery: it is the eucharist."[8] What the monk practices with crystal clarity aids the laic in understanding his or her own liturgical asceticism. Let us try an example. We know that the monks embraced poverty in the desert, and John Climacus defines poverty this way: "The poverty of the monk is resignation from care."[9] The monk has done the more dra-

7. Maximus, "Difficulty 10," in Louth, *Maximus the Confessor,* 118.

8. John Zizioulas, *Being as Communion* (Crestwood, N.Y.: St. Vladimir's Seminary Press, 1985), 63n66.

9. John Climacus, Step 17, "On Poverty," *The Ladder of Divine Ascent,* 189.

matic, startling resignation by leaving home, civitas, marriage, and the prospects of procreation, but the laic also has cares to resign from. The laic must also practice this kind of poverty. The amount of resignation held by a tall, narrow container can also be held by a broad, flat receptacle, as you will find by pouring water from a dinner glass onto a dinner plate. The desert ascetic's discipline is the more excellent for being taller and narrower, and so it has been lauded by tradition; the secular ascetic's discipline is more diffuse because he or she is commanded by the Creator to oversee many responsibilities without being entangled in worldly cares. The laic must also avoid avarice, envy, vainglory, and the like in every case. Thus Kavanagh concludes,

> The monk is simply a baptized Christian whose witness or *martyria* is identical with the witness of every other baptized Christian. The monk's ministry or *diakonia* among his or her baptized peers in faith is to manifest the costs and radical conditions of Christian discipleship in Christ for all. Both witness and ministry are common to all Christians, including monks. But the *mode* of monastic witness and ministry in and for the community of the baptized is peculiar. It is said to be that of a *homo spiritualis* who has attained a high degree of spiritual discipline and insight by the practice of asceticism, the most distinguishing quality of which is *puritas cordis*—Cassian's phrase for Evagrius' concept of *apatheia*.[10]

When things are enlarged, they are often easier to see, and this is a service the monk gives to the Church. A small object lit from behind can extend a nearly limitless shadow if projected upon a flat landscape stretching without break to the horizon—say, for example, across a desert landscape. The monk's poverty in the desert is a shadow of the baptismal liberty from avarice cast upon the vast desert landscape, which, by being elongated and exaggerated, is easier to understand.

From among all the baptized ascetics there are some ascetics who make a vow; they are professed; it would not be inappropriate to call them professional ascetics.

10. Kavanagh, "Eastern Influences on the Rule of Saint Benedict," 59.

Now, the monk is called a "professional of prayer" because he has left everything behind and freed himself to join Jesus in his prayer. In his vicarious prayer, standing like Moses on the mountain, the monk gathers all peoples around Jesus in the same worship; thus it is the monks, before anybody else, who realize the icon of the "Church at prayer," the Bride of Rev. 22:17, who unceasingly cries for the coming of the Glory of Unity, radiation of the unity of the Most Holy Trinity, model of all reality and unity.[11]

All vocations to holiness begin with baptism into Christ, who is the light of the world and contains within himself all apostolates, as white light contains all the colors of the rainbow. All paths to holiness are baptismal refractions of the divine light into a spectrum of vocational colors. Therefore, Andrew Louth can say that

Maximus' ascetical theology in principle applies to all Christians. Although most of the writings that developed this ascetical theology in the Byzantine world were for monks and by monks (and Maximus himself was a monk), what is being discussed is something that takes place in the life of any Christian who strives to be faithful to his baptism.... "Baptized in Christ through the Spirit we receive the first incorruption according to the flesh. Keeping this original incorruption spotless by giving ourselves to good works and by dying to our own will, we await the final incorruption bestowed by Christ in the Spirit" (*Centuries on Theology* I.87).[12]

Sometimes one finds a modern laic who is uncomfortable with his or her lay status, and he or she tries to exalt himself or herself by denigrating monasticism, but this is not the general instinct of tradition. We are not normally cowed by our heroes.[13] People normally tell stories of heroes to be inspired, not to be hu-

11. Archimandrite Boniface Luykx, *Eastern Monasticism and the Future of the Church* (Stamford, Conn.: Basileos Press, 1993), 31. I can also picture the smile on his face when he repeated this in a personal conversation. "My men work hard at their prayer. They are professionals."

12. Louth, *Maximus the Confessor*, 35.

13. Chesterton said, "Any human tradition would make more of the heroes who suffered for something than of the human beings who simply benefited by it. But that does not alter the fact that there are more human beings than heroes; and that this great majority of human beings has benefited by it"; see "The Feasts and the Ascetic," *The Thing: Why I Am a Catholic*, in *G. K. Chesterton: Collected Works*, 3.237–38.

miliated, and people do not normally feel shamed upon meeting a hero. Christians have honored martyrs without feeling inadequate because they were not martyred themselves; it should be the same with the martyrdom of the monk. Yes, the tradition unhesitatingly affirms that salvation may be attained in the world. Yes, there are frequent stories in which a monk is humbled by finding a person in the city who is an equal or superior. ("It was revealed to Abba Anthony in his desert that there was one who was his equal in the city. He was a doctor by profession, and whatever he had beyond his needs he gave to the poor, and every day he sang the Sanctus with the angels.")[14] Yes, it is freely admitted that Mary needs Martha.

A brother went to visit Silvanus on Mount Sinai. When he saw the brothers hard at work, he said to the old man, "'Labour not for the meat which perisheth" (John 6:27) and "Mary hath chosen the best part" (Luke 10:42)." Silvanus said to his disciple Zacharias, "Put this brother in a cell where there is nothing." When three o'clock came, the visitor kept looking at the door, to see when they would send someone to invite him to eat but no one did so. So he got up and went to Silvanus and said, "Abba, don't the brethren eat today?" He said, 'Yes, they have eaten already." The brother said, "Why didn't you call me?" He replied, "You are so spiritual you do not need food. We are earthly, and since we want to eat, we work with our hands. But you have chosen the good part, reading all day, and not wanting to take earthly food." When the brother heard this he prostrated himself in penitence and said, "Forgive me, abba." Silvanus said, "I think Mary always needs Martha, and by Martha's help Mary is praised."[15]

Nevertheless, Mary has chosen "the better part." The words Jesus gave about Mary do contain a pearl worth diving for, and they cannot be dismissed as easily as saying that the two vocations are identical. Since it may be a challenge for some modern persons to grasp the grammar by which it can be said that two states can be equal in merit but the labor of one is more excellent, we are

14. Alphabetical Sayings, Anthony the Great 24.
15. Systematic Sayings, 10.69.

going to turn in this chapter to consider how the tradition has presented Mary and Martha.

Here is the Lucan account in chapter ten.

> Now as they went on their way, he entered a certain village, where a woman named Martha welcomed him into her home. She had a sister named Mary, who sat at the Lord's feet and listened to what he was saying. But Martha was distracted by her many tasks; so she came to him and asked, "Lord, do you not care that my sister has left me to do all the work by myself? Tell her then to help me." But the Lord answered her, "Martha, Martha, you are worried and distracted by many things; there is need of only one thing. Mary has chosen the better part, which will not be taken away from her."[16]

Augustine deals with the relationship between the two sisters by saying that when Christ delivers up the kingdom to God, then there will be a joy never taken from us, and Mary foreshadows a similitude of a joy that consists of "sitting at the feet of the Lord, and earnestly listening to his word" and "resting as she did from all business, and intent upon the truth."[17] Life now does not fully permit this heavenly delight, yet she "prefigure[s] that which shall be for eternity." The work that Martha did was necessary business, Augustine says, a good and useful business, yet it is work that will one day pass away. So Jesus was not rebuking Martha for doing something wrong, he was placing her temporal work against the backdrop of eternity.

> He did not say that Martha was acting a bad part; but that "best part that shall not be taken away." For that part which is occupied in the ministering to a need shall be taken away when the need itself has passed away. Since the reward of a good work that will pass away is rest and that will not pass away. In that contemplation, therefore, God will be all in all; because nothing else but Himself will be required, but it will be sufficient to be enlightened by and to enjoy Him alone.[18]

16. Luke 10:38–42.
17. Augustine, *On the Holy Trinity*, book 1, ch. 10.
18. Ibid.

This approach is different from scores of homilies that turn the text into a moral lesson. Since Mary appears to be complimented, and Martha appears to be chastened, the homilist feels that Martha must have committed some fault to draw Jesus' rebuke upon her, and speculates she grumbled in the kitchen with an unchristian spirit. Augustine did not take this route, and neither do most others commentators. Martha did a good thing. But there is a more excellent thing. The episode does not contrast something bad with something good, it contrasts something good with something greater.

Cassian records a conversation with Abba Moses about this passage, and this elder also instructs Cassian that "Martha was indeed devoting herself to a holy service, ministering as she was to the Lord himself and to his disciples."[19] He acknowledges that when Martha called Mary for help, "[s]he was calling her not to a disreputable task, to be sure, but to a praiseworthy service."[20] Hospitality and charity are demanded for a guest, and this is laudable. Yet what does Martha hear from the Lord?

> "Mary has chosen the good part, which shall not be taken away from her." You see, then, that the Lord considered the chief good to reside in theoria alone—that is, in divine contemplation. Hence we take the view that the other virtues, although we consider them necessary and useful and good, are to be accounted secondary because they are all practiced for the purpose of obtaining this one thing.[21]

When Jesus points this out, Abba Moses does not conclude he is disparaging Martha. "For when he says: 'Mary has chosen the good part,' although he says nothing about Martha and certainly does not seem to reprimand her, nonetheless in praising the former he asserts that the latter occupies a lower position."[22] Why? Why is the contemplative life more excellent? Not because Martha's work is not important, and not because Mary is doing her work better than Martha is doing hers, but rather because Mar-

19. Cassian, *Conferences*, 1.8.1.
20. Ibid.
21. Ibid.
22. Ibid.

tha's work will end, but Mary's will not. So Abba Moses concludes chapter 8 by saying, "To minister to the body is a transitory work: to listen to his word is the work of eternity."[23] Then he continues in chapter 10.

> I did not say that the reward of the good work would be taken away.... But I am saying that the action, which either bodily necessity or a requirement of the flesh, or the inequity of this world calls for, will be taken away.... We consider the exercise of the aforesaid works to be necessary, because without them the heights of love could not be scaled.... The things that you refer to as works of piety and mercy are necessary in this age, as long as inequity continues to dominate.... But this will cease in the world to come, where equity will rule and when there will no longer exist the inequity that made these things obligatory. Then everyone will pass over from this multiform of practical activity to the contemplation of divine things in perpetual purity of heart.[24]

Abba Moses doesn't say Martha's *reward* won't be eternal, he says her *work* is not eternal. The sisters are not different, their work is different. Similarly, we are not comparing the sincerity of the monk to the sincerity of the laic; and we are professing that the laic's righteousness can earn a heavenly reward; but the laic's work will come to an end and the monk's will not. The monk is doing heaven early—but, of course, "early" is only a temporal metaphor by which to contrast one aeon with another.

Makarios of Egypt also uses the incident with Mary and Martha to point out that prayer is superior to every virtue and commandment. He is therefore also uninterested in finding fault with Martha's actions. Jesus made his remark "not in order to disparage acts of service, but so as to distinguish clearly what is higher from what is lower. For how could He not give His sanction to service when He Himself performed such service in washing His disciples' feet."[25] How could Jesus not give his sanction to Martha's service when one day he himself would

23. Ibid., but here using Owen Chadwick's translation in *Western Asceticism*.
24. Ibid, 1.10.3 and 4.
25. St. Makarios of Egypt, "Prayer," *The Philokalia*, 3.298.

put Martha's towel around his waist to wash his disciples' feet, and command them to do the same? Yet those same disciples later came to understand (Makarios says it was in Acts 6) that it was not right for them "to abandon the word of God in order to serve at table," that they should "put first things before secondary things, although they recognized that both spring from the same blessed root."[26]

We will look at one final treatment of Mary and Martha, this one centuries later (the fourteenth), in another place (Europe), and another language (Middle English). The anonymous author of *The Cloud of Unknowing* also begins where many modern homilies fail to begin, that is, by admitting that "certainly Martha's chores were holy and important. (Indeed, they were the works of the first degree of the active life.)"[27] Yet there has never been a creature who does not approach God through the lofty *cloud of unknowing,* "and it was to this very cloud that Mary directed the hidden yearning of her loving heart. Why? Because it is the best and holiest part of the contemplative life possible to man and she would not relinquish it for anything on earth."[28] Martha's work was "important and valuable to her spiritual development,"[29] but she must understand that it is not the highest work possible. The author of *The Cloud* wants to bring his readers to realize there is a ladder to heaven that consists, first, of an upright Christian life that is predominantly active; second, of meditation upon spiritual truths regarding our own sinfulness; and, third, of entering a dark cloud of unknowing. "The first and second parts are good and holy but they will cease with the passing of this mortal life. For in eternity there will be no need for the works of mercy as there is now."[30] Yet, the remarkable fact is that eternal life can begin now, already, and this is what Mary symbolizes. This is why

26. Ibid.

27. *The Cloud of Unknowing,* translated by William Johnston (New York: Image Books, Doubleday, 1973), 71.

28. Ibid.

29. Ibid., 75.

30. Ibid.

her activity is lauded as primary. "If God is calling you to the third part, reach out for it; work for it with all your heart. It shall never be taken from you, for it will never end. Though it begins on earth, it is eternal."[31]

This leads us to refrain from either defending the laic by debasing monasticism, or defending the monk by arguing some utilitarian purpose for monasticism. Sometimes one hears such a defense of the monastic life, a toothless defense that points out the contributions that monks have made to this world. Kallistos Ware is not impressed. "They fled, not in order to prepare themselves for some other task, but out of a consuming desire to be alone with God … for the monk helps the world not primarily by anything he does and says, but by what he is, by the state of unceasing prayer which has become identical with his innermost being."[32] The monks help the world when they are permitted to be what they are: a lamp of this eternal light whose purpose is to shine. "Acquire peace," said Seraphim of Sarov, "and thousands around you will be saved,"[33] because "the true aim of our Christian life consists in the acquisition of the Holy Spirit of God."[34] The full consequence of what he intends is revealed in the famous eye-witness account by A. N. Motovilov of Seraphim's illumination with which we concluded the last chapter. When Motovilov sees the light emanating from Seraphim's face, the laic also experiences the divine peace, sweetness, joy, warmth, and smell that radiate from the monk. Seraphim tells him why this is so.

The fact that I am a monk and you are a layman is utterly beside the point. What God requires is true faith in Himself and His Only-begotten Son. In return for that the grace of the Holy Spirit is granted abundantly from on high. The Lord seeks a heart filled to overflowing with

31. Ibid., 77.

32. Kallistos Ware, "The Spiritual Guide in Orthodox Christianity," *The Inner Kingdom*, in *The Collected Works* (Crestwood, N.Y.: St. Vladimir's Seminary Press, 2001), 1.132.

33. St. Seraphim of Sarov, in Archimandrite Lazarus Moore, *St. Seraphim of Sarov* (Blanco, Texas: New Sarov Press, 1994), 46.

34. Ibid., 169

love for God and our neighbor; this is the throne on which He loves to sit and on which He appears in the fullness of His heavenly glory.[35]

The path to this hesychasm is revealed by the cross, which is why the ascetic in the desert and the ascetic in the world must both die a preemptive mortification to everything that would hinder unceasing prayer. The Ascetical Fathers frequently repeat this lesson in order to drive it home to the fledgling monks. John the Short describes the perfect monk by saying "[h]e would live as though buried in a tomb and already dead, every day feeling death to be near him."[36] When a relative in the world dies and tries to give Arsenius an inheritance, he replies, "I died before he did. Now that he is dead, how can he make me his heir?"[37] And when envy rears its head, Abba Poemen had to be reminded of his state. "Paesius, the brother of Poemen, loved one of the monks and Poemen did not like it. So he went and visited Ammonas, and said to him, 'My brother Paesius loves someone else and I don't like it.' Ammonas said to him, 'Poemen, are you still alive? Go and sit in your cell, and think to yourself that you have been in your grave a year already.'"[38] However, monks are not the only persons dead to sin and alive to God in Christ Jesus. In the waters of baptism every Christian has died to sin, Satan, and self, and must now ascetically substantiate that sacramental death in his or her life. Monks are not the only ones trained in death: all the little neophytes caught by Christ in the baptismal font are dead. He has taken one rusty nail out of his hand and bent it into a fish hook to catch us—but some he throws back into the world! Archimandrite Sophrony speaks of the Apostles sojourning in eternity while they were still here on earth. To those to whom it was given to see the Kingdom of God come with power before they tasted death, a different perception of the world was also given. These are the ways of the Lord.

35. Ibid., 203.
36. Systematic Sayings, 1.8.
37. Systematic Sayings, 6.2.
38. Systematic Sayings, 16.8.

To begin with, He seeks us, reveals His "Face" to us, draws us into His eternity. Then he may return us to the framework of time. There would seem to be no sense in this return other than to entrust us to manifest in our life the knowledge given to us of the I AM, and bear witness to His love for us. We ourselves, however, feel our return as an "absence from the Lord," as a withdrawal of grace, and we weary under the burden of the mortal body. The craving to restore the lost fullness of union with God urges one to spiritual effort, which ... becomes an ascetic science, an art, a culture. In our age this culture is largely abandoned or forgotten.[39]

The laic in the city should become as dead to sin as the hermit in the desert, for the laic has been thrown back into the world to obey the King's commands: beget justice, spiritualize creation, sit on the throne as royal *homo adorans,* and gather up the cosmos into the liturgical ascent to God. Turning from the passions is "the path that leads to the discovery of the Good," says Gregory of Nyssa. "And all the other things which attract men's love—no matter how much we may think them good and worthy of effort and possession—all these things we must transcend, for they are merely transitory and too insignificant to absorb our capacity for love."[40]

The monk lives as already dead to the possessions of the world, but the laic must live with similar faith so that when the last trumpet sounds he will drop the goods of this world without a moment's hesitation, fold up his tabernacle of clay, and enter into glory. Fr. Hugo Rahner says the Christian lives at "the exact midpoint between heaven and earth,"[41] the only place from which one can "accept and lovingly embrace the world as God's handiwork, and, at the same time, toss it aside as a child would toss a toy of which it had wearied, in order to soar upward into the 'blessed seriousness' which is God alone."[42]

39. Archimandrite Sophrony, *The Monk of Mount Athos: Staretz Silouan* (Crestwood, N.Y.: St. Vladimir's Seminary Press, 1973), 83.

40. Gregory of Nyssa, *From Glory to Glory,* 108.

41. Hugo Rahner, S.J., *Man at Play* (New York: Herder & Herder, 1972), 39.

42. Ibid., 40.

This obligation of liturgical asceticism is jointly practiced, but in different ways. And so the "athletes," the "professionals" have things to teach the ascetics in the world, but sometimes the laic can jar the monk into clarity of mind. Evagrius counsels,

> Better a gentle worldly man
> than an irascible and wrathful monk.[43]

One cenobite learned it the hard way when he tried the eremitic life prematurely. Being restless and often irritated in his community, he resolved to go and live by himself where he would "not be able to talk or listen to anyone and so I shall be at peace, and my passionate anger will cease."[44] So he went out to a cave alone, intending to be a hermit. One day when he filled his jug with water, it spilled; and then a second time; and on the third time "he snatched up the jug and smashed it. Coming to his senses, he knew that the demon of anger had mocked him, and he said, 'Here am I by myself, and he has beaten me. I will return to the community. Wherever you live, you need effort and patience and above all God's help.' So he got up, and went back."[45] It can be a seduction to think one can alter the environment instead of the heart, and that temptations will cease if only one gets some geographical distance from the cause of the temptation. No ascetic went into the desert with the idea that they would find it easier.

Another monk once asked in prayer to see a man as good as he is. God obliged. An angel revealed that he had not yet become like a certain gardener in a certain city, so the monk set off to find the laic, and pestered him until the modest gardener told him about the manner of his life.

> I usually eat late in the evening and when I finish, I set aside only what I need for my food, and the rest I give to those in need, and if I am host to any of God's servants, I give it to them. And when I get up in the morning, before I sit down to work, I say, "This city, from the least to

43. Evagrius, *Ad Monachos*, 34.
44. Systematic Sayings, 7.33.
45. Ibid.

the greatest, will enter the Kingdom because of their righteousness, but I alone will inherit punishment on account of my sins." And again in the evening when I go to sleep, I say the same thing.[46]

The monk weighed the practice in his mind and concluded that it was good, but not so good as to surpass his own labors. Had the angel been mistaken? He, too, had controlled his appetite, given to people in need, accused himself of sin, and prayed for others, just as this gardener did. Things finally came clear that evening. When they sat down at table they heard people in the street singing songs, since the gardener lived in a public place.

Therefore the old man said to him, "Brother, wanting as you do to live according to God, how do you remain in this place and not be troubled when you hear them singing these songs?" The man said, "I tell you, Abba, I have never been troubled or scandalized." When he heard this, the old man said, "What, then, do you conceive in your heart whenever you hear these things?" And he said, "That they are all going to the Kingdom." When he heard this, the old man marveled and said, "This is the practice which surpasses my labor of all these years." In apology he said, "Forgive me, brother, I have not yet approached this standard." And, without having eaten, he withdrew again in to the desert.[47]

A heart of charity toward others is the reason for the *scopos* the monk practices, and this anonymous monk finds it inside the heart of this gardener in the city. One cannot always see it in practice, which is why Maximus distinguishes an "outer monk" and an "inner monk."

The one who has renounced things such as a woman, wealth, and so forth, has made a monk of the outer man but not yet of the inner. The one who renounces the passionate representations of these things makes a monk of the inner man, that is, of the mind. Anyone can easily make a monk of the outer man if he really wishes to, but it is no small struggle to make a monk of the inner man.[48]

46. Columba Stewart, *The World of the Desert Fathers* (Fairacres, Oxford: SLG Press, 1986), 13.

47. Ibid.

48. Maximus the Confessor, *The Four Hundred Chapters on Love,* 4.50.

Paul Evdokimov follows this train of thought, defining *interiorized monasticism* as a wisdom that derives from a joyous and impatient expectation of the eschaton. This attitude of hope concerns every Christian. "When the Fathers spoke, they addressed all the members of the Church, without any distinction between clergy and laity. They spoke to the universal priesthood."[49] Evdokimov then quotes Tikhon of Zadonsk, writing to Church authorities: "Do not be in a hurry to multiply the monks. The black habit does not save. The one who wears a white habit and has the spirit of obedience, humility, and purity, he is a true monk of *interiorized monasticism*."[50]

These stories do not exist in order to show up some hypocrisy of the monk, or raise the status of laics in some sort of jealous competition. Rather they exist to remind the monk that exterior activities alone are not enough.

> Abba Sisoes was living for a time on the mountain of Abba Anthony, and his disciple was a long time coming, so he did not see anyone for ten months. Now while he was walking on the mountain he met a Pharanite who was hunting wild animals. The old man said to him, "Where have you come from? And how long have you been here?" He replied, "indeed, Abba, I have been eleven months on this mountain and I have not seen anyone except you." Hearing this the old man entered his cell and beat his breast saying, "Look, Sisoes, you thought you had done something special but you have not even equaled this layman."[51]

Ascetic writers frequently remind their readers that even after the monk's flight from the world to God, he must still confess that it is also possible to reach the same transcendent God through the world. Symeon the New Theologian deals with it at length, saying, "[s]o it is possible for all men, brethren, not only for monks but for laymen as well, to be penitent at all times and constantly, and to weep and entreat God, and by such practices to acquire all other

49. Evdokimov, *Ages of the Spiritual Life*, 137.
50. Ibid., 139, quoting Guippius, *Saint Tykhone de Zadonsk*.
51. Alphabetical Sayings, Sisoes 7.

virtues as well."[52] Symeon then references John Chrysostom's discourses on Psalm 50 to bear witness to the fact.

> In his discourses on David ... he asserts that this is possible for one who has wife and children, men and women servants, a large household, and great possessions, and who is prominent in worldly affairs. Not only is he able daily to weep and pray and repent; he can also attain to perfection of virtue if he so wishes. He can receive the Holy Spirit and become a friend of God and enjoy the vision of Him.... All the things they acquired during their lifetime they used with piety, not as though they owned them, but rather like servants of the Master.... For this reason they have become glorious and illustrious even in this present life, and now and to endless ages they will become even more glorious and illustrious in the kingdom of God. If instead of being timid, slothful, and despisers of God's commandments, we were zealous, watchful, and sober, we should have no need of renunciation or tonsure or the flight from the world. So listen to me, that you may be persuaded of what I have to say![53]

Evdokimov also cites a passage from Chrysostom saying that Christ orders all people to follow the narrow path. Therefore, the Golden Mouthed concludes, "The monk and the lay person must attain the same spiritual heights," and upon this remark Evdokimov comments: "In fact, according to the great teachers, the monastics were only those who wished 'to be saved,' those who 'led a life according to the Gospel,' who 'sought the one thing needful,' and 'did violence to themselves in all things.' It is quite evident that these words exactly define the state of every believing lay person. St. Nilus thought all monastic practices were required of people in the world."[54]

This would require us to hear certain words, words that we currently associate only with monks, in a new and larger way. We have already seen John Climacus define poverty as "resignation from care." Isaac the Syrian can build on that by refining the definition of possessiveness in such a way that it convicts the per-

52. Symeon the New Theologian, *The Discourses*, 93.

53. Ibid., 94

54. Evdokimov, *Ages of the Spiritual Life*, 137.

son in the world, too. "Do not imagine that merely the possession of gold and silver is possessiveness; rather, it is the acquisition of anything whatever which your will clings to."[55] Wills can cling to things while living in the world or in the desert. One can possess the thing but not cling to it; one can throw it down but still cling to it in one's heart. Abba Moses astutely notices that some monks who have forsaken "very great riches in this world—and not only large sums of gold and silver but also magnificent properties—being disturbed over a penknife, a stylus, a needle, or a pen."[56] And as if to convict the academic who might write about asceticism, he adds, "And often some people hold on to a book so tightly that in fact they do not easily permit another person to read or touch it, and hence they bring upon themselves occasions of impatience and death precisely when they are being urged to acquire the rewards of patience and love."[57] Evdokimov presents the challenge of the ascetical life to laics by broadening several terms to a point where they are included, too.

> *Poverty* frees from the ascendancy of the material. It is the baptismal transmutation into the new creature. *Chastity* frees from the ascendancy of the carnal. It is the nuptial mystery of the *agape*, the marriage covenant in divine love. *Obedience* frees from the idolatry of the ego. It posits our relationship as children of the Father. All, whether monks or not, must ask God for these things in the tripartite structure of the Lord's prayer: *obedience* to the will of the Father, the *poverty* of one who is hungry only for the substantial and eucharistic bread, and *chastity*, the purification from evil.[58]

Because the inaugurated eighth day is lived in supernatural charity, known in revealed faith, and believed with sustained hope, therefore all Christians make ascetical renunciation—whether as a permanent state of life (professed vow), or as a regular manner of life (the laic still in the world).

55. Isaac the Syrian, Homily 4, *The Ascetical Homilies*, 30.
56. Cassian, *Conferences*, 1.6.1.
57. Ibid.
58. Evdokimov, *Ages of the Spiritual Life*, 139.

The nineteenth-century Russian monk Fr. Ignatius Brianchaninov compares the two kinds of liturgical ascetics to flowers, and says each has its own merit. "The monk can be compared to a hot-house flower and the layman to a field flower."[59] The field flower is heartier, more rugged in its constitution, while the hot-house flower, although it must be more carefully watched, reaches a special beauty.

> In the fields it is impossible to find such beautiful and precious flowers as may be seen in a hot-house; but on the other hand hot-house flowers need special care; they cannot bear changes of weather; a slight fall in temperature may damage them, whereas the field flowers need neither care nor attention; they grow wild, and easily bear changes of temperature. All the holy Fathers order monks to exercise the strictest watchfulness over themselves, and to be always on their guard. An apparently insignificant circumstance may be for a monk an occasion of the greatest temptation, and even a fall. A careless touch, a casual glance have suddenly changed the whole state of a monk's soul, all his innermost feelings, even his way of thinking, as has been proved by unfortunate experiences.[60]

Such comments reveal that the tradition understands the monk to be a resource for the lay liturgical ascetic, and it is evident that only in rare cases was a hermit so isolated as to have had no impact whatsoever on the world around him. From Anthony the Great to Seraphim of Sarov, the pattern was to spend decades alone, in battle, but then come forth and receive seekers. Even more often, the seekers come to the monk; Pachomius describes laypeople coming out to the isolated monasteries like bees from a hive. The monk and the laic do not exist in isolation from one another, doing "parallel play," as psychologists like to call it when children of a certain age do not notice what other children are doing around them. Evdokimov says the monk has a ministry to the faithful.

59. Ignatius Brianchaninov, *The Arena: An Offering to Contemporary Monasticism* (Madras, India: Diocesan Press, 1970), 273.

60. Ibid.

Asceticism concentrates our attention and begins by an experimental phenomenology of our human interior. It was necessary to materialize and personalize the perverted elements of a being, the hateful ego with its self-love, the doubter and the demonic counterpart. Above all, it was necessary to completely eradicate them, to "vomit" them, and to objectify them, in order to look them in the face, detached and exteriorized.... *The Fathers of the desert have carried out this operation once for all and in place of all....* They have stripped humanity of its masks, and they have put a face and a name to every obscure element of evil.... After this revelation, the one going to confession knows what must be done and what is going to happen. Each time he or she repeats the experience of the desert Fathers.[61]

This self-inspection is presented as the very purpose for going into the desert. Once there were three serious men who became monks, and one of them chose to make peace between people who were angry, the second chose to visit the sick, and the third went away to be quiet in solitude. The first discovered he could not stop all quarrelsomeness; the second was overwhelmed by the sick and unable to carry out his purpose to the full.

So the two went away to see him who had withdrawn into the desert, and they told him their troubles. They asked him to tell them how he himself had fared. He was silent for a while, and then poured water into a vessel and said, "Look at the water," and it was murky. After a little while he said again, "See now, how clear the water has become." As they looked into the water they saw their own faces, as in a mirror. Then he said to them, "So it is with anyone who lives in a crowd; because of the turbulence, he does not see his sins: but when he has been quiet, above all in solitude, then he recognizes his own faults."[62]

Apatheia is water without ripples so the mind can reflect—and reflect upon—images of truth. But this deep interior reflection is not narcissistic. Makarios imagines the monk finding treasure for the whole Church.

61. Evdokimov, *Ages of the Spiritual Life*, 124–25.
62. Systematic Sayings, 2.16.

Take the example of divers who swim in the bottom of the sea and risk death in the water in order to find there pearls for a royal crown and purple dye. In similar fashion there are also those who live the eremitical life. They leave the world, stripped of everything, and descend into the depths of darkness. And from there they gather up and take back precious stones fit for the crown of Christ, for the heavenly Church, for a new world, for a lighted city and an angelic people.[63]

The monk serves the Church. The gentle soul, which loves freely and without prejudice and from out of a healthy state, cannot be explained: it must be shown. That is the reason why Christian tradition has honored and maintained the Desert Fathers' collections. These stories are like snapshots of *apatheia*. So long as Christians have held this desire, they have repeatedly returned to this collection; and when they have stopped turning to this collection it may be taken as a warning sign to our spirituality. We will take but three examples to illustrate the point, examples concerning avarice, anger, and lust.

First, what would a person look like who was in control of avarice? Two old men, after living together for many years in one cell, realized that they were ignorant of one experience common in the world: "never had there risen even the paltriest contention between them." So they laid the groundwork for an experiment. "Let us have one quarrel the way other men do," said one. The other replied, "But I do not know how one makes a quarrel." The first explained his understanding. "Look, I set a tile between us and say, 'That is mine,' and do thou say, 'It is not thine, it is mine.' And thence arises contention and squabble." So they retrieved the tile and set it between them and the first said, "That is mine." The second replied, "I hope that it is mine." The first rebutted, "It is not thine: it is mine." At this point the experiment unraveled, for the second forgot himself and said "If it is thine, take it."[64]

63. Pseudo-Macarius, Homily 15, in *The Fifty Spiritual Homilies and The Great Letter* (New York: Paulist Press, 1992), 128.

64. Systematic Sayings, 17.12. Here I am using Helen Waddell's translation, *The Desert Fathers* (Ann Arbor: University of Michigan Press, 1936), 142.

Second, what would a person look like who controlled irritability? One day Abba John was going up to Scetis with some other brothers, and their guide lost his way in the night. The brothers said to Abba John, "What shall we do, in order not to die wandering about, for the brother has lost the way?" The old man knew the right way himself, but reasoned, "If we speak to him, he will be filled with grief and shame." So instead he proposes "I will pretend to be ill and say I cannot walk any more; then we can stay here till the dawn." The others offered to stay with him, and "they sat there until the dawn, and in this way they did not upset the brother."[65] In the gentle soul, the passion of irascibility would be overcome by the still stronger force of gentleness. Although our culture perceives meekness as spinelessness, John Climacus calls it "a rock looking out over the sea of anger which breaks the waves which come crashing on it and stays entirely unmoved."[66] The angry person he compares to a "voluntary epileptic" who breaks out into involuntary convulsions of anger. The *apathetic* person, who withstands waves of anger, is the stronger one.

Third, what would a person look like who was in control of lust? This story comes from "The Life of St. Pelagia the Harlot."[67] Bishop Nonnus came to a conclave at Antioch, and while he was teaching, "Lo! On a sudden she that was the first of the actresses of Antioch passed by; first of the dancers was she ... [and] so decked that naught could be seen upon her but gold and pearls and precious stones: the very nakedness of her feet was hidden under gold and pearls."[68] When the other bishops saw her ride by shamelessly, "bare of head and shoulder and limb, in pomp so splendid, and not so much as a veil upon her head or about

65. Alphabetical Collection, John the Short 17.

66. John Climacus, Step 8, "On Placidity and Meekness," *The Ladder of Divine Ascent*, 147.

67. "The Life of St. Pelagia the Harlot." These quotations are taken from Helen Waddell's translation, 178–79. It is also found in Benedicta Ward, *Harlots of the Desert: A Study of Repentance in Early Monastic Sources* (Kalamazoo, Mich.: Cistercian Publications, 1987).

68. Ibid., 178.

her shoulders, they groaned, and in silence turned away their heads as from great and grievous sin. But the most blessed Nonnus did long and most intently regarded her: and after she had passed by still he gazed and still his eyes went after her."[69] He turned to the bishops and asked, "Did not the sight of her great beauty delight you?" The other bishops did not answer. Nonnus sank his face upon his knees, over the Bible he held in his hands, and tears fell upon his breast, and he repeated the question. They maintained their silence. And he said, "Verily, it greatly delighted me, and well pleased was I with her beauty; whom God shall set in presence of His high and terrible seat, in judgment of ourselves and our episcopate."[70] How so? Bishop Nonnus challenged his confreres to consider how many hours this woman spent on her body's beauty, that it not disappoint her lovers. Yet her lovers are here today and gone tomorrow, and her own beauty will fade, while they have an immortal Lover, a Father Almighty in heaven, and they have the promise of eternal riches. The bishop was grieved that even having been given a promise to one day have a vision of the Bridegroom upon whom the Cherubim dare not look, "we adorn not, we care not so much as to wash the filth from our miserable souls, but leave them lying in their squalor," so when he returned to his room, the good bishop flung himself on the floor and wept, saying, "Lord Christ, have mercy on a sinful man and an unworthy, for a single day's adorning of a harlot is far beyond the adorning of my soul. With what countenance shall I look upon Thee?"[71] Everything in the world—everything!—directs the righteous, ordered man to the Kingdom of God, and stirs his hunger for it.

The list of examples could go on, both from the fourth century and from contemporary times.[72] They are hypostasized dis-

69. Ibid.

70. Ibid., 179.

71. Ibid.

72. For contemporary examples, see Archimandrite Cherubim, *Contemporary Ascetics of Mount Athos,* 2 vols. (Platina, Calif.: St. Herman of Alaska Brotherhood Press, 1991),

passion, living icons in the desert, *apatheia* rendered visible. The Fathers are ascetical apparitions of the same *apathetic* life that is incumbent on all who bear baptism's *sacramentum*. Because we cannot learn *apatheia* in theory, it must be shown to us by a spiritual father or mother, and then, says Archimandrite Boniface Luykx, the exemplars lift us up.

All human activity, directed toward a transcendent goal and meant to build up community, needs an exemplar as its model and incentive, a model that incarnates, as in a life-giving root, the principal values that this community is meant to materialize in its myths and institutions. Such a paradigm works as a constant presence or anticipation of the goal as if already attained, and hence as a norm for living, an "uplifter to hang on to"; a boost to spur us on and to inspire us.[73]

He adds that Christian monasticism wants nothing else but to reach human perfection by living the core of the Gospel. For that reason, "monasticism represents the fullness of the Church, anticipating the fulfillment of the Kingdom of God."[74] The fullness of the Church comes to us through two channels, he suggests: hierarchical and charismatic. The sacraments and monasticism are the institutional and charismatic channels through which the life of Christ flows to the Church.

For the East, monastic "profession" is a *true consecration that affects the whole person and his entire life*. It is effected by the consecratory powers and actions of a solemn liturgical celebration by the Church, enacted by the priestly ministry of the Abbot or hierarch of the place; it is "existential," as is any sacramental action, in sacramentals as well as in

---

Archimandrite Ioannikios Kotsonis, *An Athonite Gerontikon: Sayings of the Holy Fathers of Mount Athos* (Thessaloniki, Greece: Holy Monastery of St. Gregory Palamas, 1997), and Hieromonk Alexander Golitzin, *The Living Witness of the Holy Mountain: Contemporary Voices from Mount Athos* (South Canaan, Pa.: St. Tikhon's Seminary Press, 1996).

73. Luykx, *Eastern Monasticism*, 55. He continues by explaining where this knowledge belongs in theology. "Since this exemplar is a final cause, it must be envisioned and treated first, so that it may mobilize and concentrate our striving and organizing powers and thus build up the community, according to the Aristotelian (and Thomistic) schema of cause: *finis primus in intentione, sed ultimus in executione* (the goal is the first to be intended, yet the last to be attained)."

74. Ibid., 57.

sacraments. Its purpose and effect are to "verticalize" the whole person for living a life out of the Gospel in a radical manner, as the living sacrifice of a person who exists for God alone, as the practical expression of the Mystery of the church and of her primary vertical (contemplative) dimension which he *celebrates* henceforth as a "professional, as one who truly belongs there."

This inner change happens by a renewed outpouring of the Holy Spirit—as it were a renewed Christian initiation; that is why monastic consecration is said to have the effects of a new baptism.[75]

Monasticism is "the pneumatic 'organism' of the Church"[76] which reminds us that the Church is not simply an institution but a mode of existence, a manner of being. Monasticism is the carrier of Tradition on the charismatic level, as the magisterium is the carrier of Tradition on the hierarchical level. Sometimes the monk's existential holiness corrects decisions made at the hierarchical level, even as the hierarchs oversee monastic life, but Luykx says their relationship is ultimately complementary, not antagonistic. They are two channels of the same life.

This charismatic character of monasticism and its standing in the heart of Christianity do not imply any anti-hierarchical attitude; rather the opposite. Both, according to Vatican II, stem in organic continuity from the Apostolic Community through the continued working of the Holy Spirit: the hierarchy, by the sacramental continuity of apostolic succession; and religious life, by pneumatic continuity of the evangelical counsels [Lumen Gentium, no. 43].... Both this sacramental and charismatic relation between hierarchy and monasticism as two essential channels of life in the Holy Spirit has always been the undergirding power for the monks being the champions of orthodoxy. Another guarantee of orthodoxy was the fact that most of the Church Fathers and leading bishops were monks themselves, or closely linked with them.[77]

We have attempted here to present the monk and the laic as coworkers in the vineyard. They share the same human nature, have the same vices to conquer and the same virtues to achieve,

75. Ibid., 85–86.
76. Ibid., 76.
77. Ibid., 81–82.

they are directed to the same purity of heart that will enable them to see God, their spiritual vocation comes from the same baptism, it is the same kingdom they seek, they both cry tears of repentance, they are both instructed to serve their neighbor even to the point of laying down their life. But they travel different roads because God treats each person as an individual. John Climacus sees this as a cause for humility:

> God in his unspeakable providence has arranged that some received the holy reward of their toils even before they set to work, others while actually working, others again when the work was done, and still others at the time of their death. Let the reader ask himself which one of them was made more humble.[78]

There is only one God, one salvation, but we are individuals and so asceticism must be individually crafted to suit each one. "There are many roads to holiness (and to hell). A path wrong for one will suit another, yet what each is doing is pleasing to God."[79] At the final judgment Christ will come to draw all holiness to himself, like a magnet; asceticism is the process of scraping off rust that prevents Christ from attracting us. Asceticism is the process of finding Christ attractive: it is erotic training. Asceticism is training for beatitude by learning to be attracted to Christ's life. We do not prepare for monasticism, we prepare for beatitude, but monasticism is what it costs to display beatitude now, existentially, in this old age, and the monk pays that price in love for mankind.

The same price will be exacted of both the monk and the laic: death. We must die to enter the Kingdom; that's why we're baptized. Asceticism is the link between baptism and beatitude for Olivier Clement.

> We have to learn—and this is the whole meaning of ascesis—to get round obstacles, to tear away dead skin, to let the very life of Christ arise

78. Ibid., 241.
79. John Climacus, Step 26, "On Discernment," *The Ladder of Divine Ascent*, 243.

in us by the power of his resurrection. Each present moment has to become baptismal: a moment of anguish and death if I seek to cling to it and so experience its non-existence, but a moment of resurrection if I accept it humbly as "present" in both senses of the word.

The exploration of this potential for resurrection was made in the deserts in the early Church, but Clement wonders where the real deserts are today.

The monk is one who of his own choice descends to death, who explores it during this life (in the desert, in the tombs—but where are the real deserts today?). The monk wears himself out sharing Adam's mourning and exile. His aim is to abandon himself without further delay to Christ who has conquered death: to see clearly in hell the dawn of baptism, and already here below to become aware of his own resurrection in the Risen One.... All the baptized are called, in one way or another, to take this monastic journey, in order to understand that their death is behind them; they have no more to fear from death of the body.[80]

80. Clement, *The Roots of Christian Mysticism*, 106–7.

6 THE FACE OF ASCETICISM

The teleological end of liturgical asceticism is to be further conformed to Christ, riding upward on baptism's artesian fountain. Gregory of Sinai understands this to come about by applying each moment in the life of Jesus to our spiritual journey.

> Everyone baptized into Christ should pass progressively through all the stages of Christ's own life, for in baptism he receives the power so to progress, and through the commandments he can discover and learn how to accomplish such progression. To Christ's conception corresponds the foretaste of the gift of the Holy Spirit, to His nativity the actual experience of joyousness, to His baptism the cleansing force of the fire of the Spirit, to His transfiguration the contemplation of divine light, to His crucifixion the dying to all things, to His burial the indwelling of divine light, to His resurrection the soul's life-quickening resurrection, and to His ascension divine ecstasy and the transport of the intellect into God. He who fails to pass consciously through these stages is still callow in body and spirit, even though he may be regarded by all as mature and accomplished in the practice of virtue.[1]

1. Gregory of Sinai, *Further Texts, The Philokalia*, 4.253.

The mysteries of Christ were first lived by him, but he lived them as a man so that other human beings may live them in union with him. Liturgical asceticism is being conformed to Christ, our souls becoming an image of the image of God. Symeon the New Theologian assures us that "in the future life a Christian will not be tested as to whether he renounced the world, whether he fasted, whether he performed vigils, whether he prayed, whether he wept, or performed any other such good deeds in the present life; but he will be carefully tested as to whether he has some kind of likeness to Christ, as a son to his father."[2]

This is why it has seemed appropriate to call this asceticism liturgical. Christianity is not a creed, or institution, or cultic activity, or doctrine— although it includes all of these—Christianity is Christ's life lived in us,[3] and Christ's entire life and mission was ascetical, as Matthew the Poor indicates:

> The divine incarnation in itself may be taken as the highest expression of ascetic action, for it required the greatest possible degree of humility. The Son of God carried this out in Himself by deliberately relinquishing all the glory of His divinity and taking the form of a humble slave, a rejected servant.
>
> Moreover, as a direct result of this, as the human will was totally united with the divine will, Christ completely conformed the human mind to the mind of God. This in itself may also be considered an act of asceticism, in the sense that it was an act of obedience by which Christ demonstrated definitively and practically His Sonship to God.
>
> Asceticism is that constant working toward conforming the human will and mind to the will and mind of God. This definition is a guide for the ascetic life itself, for it indicates that every ascetic act that does not conform to the will of God is dogmatically erroneous.[4]

2. Symeon the New Theologian, *The First Created Man: Seven Homilies by St. Symeon the New Theologian* (Platina, Calif.: St. Herman of Alaska Brotherhood, 1994), 54.

3. For a Thomist's view of this, see the conferences of Dom Columba Marmion, summarized in Fagerberg, "*Theosis* in a Roman Key? The Conferences of Columba Marmion," *Antiphon* 7, no. 1 (2002): 30–39.

4. Matthew the Poor, *The Communion of Love* (Crestwood, N.Y.: St. Vladimir's Seminary Press, 1984), 88–89.

Christian asceticism is made possible by the hypostatic union in the Incarnation. Therefore asceticism permeates within our definition of liturgy as the perichoresis of the Trinity kenotically extended toward us to invite us to a life that climbs a ladder of divine ascent. Christ is the source of our liturgy, our theology, and our asceticism. What Christ is by nature, we are to become by grace. The union of God and man in the person of Jesus (a hypostatic union) is the source of Christian liturgy (with all its sacramental graces and sacrificial offering), and Christian asceticism (as the discipline that leads to total participation in Christ), and Christian theology (a knowledge of *Theos* possessed by the *Logos* and shared with us). Liturgy, theology, and asceticism interpenetrate. (1) Asceticism that is liturgical-theological is a battle with the passions so that we might be prepared for theological encounter with God. (2) Liturgy that is ascetical-theological works an adjustment in the mind that prepares the subject for theological encounter with God. (3) Theology that is liturgical-ascetical is the presence of deifying power whereby we experientially know God. These are three atoms in one molecular structure: remove one, and you will not have the same Christian molecule. And if any element is isolated from the other two, it will no longer be the same, either. When the three are connected at the molecular level, then asceticism is more than morality, theology is more than a human science, and liturgy is more than human religious ceremony. In this chapter we will begin by considering the necessity of keeping a fruitful tension between these three, before asking where their integrated harmony can be seen. (The answer to that question will be: in the saints and their icons, and in Mary as liturgical person.)

First, when the three are kept in fruitful tension we discover that asceticism is more than morality. This asceticism is a liturgical activity, whether for monk or laic, because its goal is deification. The end of Christian asceticism is sanctity, and sanctity is a liturgical fruit, not a moral accomplishment. Athanasius Pekar describes the contrast by saying "*Moral Theology* is the study of the commandments; *Ascetical Theology* is the science of Christian perfection."[5] Christian asceticism involves the energies of the Holy Spirit at work through the sacramental life of the Church, a theme that Andrew Louth identifies in Maximus:

> Here lies the importance of monasticism for Maximus, not that sanctity is confined to a monastic elite, but sanctity is the goal of the ascetic struggle that monks have set themselves to pursue without distraction, just as sanctity is the goal of any Christian's life. But sanctity is not simply a matter of ascetic struggle: it is a response to God's presence among us in the Incarnation, a presence that can be experienced through the Sacraments, pre-eminently the Eucharist.[6]

We are positing a distinction between morality, on the one hand, and liturgical asceticism stemming from the divinizing energies of God, on the other. This difference between morality and saintliness on the side of the cure is the same as the difference between immorality and sinfulness on the side of the disease. We grant that there is a moral element to the liturgist's asceticism, but moral improvement and a better human character is not the main *telos* of liturgical asceticism; its *telos* is deification. The face of liturgical asceticism is not Marcus Aurelius but Anthony the monk. And because liturgical asceticism strives to attain to deification, moral reasoning alone cannot understand it, as Evdokimov confirms. "Asceticism has nothing to do with moralism. The opposite of sin is not virtue but the faith of the saints. Moralism exercises natural forces, and its fundamental voluntarism submits human behavior to moral imperatives."[7] He goes on to say that an ethical system is fragile and ineffective

5. Athanasius Pekar, O.S.B.M., *The Perfect Christian*, 44n15. Elsewhere (ibid., 31), Pekar describes the unified Christian faith as having been worked out along three great theological branches, emerging as "1) exegesis—the science of interpreting Holy Scripture, 2) dogma—the philosophical definition and explication of the truths of the faith and 3) asceticism—the systematic exposition of the evangelical principles of Christian life."

6. Louth, *Maximus the Confessor*, 23.

7. Evdokimov, *Ages of the Spiritual Life*, 163–64.

because it is not a source of life, that moral and sociological principles are powerless to overcome sorrow or loneliness, and that principles alone lack the power to tell a paralytic to get up and walk, they cannot pardon, absolve, wipe out of fault, or raise the dead. "The 'virtue' of the ascetics has an entirely different resonance and designates the human dynamism set in motion by the presence of God."[8]

Put bluntly, and a little unfairly, but in a way that may nevertheless be useful for the sake of clarity, we may say that it is a moral act to renounce something if it is bad, but it is an ascetical act to renounce something even if it is good. This is Mary speaking to Martha, again. Morality urges renunciation of those things injurious to a person, such as if an alcoholic gives up wine, but an ascetic does not give up wine for the moral reason that he thinks wine is bad; in fact, the ascetic thinks wine is good but the monk may give it up in his state of life, and the laic may give it up during Lent. We are not talking about a morality here, we are talking about the asceticism that capacitates a person for liturgy. It is the asceticism that liturgy directly inspires.

The practices of liturgical asceticism are therefore hard to explain to either the pagan hedonist, who does not know why someone would abstain from wine if it is a good thing, or to the puritan prohibitionist, who thinks of wine as a bad thing. They both miss the mark. When Abba Macarius was among the brothers he had a rule that "if wine could be had, he used to drink it for the brothers' sake: and then, for one cup of wine he would go without water for a whole day. And the brothers, wanting to refresh him, used to give him wine. And the old man took it with joy, so as later to crucify himself"[9] His disciples finally had to secretly intervene with his hosts to stop them from offering it. The ascetic knows the paradox that no thing is bad (contra the teetotaler), but

8. Ibid.

9. Systematic Sayings, 4.26; also Alphabetical Sayings, Macarius 10.

the ascetic also knows that interior discipline is done by means of exterior things (contra the dualist). The lesson all ascetics learned is that if we let ourselves do everything that is permitted, we will soon grow lax and do what is not permitted. The mistake of reading the ascetical discipline through moral eyeglasses accounts for the confusion experienced by many in their first contact with a desert Abba or Amma. In a moral system, a good action should be done by everyone, all the time, and a bad action should be forbidden to everyone, all the time, and yet the Sayings seem to be filled with exceptions, exceptions that appear to pile up into contradictions if they are applied generally. The explanation, of course, is that the discipline cannot be applied generally because the asceticism is done for the personal growth of an individual, and an individual's needs are kept secret from prying eyes. Grace works individually, one by one. Asceticism is the most intimately private act a person can do (like dying), one that takes place between that person and God in the hidden recesses of a heart that is undergoing purification.

The commandment to love one's neighbor trumps every ascetical practice, but the commandment does not permit us to grow lax on that account. Using charity as an excuse to relieve oneself of ascetical discipline is a hypocritical kind of charity. My neighbor calls for one sort of behavior from me, my sins call for another. One imposes a discipline on oneself that one would not necessarily impose on another.

Once Silvanus and his disciple Zacharias arrived at a monastery. The monks made them eat a little before they went on their way. When they left, the disciple saw a pool by the wayside and wanted to drink. Silvanus said, "Zacharias, today is a fast." Zacharias said, "But surely we have already eaten today, abba?" The hermit said to him, "We ate their meal out of love for them, but when we are on our own let us keep our fast, my son."[10]

10. Systematic Sayings, 4.40.

The battle occurs on a different plane than the moralist can know, because it is neither between good and bad, nor between soul and body, it is between our holiness and Satan's envy. Once a monk questioned Abba Sisoes whether it was overindulgence to drink three cups of wine in the meeting of monks on Saturday and Sunday. He replied, "If Satan is not in it, it is not much."[11]

Liturgical asceticism could not have existed before the Incarnation any more than icons. But from the Incarnation onward there is a new state of affairs. A young man asked Jesus what he must do to inherit eternal life, and when he was told he should obey the commandments he protested that he had done so since his youth. We do not read that the young man was wrong in saying so; Jesus does not confront him with some secret moral failing that the young man had overlooked in himself; Jesus does not appear to chastise him. Rather, "Jesus, looking at him, loved him and said to him, 'You are lacking in one thing. Go, sell what you have, and give to the poor and you will have treasure in heaven; then come, follow me'" (Mark 10:21). After obedience to the commandments comes a yet more radical invitation, and accepting it requires a spiritual prowess that was prepared for by obedience to the very commandments he is now told to excel. He is to choose the more excellent way by a liturgical asceticism that exceeds moral asceticism with a transcendent recklessness. In Olivier Clement's words, "Ascesis is not obedience to some abstract categorical imperative. It frees human nature to follow its deep instinct to ascend towards God."[12] "Christian ascesis is not only or even especially moderation, self-control, wisdom. It is the folly of those who in Christ fling themselves into the furnace of the spirit, of those who themselves have something in common with fire."[13]

Second, when the three are kept in fruitful tension we dis-

11. Alphabetical Sayings, Sisoes 2.
12. Clement, *The Roots of Christian Mysticism*, 132.
13. Ibid., 144.

cover that theology is more than a human science. The kind of *theologia* being spoken about here stands at the end of a long process of being conformed to Christ through the liturgical rhythms of the Church. Theology does not begin in the card catalogue, it begins in fasting, and the end of theology is not becoming a professor, it is becoming a saint. The starting point for liturgical theology is *dogma,* if we understand that the word the way Basil does. In his apology for the divinity of the Holy Spirit, Basil explains that Church teaching has come down to us in both a written and an oral form, and says "[b]oth sources have equal force in true religion. No one would deny either source.... If we attacked unwritten customs, claiming them to be of little importance, we would fatally mutilate the Gospel ... or rather, we would reduce the Gospel teaching to bare words."[14] Those teachings of the Church that are publicly proclaimed Basil calls *kerygma,* and those which are reserved to members of the household of faith Basil calls *dogma.* "His use of terms is peculiar," admits Fr. Georges Florovsky.

> *Kerygmata* were for him what in the later idiom was usually denoted as "dogmas" or "doctrines"—a formal and authoritative teaching and ruling in the matters of faith—the open or public teaching. On the other hand, *dogmata* were for him the total complex of "unwritten habits," or, in fact, the whole structure of liturgical and sacramental life.... In any case, one should not be embarrassed by the contention of St. Basil that *dogmata* were delivered or handed down, by the Apostles, *en mysterion.* It would be a flagrant mistranslation if we render it as "in secret." The only accurate rendering is: "by the way of mysteries," that is—under the form of rites and (liturgical) usages, or "habits."[15]

We understand by undergoing liturgical mysteries. The examples of dogma Basil gives include such things as signing catechumens with the cross, the words used in the invocation over

14. Basil, *On the Holy Spirit,* para. 66.

15. Georges Florovsky, "The Function of Tradition in the Ancient Church," in *Bible, Church, Tradition: An Eastern Orthodox View,* vol. 1 of *The Collected Works* (Belmont, Mass.: Notable & Academic Books, 1987), 86.

the Eucharistic bread and cup, facing east for prayer, blessing baptismal water and oil, triple immersions, the renunciation of Satan, standing for prayer on Sunday, and calling the first day of the week the eighth day. Theology comes by way of the mysteries' *lex orandi.*

Andrew Louth compares Basil's distinction to one Dionysius makes between the ineffable and the knowable:

> Basil's distinction between *kerygma* and *dogma* seems then to amount to this: *kerygma* is the Church's preaching of the gospel, it is something proclaimed, it seeks to awaken faith in those who do not believe, it seeks to persuade, to convert; *dogma,* on the other hand, is the experience of the mystery of Christ within the bosom of the Church, which is to be kept secret from those outside, from those who do not have faith—it is a growing understanding of the faith mediated through the experience of the liturgy of the Church and a deeper grasp of the hidden significance of the Scriptures. This distinction seems very close to Denys's "twofold tradition of the theologians." The hidden, inner dimension of theology is a matter of experience.... It is a matter of a lifetime's experience of prayer and worship within the bosom of the church.[16]

A person knows this kind of dogmatic theology by experiencing it within the bosom of the Church. Theology comes out of a liturgical body that is in communion with God. When the Christian heart beats in sympathy with the divine perichoresis, then conversion makes the heart into a theological organ. And without this cardial renewal, the *nous* that has descended into the heart cannot conduct theology. Louth deals with this beautifully in another place where he uses the category of "the tacit" to explain himself. "The silence of the tacit makes immediate contact with the silence of prayer: and prayer is seen in the Fathers to be, as it were, the amniotic fluid in which our knowledge of God takes form."[17] But being surrounded by such a liturgical fluidity comes at a conditional cost, he adds, "For the Fathers knowledge of God,

16. Andrew Louth, *Denys the Areopagite* (Wilton, Conn.: Morehouse-Barlow, 1989), 27.
17. Louth, *Discerning the Mystery,* 65.

and his love for us in Jesus Christ, could only be found within the tradition of the Church.... Participation in the tradition of the Church meant for the Fathers acceptance of the Church's rule of faith."[18] Liturgical asceticism is the *lex* of the Church's *orandi*.

This is theology that fills both mind and body. The capacity for theology depends upon a renewed mind, a *meta-nous*, which is brought about by the energy of the Holy Spirit. The Holy Spirit is the primary actor in this, bringing the Church and her children into the new age, and making theologians of them. Metropolitan Hierotheos cites examples of this theme:

> According to St. Maximus there is an attraction between a pure nous and knowledge. [St. Maximus, *Philokalia*, 2.56, 32]. The Holy Spirit finds the pure nous and "initiates it accordingly into the mysteries of the age to be" [Maximus, St. Thalassios, *Philokalia*, 2.329]. In this way the person becomes a theologian. For theology is not given by human knowledge and zeal, but by the work of the Holy Spirit which dwells in the pure heart. The nous which has been purified "becomes for the soul a sky full of the stars of radiant and glorious thoughts, with the sun of righteousness shining in it, sending the beaming rays of theology out into the world" [Nicetas Stethatos, *Natural Chapters*, ch. 67].... Real theology is not a fruit of material concentration but a manifestation of the Holy Spirit. When a man's nous is purified then he is illuminated and if his nous has the capacity, that is, wisdom, he can theologise. Therefore we say that his whole life, even his body itself, is theology. The purified man is wholly a theology.[19]

This is an unusual grammar to those who think of theology exclusively as a mental activity done in university departments housed down the hall from the sociology and biology departments. It is a startling proposition to think that theological *episteme* stands upon *askesis*: what we know depends upon the kind of person we are. "For Clement of Alexandria, *gnosis* is 'that light which is kindled in the soul as the result of obedience to the com-

18. Ibid., 64.

19. Metropolitan Hierotheos, *Orthodoxy Psychotherapy: The Science of the Fathers* (Levadia, Greece: Birth of the Theotokos Monastery, 1994), 147.

mandments.'"[20] Therefore, liturgical theology supposes that *theologia* is not just knowing, rather it is better understood as a kind of participation, at which point our whole self becomes theology, or what Abbot Vasileios calls a *theologian soul.* "True theology is always living, a form of hierugy, something that changes our life and 'assumes' us into itself: we are to become theology. Understood in this way, theology is not a matter for specialists but a universal vocation; each is called to become a 'theologian soul.'"[21] Each laic is to become an ascetic, even if not of the monastic variety; each laic participates in the baptismal priesthood, different from the clerical priesthood; and Mrs. Murphy is called to become a theologian, the title used differently of her than it is used in the academy. Becoming this kind of theologian carries the cost of liturgical asceticism. This *theologia* participates in the circulation of love (*perichoresis*) that flows between Father, Son, and Holy Spirit, which is the apex of the very prayer being sought by the ascetic. There is no true knowledge without love, which is why Evagrius says *praktike* attains to *apatheia,* and *apatheia* has a child called *agape,* and agape keeps the door to deep knowledge. *Theologia* is this deep knowledge after *praktike* and *physike.*

Third, when the three are kept in fruitful tension we discover that liturgy is more than human cult.[22] Liturgy is not one of Adam's religions, liturgy is participating in the cult of the New Adam. By the light which bursts out the doors of the temple to flood the world in transfiguring light, the liturgist sees the cosmos theologically, as gift from God and raw material for eucharist; it sees man and woman finally, fully, in their role as cosmic priests; it sees time no longer as a drain pool into nothingness, but rather as a training school for eternal happiness. Liturgical

20. Spidlik, *The Spirituality of the Christian East,* 328, quoting Clement's *Stromata,* 3.5.44.

21. Archimandrite Vasileios, *Hymn of Entry: Liturgy and Life in the Orthodox Church* (Crestwood, N.Y.: St. Vladimir's Seminary Press, 1984). 27.

22. Such was my intention in my earlier writings when distinguishing "liturgy" from "*leitourgia,*" or distinguishing "thin liturgy" from "thick liturgy."

theology is not looking at the liturgy, it is looking through the liturgy to see the world in its course of transfiguration. Mrs. Murphy is capacitated to do this by her liturgical asceticism, and for that reason she is a liturgical theologian. It is a kind of wisdom of the heart, not merely a knowledge of the mind, and so one approaches liturgy with a different expectation. Liturgical ceremony is attached to something greater, something beyond our rational comprehension, though not beyond our mystical participation. The massive reality that undergirds our ceremonies turns out to be the same reality that supports our very existence and beckons us to beatitude.

Liturgy is the mystery of salvation being accomplished, and the public, liturgical cult that we can see is only like the tip of an iceberg. The visible cult is the part of liturgy we can see above the water line, but the ritual is actually connected to a massive work of God below the sacramental water line. We don't object to using the term "liturgy" to mean the public collection of official services, rites, ceremonies, prayers, and sacraments of the Church, but what is the deeper reality that lies below the ceremonial surface? To discover what this cult is connected to would be to discover connections between cult and cosmos, sacred and profane, Church and world, ritual liturgy and lived liturgy—a connection between liturgy, theology, and asceticism. Liturgy is not the activity of the Jesus club, it is a work of God that stretches from the alpha to the omega. It is cosmic in scale and eschatological in ambition. Sanctification radiates out from man to the created world, as Leonid Ouspensky observes. "It is the nature of holiness to sanctify that which surrounds it. It is in man and through man that the participation of all creatures in the divine eternal life is actualized and made manifest. Just as creation fell with the fall of man, so it is saved by the deification of man."[23]

23. Leonid Ouspensky, *Theology of the Icon* (Crestwood, N.Y.: St. Vladimir's Seminary Press, 1992), 1.187. This first volume was originally published alone as *Theology of the Icon* (Crestwood, N.Y.: St. Vladimir's Seminary Press 1978). In 1992 it was re-

This process reverses the fall of Adam and the cosmic catastrophe that ensued, so here, then, is the job description of the liturgical ascetic: reverse the Fall! Or, in words Andrew Louth uses to summarize the thought of Maximus, "the ascetic struggle involved in responding to God is not simply an individual matter, it is part of the process of overcoming the divisions that have shattered the cosmos as a result of the Fall—ascetic struggle has cosmic significance and this is made manifest in the drama of the liturgy."[24] Maximus spoke of five divisions of being that *anthropos* should have held united. When man and woman failed their vocation of coherence, then instead of holding in union (symbolically) what would be divided (diabolically), they added to the alienation that creation experiences. First, the created was divided from the Uncreated (we no longer find our end in God); second, what was perceived by the mind was divided from what was perceived by the senses (we look without seeing); third, heaven was divided from earth (the angelic and earthly creations go their separate ways); fourth, paradise was divided from the inhabited lands (Eden, our original home, is far from our current place of toil); fifth, the division of man and woman appears (the need for reproducing the species through sexual union is a sign of death's reign over every generation).[25] The human being in creation is

published as vol. 1, with its ten essays and some parts newly translated, and vol. 2 contained an additional eight essays. This chapter, "The Meaning and Content of the Icon," appears always as chapter 10 and is the finest piece written on the correlation between the theological basis and the artistic canons of iconography.

24. Louth, *Maximus the Confessor,* 23.

25. Here it is in Maximus's own words. "[The saints] say that the substance of everything that has come into being is divided into five divisions. The first of these divides from the uncreated nature the universal created nature, which receives its being from becoming. . . . The second division is that in accordance with which the whole nature that receives being from creation is divided by God into that which is perceived by the mind and that perceived by the senses. The third is that in accordance with which the nature perceived by the senses is divided into heaven and earth. The fourth is that in accordance with which the earth is divided into paradise and the inhabited world, and the fifth, that in accordance with which the human person, which is the laboratory in which everything is concentrated and in itself naturally mediates between the extremities of each division, having been drawn into everything in a good and fitting way through becoming, is divided into male and female"; see *Difficulty 41* in Louth, *Maximus the Confessor,* 156.

what Maximus calls "the laboratory in which everything is concentrated," because, Louth explains, "human beings are found on both sides of each division: they belong in paradise but inhabit the uninhabited world; they are earthly and yet destined for heaven; they have both mind and senses; and though created, they are destined to share in the uncreated nature by deification. All the divisions of the cosmos are reflected in the human being, so the human being is a microcosm."[26] Therefore the celebration of liturgy has cosmic consequences, but humanity's lordship over creation can only be exercised correctly by the priest-king if our appetites are in order. In Kavanagh's pithy phrase, liturgy is doing the world the way it was meant to be done.

Liturgy is the activity of the Second Adam who shares his sacrificial action with the Church, his body, but the cost of participating in this spiritual activity is taking the death plunge to the bottom of the baptismal font and emerging revivified by the Spirit of God. Before the Father of all, the Son makes an action on behalf of all, and the spiritual liturgy is the flow of divine life reaching to earth and regenerating life in a new age. This is the age of the Church, and liturgy is the Church in motion; the Church's liturgy is the Holy Spirit pulsing with life through her. To say that the worship of the Church is spiritual is to say it belongs to the spiritual age, the renewed age, the age of the Holy Spirit in which a ladder of divine ascent was erected. Above all other definitions, says Olivier Clement, "the Church is the power of resurrection, the sacrament of the Risen One who imparts his resurrection to us; the new Eve, born from Christ's open side as Eve was born from Adam's rib.... In its deepest understanding the Church is nothing other than the world in the course of transfiguration, the world that in Christ reflects the light of paradise."[27] In the liturgy the world is reborn from the amniotic fluid of prayer, and if

26. Louth, *Maximus the Confessor*, 73.
27. Clement, *The Roots of Christian Mysticism*, 95.

asceticism has a reputation for being painful, it is only because in liturgical asceticism we are experiencing our birth pangs. A new creation is birthed from the womb of the Church, visible to eyes of faith. The Kingdom of God is among us because Jesus is the Kingdom of God, and Jesus remains among us. Jesus is both seated at the right hand of his Father and he resides amongst his people: this is how he is mediator between heaven and earth, accomplished in his own risen God-manhood. And by means of the Holy Spirit's activity in the Church Christians are incorporated into his *leitourgia* of reconciliation.

In summary, the three elements of liturgy, theology, and asceticism interplay and interpenetrate to bring a person to holiness. Liturgy and asceticism give birth to a theologian soul who has communion with the *Theos* through the *Logos*; theology and asceticism give birth to a liturgical person who stands aright, stands with fear, who attends the holy oblation; and liturgy and theology give birth to an ascetic who strives upward by breaking free of passionate tendrils that would bind him to the world. Theologians, ascetics, and liturgists populate the Church. Their paradigm is Mary and the saints. We would like to turn now to how the holiness of the saints is made visible in icons, and then finally conclude with Mary as liturgical person.

A new theological countenance is formed in the Christian. This is possible because Christ was God and man united hypostatically, the union of two natures in one *hypostasis* (person). Thus did God receive a face, which is where Gennadios Limouris begins his definition of icon:

> The icon, then, is the Christ, the God who became a face. Then it is also the faces of all the friends of God who are our friends and who insist on including us in their circle. And already, the icon represents the Kingdom of God.... The Kingdom of God is anticipated, either starting from the beauty of the world, though this is an ambiguous beauty, or starting from certain faces, certain old faces, fashioned by a long life, faces which have not been plunged into resentment or bitterness or the fear of death, faces of those who do not flinch as they approach death, faces

that know precisely where they are, and have found again the mind of a child.[28]

Icons are ascetical products for several reasons: in an icon of Christ we come face-to-face (literally) with the source of dispassion; in the icons of the saints we behold someone who has attained *apatheia*; the iconographer only writes the icon after ascetical prayer and fasting; the eye required to behold an icon must be ascetically cleansed; the depictions of created things radiate a glory of a world put back in order; and the icon shows something invisible. The icon pictures a person mirrored in another person (Christ mirrored in the saint) in order to encourage a third person (the one contemplating the icon) to take on the *apatheia* seen there.

The icon is an image of a hesychast at peace from the passions. And as the saint overcomes the passions within, the world around the saint also changes. "Sanctity has not only a personal, but also a general human, as well as a cosmic significance. Therefore all the visible world represented in the icon changes, becomes the image of the future unity of the whole creation—the Kingdom of the Holy Spirit."[29] The ascetic can look more deeply into the nature of things than their sensible appearances can show, and therefore even fallen nature, with which we are familiar sensually, can be used to image the new heavens and the new earth. "The ascetic experience, or rather its result, also finds here its outward expression in the severity of the often geometrical forms, in the lighting and in the lines of the folds. They cease to be disordered.... In effect, the sanctification of the human body is communicated to its clothing."[30] It is the beginning

28. Gennadios Limouris, "The Microcosm and Macrocosm of the Icon: Theology, Spirituality and Worship in Colour," in *Icons: Windows on Eternity,* compiled by Gennadios Limouris (Geneva: WCC Publications, 1990), 119.

29. Leonid Ouspensky, "The Meaning and Language of Icons," in *The Meaning of Icons,* edited by Leonid Ouspensky and Vladimir Lossky (Crestwood, N.Y.: St. Vladimir's Seminary Press, 1983), 40.

30. Ouspensky, *Theology of the Icon,* 185.

of the transfiguration of the world, its return to unity. This gives the icon its unusual appearance to the secular eye.

> Because the icon sought to spiritualize the world, the image of physical beauty was quite unsuited to express the new man in Christ. Everything that recalled the sensible world thus had to be transfigured.... This spiritualizing tendency is seen even more clearly in the details of the icon.[31]

> Byzantine art avoided the representation of nature as we see it in this world. Thus the rocks of the countryside appeared to be weightless. Buildings were often shown very sumptuously, but they and the objects in and around them were not subordinated to natural space. They often had their own individual type of perspective. In the same way, colors were not those of nature but had a meaning of their own and were integrated into the requirements of the composition. Everything was penetrated by a light which cast no shadows. This light was the divine light which was communicated through the celestial and terrestrial hierarchies so as to be reflected, in the final degree, in the material substance of the icon.[32]

The absence of naturalism in the face and body of the saint reminds us that these dispassionate ones engaged in *theoria*. "These transfigured bodies already perceive more, and even something else, than the majority of us do: they see the spiritual and not just the physical world"[33] where order and peace inundate the icon because "men and animals, landscapes and architecture, all participate in the divine harmony."[34]

Knowledge follows from union. Transfigured creation passes before the eye of the dispassionate ascetic, like the animals passed before Adam, and the contemplative sees the true meaning and identity of each thing. This is vision by two suns, as Symeon the New Theologian said, by someone who possesses

31. Egon Sendler, *The Icon, Image of the Invisible: Elements of Theology, Aesthetics and Technique* (Torrence, Calif.: Oakwood Publications, 1992), 62.

32. Ibid., 64.

33. Michel Quenot, *The Icon: Window on the Kingdom* (Crestwood, N.Y.: St. Vladimir's Seminary Press, 1991), 97.

34. Ibid., 101.

both a physical and a spiritual eye. To show this, the icon attempts to portray not only the matter, but also the reality—which are not identical, despite what positivism has claimed.[35] The icon shows what the cosmos is, and not just what it is made of, because what the contemplative sees is the essence of things, and not only their visible aspect.

To help explain this enigma, Pavel Florensky provides a fascinating metaphor that is worth our attention. Florensky was a Russian Orthodox priest, philosopher, and scientist of the twentieth century (born 1882, martyred under Stalinism in 1937). He knew the physics of this world, having entered the Physics and Mathematics Department of Moscow University as a young prodigy, but after graduation he refused a post offered to him. He also turned his back on his agnostic youth to join the Orthodox faith at age twenty-one, and was ordained at age twenty-nine. If we may say so, he left physics for *physike*. He wrote about icons in a little book entitled *Iconostasis,* and in it we find this interesting illustration. He begins by asking us to imagine being given the task of sketching a picture of a magnet.

> Consider. If an artist in depicting a magnet were to be satisfied with showing merely the visible aspect (I mean, here, visible and invisible in the common way of speaking), then he would be depicting not a magnet but merely a piece of steel; the real essence of the magnet—that is, its force-field—would go not only unrepresented but also unindicated (though undoubtedly we would simply imagine it into the representation).[36]

35. In the *Chronicles of Narnia,* one of the sons of Adam meets a star so old that he is at rest, and now eats a fireberry every day from the valley of the Sun which takes away a little of his age until he becomes strong enough to rejoin the celestial dance again. The boy marvels at meeting a retired star, and comments that in his world a star is only a huge ball of flaming gas, to which the star replies, "Even in your world, my son, that is not what a star is but only what it is made of"; see C. S. Lewis, *The Voyage of the Dawn Treader* (New York: Mcmillan, 1970), 180.

36. Pavel Florensky, *Iconostasis* (Crestwood, N.Y.: St. Vladimir's Seminary Press, 1996), 127.

By drawing a two-dimensional picture of a block of metal we would not have gotten to the essence of the magnet yet, which is its force-field. "When we speak of a magnet, we *mean* the force-field along with the piece of steel—but we don't mean the opposite: a piece of steel and, secondarily, a force-field."[37] We can draw a bar of steel, but how can we draw magnetism?

Perhaps someone will suggest that the artist draw some kind of force-field but Florensky says that would create a "visual lie," because we would have visibly drawn a force that is invisible.

> If an artist were to use some physics textbook in depicting the force-field as something visually equal to the steel of the magnet, he would thereby be mingling thing and force, visible and invisible, in his representation, and in doing so he would be fashioning a visual lie about the thing as well as misrepresenting the definitive characteristics of the field (i.e., its invisibility and its activating power); hence, he would be showing two untruths about the magnet in his depiction, none of which is the magnet.[38]

Therefore, if the magnetic force is indicated, it must be indicated in some different way from how the visible bar of steel is indicated. So Florensky concludes:

> Clearly, in depicting a magnet both the field and the steel must be shown; but their depictions must also be incommensurate, showing that the magnet's two dimensions belong to two different planes.... I dare not try to instruct the artist in how actually to represent this unmingled mingling of two planes of existence; but I am entirely certain that figurative art has the capacity to do it.[39]

If we put lines on our drawing coming out of the ends of the magnet to indicate the force-field, somehow they should be depicted in a way that is incommensurate with the lines we used to draw the magnet. The lines representing the visible bar should somehow look like different from the lines representing the invisible force-field. Perhaps they could be made wavy to indicate

37. Ibid.

38. Ibid.

39. Ibid.

that these are not the lines of a solid object; perhaps they can suspend in the air, unattached to the bar. At any rate, the straight line and the squiggly lines would have to be shown to be incommensurate lines.

Florensky's point in all this is that an iconographer faces the same challenge, if not an even greater one. The illustrator was faced with the dilemma of drawing neither steel nor magnetism, but magnetized steel. The iconographer is faced with the challenge of drawing neither a person nor divinity, but a deified person. As Ouspensky says, "The icon indicates holiness in such a way that it need not be inferred by our thought but is visible to our physical eyes."[40] Yet how can one draw "holiness" any more than one could draw "magnetism?" The latter is at least a physical force, a created energy, while the former is a supernatural energy, an uncreated light. This leads Florensky to conclude that what we seek is the "representation of the invisible dimension of the visible, the invisible understood now in the highest and ultimate meaning of the word as the divine energy that penetrates into the visible so that we can see it.... Analogically, then, we can say this: the form of the visible is created by these invisible lines and paths of divine light."[41]

The icon looks "odd" because it sketches paths of divine light. The iconographer is not trying to draw a person, and is not trying to draw an abstract depiction of holiness, rather the iconographer is trying to draw a holy person. Both the representable thing—the saint—and the unrepresentable thing are to be represented. We will leave it to an art historian to detail the way icons accomplish this by using color, the layering of egg tempera, geometric standards, stylized noses and eyes and fingers, gravity-defying cloth, inverse perspective, open-air houses, gold leaf, light and absent shadows, and so on. A theological understanding of the icon shows that "the artistic forms were restructured so as to re-

40. Ouspensky, *Theology of the Icon*, 162.
41. Florensky, *Iconostasis*, 128.

flect not the appearance or the material envelope of beings but their essence, their spiritual core, their eternal truth. We borrow the human form from natural reality, but we submit this form to a special geometric, rhythmic, and chromatic system which is more capable of suggesting interiority, that is, the spiritual and divine essence."[42] The icon brings together liturgy, asceticism, and theology in a visible manner that is "both a means and a path to follow. It is itself a prayer. Visibly and directly, it reveals to us this freedom from passion about which the Fathers speak."[43] The icon is commonly described as a window into heaven, but it would seem more accurate to describe it as a door, for it invites an act on our part: step forward. The icon is an image of an ascetic, and when we see *apatheia* in the saint's face, and Taboric light upon their environment, and the uncreated light suffusing their bodies, we are seeing a liturgical person in *theologia*.

The icon is an ascetic aesthetic. The latter word comes from *aisthetikos,* meaning "sensitive," from *aisthanesthai,* meaning "to perceive, to feel." Something aesthetic is something perceptible. What the icon is trying to make perceptible is holy beauty. And for a sinner the way to that holiness is through asceticism. That is why the book which is simply in love with beauty (the *Philokalia*: *philo,* love; *kalia,* beauty) tells us how to overcome the passions. The *Philokalia* contains instructions for becoming a true human being, and something cannot be beautiful unless it is true, and the *Philokalia* tells us how to become truly human. Plato said that beauty is the splendor of truth (from *splendere,* "to shine"). When truth shines, there is beauty. But Evdokimov cautions that such splendor is only "inherent in truth which does not exist in the abstract. In its fullness, truth requires a personalization and seeks to be enhypostazied [sic], that is, rooted and grounded in a person."[44] Truth won't be fully splendored until it is manifested

42. Sendler, *The Icon, Image of the Invisible,* 117.
43. Ouspensky, *Theology of the Icon,* 181.
44. Evdokimov, *The Art of the Icon,* 24.

at the highest created level, which is personhood. In other words, the highest truth, the fullest beauty, the greatest good must shine forth from a person. Abstract truth must be splendored in person. Hence the Incarnation. And asceticism is nothing else but the hand of God writing the Son's countenance on our face.

However, in this we must cooperate with the Holy Spirit. The invitation to join in the perichoresis of the Trinity requires our synergy. The tradition used an aesthetic illustration to express our growth from the image into the likeness of God, and then developed it to explain our cooperation. When an artist paints a portrait of the King, he will usually first sketch an outline in charcoal. From the charcoal silhouette one can tell it is the King, but the resemblance will be much greater once the colors are painted in. So when Gregory of Nyssa notices how painters "transfer human forms to their pictures by the means of certain colors, laying on their copy the proper and corresponding tints, so that the beauty of the original may be accurately transferred to the likeness," he uses it to illustrate "that our Maker also, painting the portrait to resemble His own beauty, by the addition of virtues, as it were with colours."[45] Or, here is how Methodius speaks of it:

> Man had indeed been brought forth "after the image" of God, but he still had not yet achieved such "likeness" itself. In order to complete this task, the Word was sent into the world. First he assumed our human form, a form marred by the scars of many sins, so that we, for whom he took this form, would be enabled on our part to receive his divine form. For it is possible to achieve a perfect likeness of God only if we, like talented and accomplished painters, depict in ourselves those traits that characterized his human existence, and if we preserve them in us uncorrupted, by becoming his disciples, walking the path he has revealed to us. He who was God chose to appear in our human flesh so that we could behold, as we do in a painting, a divine model of life, and thus we were made able to imitate the one who painted this picture.[46]

45. Gregory of Nyssa, *On the Making of Man,* ch. 5, section 1.

46. Methodius, *Banquet of the Ten Virgins,* Discourse 1, ch. 4; this translation is found in Christoph Schonborn, *God's Human Face* (San Francisco: Ignatius Press, 1994), 56.

Our development from image into the likeness of God required the Word to be sent into the world, and then our cooperative participation, hand-in-hand with grace. There is a synergy between the gift of God and its reception, as this truth can also be expressed through the aesthetic illustration of adding colors to a painting. Ephrem the Syrian writes,

> For this is the Good One, who could have forced us to please Him,
> without any trouble to Himself; but instead He toiled by every means
> so that we might act pleasingly to Him of our free will,
> that we might depict our beauty
> with the colours that our own free will had gathered;
> whereas, if He had adorned us, then we would have resembled
> a portrait that someone else had painted, adorning it with his own colours.[47]

An icon is liturgical art because it is the aesthetic expression of a human being's liturgical end, namely, sanctification, holiness, sainthood. To arrive at our full humanity requires "filling in" the charcoal image of God with which we were created, in order to grow into a likeness of God through the virtues. *Graphe* means "to write": biographers "write down" the life (*bios*) of a person. With every moral act we make, or fail to make, we are each of us writing down our own lives (an *auto bios graphe*). But God is the first iconographer, and the God who wrote the law upon two tablets of stone with his finger of fire can write a new life upon hearts of stone with the finger of his Holy Spirit. At this point, the theologian does not write about God; instead, God writes the theologian. Then the saint becomes, himself, an autograph by God: written by God's own hand (a *theo graphe*).

The perfection of a human being is to liturgically join in the perichoretic dance of love (*peri, choreia*) that flows between the three persons of the Trinity. Were someone to write out (*graphe*)

47. Ephrem, *Hymns on Faith,* cited in Sebastian Brock, *The Luminous Eye: The Spiritual World Vision of St. Ephrem the Syrian* (Kalamazoo, Mich.: Cistercian Publications, 1985), 61.

the footsteps of that dance for us to learn, they would have recorded the steps of the ascetical life. Asceticism is the choreography of divine agape. Our true humanity is a liturgical posture in which the Son's love of the Father becomes ours, and the Trinity's love for every creature becomes ours, as well. Then we would look upon the poor not with human sympathy but with divine compassion, we would look at our enemies with the same urgent desire for reconciliation that God has when he looks upon us sinners, we would look at suffering and feel the same willingness to embrace the cross that Christ felt. At that moment a true personhood would shine forth; at that moment, one would be a beautiful person.

A splendor more honorable than the cherubim, and beyond compare more glorious than the seraphim was raised up from the human race. The Virgin Mary is the liturgical person par excellence, she is the archetype of liturgical asceticism, and she is the prototype of theological life. If liturgy is the perichoresis of the Trinity kenotically descended to invite our synergistic ascent into deification, then in that cult of the New Adam, Mary holds a privileged place. Fr. Jean Corbon points to this when he writes, "The Virgin Mary is the Church as it dawns in a single person."[48] Only an adequate presence of Mary in ecclesiology keeps us from thinking of the Church in exclusively institutional terms. The Church does have a structure, she does have a visible magisterium, but much more importantly the Church is response of the sort that Mary gave. What is the Church? asks Schmemann.

> On the one hand the Church is certainly structure and institution, order and hierarchy, canons and chanceries. Yet this is only the visible structure. What is its content? Is it not also, and primarily, that which is to change and to transfigure life itself? Is it not the anticipation, the "Sacrament" of the kingdom of God? Yes, the Church is structure, but the unique purpose of that structure is to be an "epiphany," to manifest and to fulfill the Church as expectation and fulfillment....

48. Jean Corbon, *The Wellspring of Worship* (New York: Paulist Press, 1988), 173.

> It is, of course, in worship that this experience of the Church is given. It is in her *leitourgia* that the Church transcends herself as institution and structure and becomes "that which she is": response, adoration, encounter, presence, glory, and, ultimately, a mystical marriage between God and his new creation. It is precisely here that Mary stands at the center—as the personification, as the very expression, icon, and content of that response, as the very depth of man's "yes" to God in Christ.[49]

As liturgical person, Mary's response is *doxological* because she offers glory to God with her whole being; it is *eucharistic* as she embodies Israel's praise and creation's thanksgiving; it is *spiritual* for having enjoyed a personal Pentecost in anticipation of the corporate Pentecost on the disciples (in both cases, the Spirit came down where Mary was); it is *theological* insofar as she enjoys a mystical union with God; it is *ascetical* insofar as her will was conformed to Christ's; it is *eschatological* for being the last of the former age and the first of the final age; and so forth. All of these are facets of the liturgical person, facets that Mary exemplifies for our instruction.

We have presented liturgical asceticism as the disciplined alignment of the self toward God, such a theocentric posture being called liturgical, and such a union with God being called *theologia*. This ascetical path to liturgical theology is made possible for the Church by Mary's continued intercession, and so monastic ascetics have always had a special affection for her—Mount Athos is called "the garden of the Virgin Mary." But to reiterate a point made throughout this work, what is true for monks specifically is true for ascetics generally (species and genus). Both the monk and the laic are animated by the liturgy, and liturgical asceticism is the life of Christ soaking ever deeper into us since our baptism began to moisten our dry, mortal bones for resurrection. "Strengthened by the presence of Christ (cf. Mt. 28:20), the Church journeys through time towards the consummation of

49. Alexander Schmemann, *Celebration of Faith: Vol. 3, The Virgin Mary* (Crestwood, N.Y.: St. Vladimir's Seminary Press, 1995), 64–65.

the ages and goes to meet the Lord who comes. But on this journey—and I wish to make this point straightaway—she proceeds along the path already trodden by the Virgin Mary."[50]

Where does this path lead? The end of a watch is to tell time, the end of a knife is to cut, the end of a human being is *theosis*. The purpose of the descending incarnation was to enable an ascending deification. To overlook that last act of the paschal mystery is to miss the purpose of the whole economy. In the Ascension, the divine nature of Jesus was not returning from whence it came after docetically discarding a temporary humanity. His human nature also ascended into heaven. But did it only concern him? That was the question. Jesus' humanity was hypostatically unified to his uncreated divine nature, but would this matter to the humanity of a created human being? That is why Mary's witness and role is so important. A human woman receives by grace what the Son of God has by nature. In the words of Vladimir Lossky, there is a deified human hypostasis to answer the incarnate divine hypostasis.

> "To have by grace what God has by nature": that is the supreme vocation of created beings.... This destiny is already reached in the divine person of Christ, the Head of the Church, risen and ascended. If the Mother of God could truly realize, in her human and created person, the sanctity which corresponds to her unique role, then she cannot have failed to attain here below by grace all that her Son had by his divine nature. But, if it be so, then the destiny of the Church and the world has already been reached, not only in the uncreated person of the Son of God but also in the created person of his Mother. That is why St Gregory Palamas calls the Mother of God "the boundary between the created and the uncreated." Beside the incarnate divine hypostasis there is a deified human hypostasis.[51]

Christ was unique, but did not wish to be alone, and Mary shows the possibility of the Church's existence in her being a deified

50. John Paul II, *Redemptoris Mater*, para. 2.

51. Vladimir Lossky, "Panagia," in *The Mother of God: A Symposium*, edited by E. L. Mascall (Westminster, London: Dacre Press, 1959), 34.

human hypostasis. In his sermon on the Nativity of the Theotokos, Gregory Palamas says, "Today a new world and a mysterious paradise have been revealed, in which and from which a New Adam came into being, re-making the Old Adam and renewing the universe."[52] Her synergistic response to the coming of God enabled the renewal of all creation, a pattern that must be repeated in each Christian life for the sake of the world, like leaven. Liturgical asceticism is walking along the balance beam that runs the boundary between the created and the uncreated. The Theotokos has opened this boundary as an arena for our training. We are not yet quit of this world, but already we are citizens of a new race, waiting a new heavens, a new earth, a new Jerusalem.

Liturgical asceticism is a preparatory phase, the training grounds for heaven, and the primitive traditions about Mary spontaneously depict her devotion to a life of preparation before becoming the mother of God. She had to be prepared to give her *fiat*. She had to become a hesychast before becoming the Theotokos. Therefore, Mary would have a natural affinity for the Temple, and the early tradition naturally assumed that the only place where Mary, herself to be a Temple for God, could possibly have lived would have been in the Temple of Jerusalem. "Where else could be better for God's tent to be pitched?" exclaims Gregory Palamas. "Surely it was absolutely necessary for the actual Tabernacle to be set up in the same place as the figurative one?"[53] The Protoevangelium of James says that at the age of three Mary was brought by her parents to the Temple of the Lord, and "she danced with her feet, and all the house of Israel loved her";[54] and the Orthodox feast of the "Entrance of the Mother of God into the Temple" sings in its vespers, "Today the Theotokos (Mother

52. Gregory Palamas, "On the Nativity of the Mother of God," in *Mary the Mother of God: Sermons by Saint Gregory Palamas* (South Canaan, Pa.: Mount Thabor Publishing, 2005), 2.

53. Gregory Palamas, "On the Entry into the Holy of Holies II," *Mary the Mother of God*, 25.

54. Protoevangelium of James, 7.

of God), the Temple that is to contain God, is being escorted into the temple of the Lord." The holiest would dwell in her, so she would dwell in the holy of holies. Fed by the hand of an angel, she was a daughter of the sanctuary because she would become sanctuary for the only begotten Son. The ark of the covenant had long since been lost, but her child would be the True Ark. What must Mary have thought when she fulfilled the law of firstborn offerings by bringing her son to the Temple after his birth and heard Simeon's song? In her heart was the desire to make an offering, and she was bringing Jesus to his Father's house (something Jesus himself would remind everyone of twelve years later) but it was her old home, too. In the Temple she lived the sacrificial life of presenting offerings, first herself, now her Son. She offered herself at the Annunciation, she offered her son in the Presentation at the Temple, and there would be one more time when she would make a sacrificial presentation of her Son, and that was as she stood beneath his cross. The Church must also, ever stand under the cross, and cannot move from that spot. The liturgist traces the sign of the cross upon himself, the theologian preaches Christ crucified even if a scandal to some and a stumbling block to others, and the ascetic learns that God's power is shown through weakness and that what seems to be Christ's defeat is actually the victory of his Resurrection.

Irenaeus writes, "The knot of Eve's disobedience was untied by Mary's obedience; what the virgin Eve bound through her disbelief, Mary loosened by her faith."[55] It is as if this small piece of temple real estate was a fenced reserve of Eden, where the human race had one last chance to get it right. Adam and Eve had forfeited their liturgical career in Eden; their appetites became confused, their passions now overwhelmed them, the voice of God that they once heard so clearly became muffled. But this time, the New Eve persevered by preemptive grace. She lived the sacrificial life humanity should have preserved. Mary, a deified human hy-

55. Irenaeus, *Against Heresies*, 3.22.4.

postasis, is the throne of a restored liturgical community. Mary is the Virgin presenting offerings, and in so doing is a model for the Church.

> There is no "icon" of the Church except the human person that has become totally transparent to the Holy Spirit, to the "joy and peace" of the Kingdom." If Christ is the "icon" of the Father, Mary is the "icon" of the new creation, the new Eve responding to the new Adam, fulfilling the mystery of love.... Thus, being the "icon" of the Church, Mary is the image and the personification of the world. When God looks at his creation, the "face" of the world is feminine, not masculine.[56]

Mary prepared for the coming of Christ; liturgical asceticism is similarly our preparation for the coming of Christ at every liturgy. John Behr calls us to notice an overlooked fact: the Scriptures do not speak about the "second coming" of Christ, they speak simply about his coming.

> From the outset, then, Christians have been waiting for the coming of their Lord: not for a "second coming" as something distinct from and other than a "first coming," but simply for his coming, his parousia, his presence. Our habitual language of a "first coming" and a "second coming" tends to separate the two: relegating the first to the past ... and projecting the second into a yet-to-be-revealed eschatological drama.[57]

Waiting for Christ's "again coming," as Behr translates the phrase from the Nicene-Constantinopolitan Creed to make his point, is a liturgical posture, and the asceticism that keeps us awake for his arrival and capacitates us to receive him when he comes (now, not only then) is liturgical asceticism. The Church is not a future work of God, says Bouyer.[58]

Mary is the prototype for the life to which *anthropos* is called. "She is, as it were, the living Image, present within time, of what

56. Schmemann, *Celebration of Faith*, 3.65.

57. John Behr, "What Are We Doing, Talking about God? The Discipline of Theology," in *Thinking through Faith: New Perspectives from Orthodox Christian Scholars*, edited by Aristotle Papanikolaou and Elizabeth Prodromou (Crestwood, N.Y.: St. Vladimir's Seminary Press, 2008), 73.

58. Louis Bouyer, *The Church of God: Body of Christ and Temple of the Holy Spirit* (San Francisco: Ignatius Press, 2011), 293.

will be brought about in us all only at the end of time. Though unique and pre-eminent, she is yet the image of what we have to become."[59] Mary's liturgical personhood and ours are intimately connected, as intimately as a mother is connected to her children. Clement said the Church is the world in its course of transfiguration, and the world in its transfiguration has yielded up Mary. The Orthodox vespers for Christmas sings:

> Each of the creatures you have made
> Brings you thanks:
> the angels, song;
> the heavens, a star;
> the Magi, gifts;
> the shepherds, wonder;
> the earth, a cave;
> the desert, a manger;
> while we bring a Virgin Mother.[60]

Liturgy is the trysting point where heaven, bending down, kisses earth, and earth, yearning upward, kisses heaven. And Mary stands at exactly that liturgical center point, herself mother and virgin. She is God's way down to man, and man's way up to God. So Schmemann comments,

> In Christ's birth, therefore, poetry and faith see not only that He comes into the world, but that the world goes out to meet Him: the star, the wilderness, the cave, the manger, the angels, the shepherds, the wise men. And at the radiant heart of this procession, as its center and fulfillment, stands Mary, the very best and most beautiful fruit of creation.... Gazing at this image and rejoicing in it, we behold the only authentic image of the true world, of true life, of the true human being.[61]

She possesses the liturgical splendor of an ascetically conformed person. The Trinity's extension of perichoresis reached all the way to the virgin's womb to produce a hypostatic union; and her

59. Louis Bouyer, *The Seat of Wisdom: An Essay on the Place of the Virgin Mary in Christian Theology* (New York: Pantheon Books, 1960), 129.

60. Hugh Wybrew, *Orthodox Feasts of Jesus Christ and the Virgin Mary* (Crestwood, N.Y.: St. Vladimir's Seminary Press, 1997), Vespers for Birth of Jesus, 25 December, p. 53.

61. Schmemann, *Celebration of Faith*, 3.34–35.

fiat is the very model of synergy. Her life was imprinted with the liturgical pattern of God's descent and man's ascent. In this sense, "Mary was not an unheard of exception, she is the masterpiece of grace."[62]

But none of these mysteries are reserved to her alone, says Gregory of Nyssa. "What came about in bodily form in Mary ... takes place in a similar way in every soul that has been made pure. The Lord does not come in bodily form, for "we no longer know Christ according to the flesh," but he dwells in us spiritually and the Father takes up his abode with him, the Gospel tells us. In this way the child Jesus is born in each one of us."[63] Mary prepared to become the Mother of God in the flesh, but every birth of faith may be considered a virgin birth, and demands an ascetical preparation which the liturgy invites. It is in this sense that Schmemann can say Mariology is "the 'locus theologicus' *par excellence* of Christian anthropology."[64] In her Virgin Motherhood the destiny of the world has already been reached. *Theosis* is union with God, and Clement says this union with God may also be expressed in terms of inward birth.

> The soul corresponds to the Blessed Virgin. It recalls the mystery of the incarnation. And the incarnation is spiritually extended to holy souls who are thereby preparing for Christ's return. All the mysteries of the Gospel are not only performed in the liturgy but take possession of us in the spiritual life. The Word is continually being born in the stable of our heart.... To ensure this birth of Christ in us is the true function of liturgical times and seasons, interpreted inwardly by ascesis, prayer and contemplation.[65]

The true end of liturgy is to arrive where Mary is. It is a place of union with God (*theologia*), and she is our help on the journey of liturgical asceticism.

62. Louis Bouyer, *The Spirit and Forms of Protestantism* (Westminster, Md.: Newman Press, 1957), 207.

63. Gregory of Nyssa, *On Virginity*; this translation is in Clement, *Roots of Christian Mysticism*, 251.

64. Schmemann, *Celebration of Faith*, 3.53.

65. Clement, *The Roots of Christian Mysticism*, 251.

CONCLUSION

It is not wrong to define liturgy as the public and official ceremonies of the Church, because that is one of the meanings the word has, but it is an inadequate and sometimes distracting definition because it directs our attention to only that part of the *leitourgia* that we see ritualized. The cultic activity of the Church is only the tip of an economy by God that has massive proportions, and breaks the surface in cult and sacrament. Liturgical theology wants to know to what is this cult connected? A successful liturgical theology would discover bonds between cult and cosmos, sacred and profane, Church and world, ritual liturgy and lived liturgy, spirituality and theology and liturgical ceremony. That last triadic combination is Schmemann's understanding of liturgical theology.

The goal of liturgical theology, as its very name indicates, is to overcome the fateful divorce between theology, liturgy and piety—a divorce which, as we have already tried to show elsewhere, has had disastrous consequences for theology as well as for liturgy and piety. It deprived liturgy of its proper understanding by the people, who began to see in it beautiful and mysterious ceremonies in which, while attending them, they take no real part. It deprived theology of its living source and made it into an intellectual exercise for intellectuals. It deprived piety of its living content and term of reference.... To understand liturgy from inside, to discover and experience that "epiphany" of God, world and life which the liturgy contains and communicates, to relate this vision and this power to our own existence, to all our problems: such is the purpose of liturgical theology.[1]

Schmemann always presented liturgy in this way. He used the Greek word *leitourgia* to identify the activity of God that occurs in cult, but cannot be an activity simply equated with cult. This "cultic antinomy," as he called it, was quite a revolutionary understanding of worship. "If Christian worship is *leitourgia,* it cannot be simply reduced to, or expressed in terms of, 'cult.' The ancient world knew a plethora of cultic religions or 'cults.' ... But the Christian cult is *leitourgia,* and this means that it is *functional* in its essence, has a goal to achieve which transcends the categories of cult as such."[2] In an antinomy, two equally necessary principles appear to stand in contradiction, but are actually aspects of one total truth. Florensky defines antinomy as a case where both the one and the other are true, but each in its own way; unity is higher than rationality.[3] Schmemann is saying that at the heart of the liturgy is an antinomy between our cultic expression of Christianity and the radical abolishment of cult.

On the one hand the Church is certainly structure and institution, order and hierarchy, canons and chanceries. Yet this is only the visible structure. What is its content? Is it not also, and primarily, that which is to change and to transfigure life itself?...

It is, of course, in worship that this experience of the Church is giv-

1. Alexander Schmemann, *Of Water and the Spirit* (Crestwood, N.Y.: St. Vladimir's Seminary Press, 1974), 12.

2. Alexander Schmemann, "Theology and Eucharist," in *Liturgy and Tradition: Theological Reflections of Alexander Schmemann,* edited by Thomas Fisch (Crestwood, N.Y.: St Vladimir's Seminary Press, 1990), 79.

3. Pavel Florensky, *The Pillar and Ground of the Truth* (Princeton, N.J.: Princeton University Press, 1997), 118.

en. It is in her *leitourgia* that the Church transcends herself as institution and structure and becomes "that which she is."[4]

Here is *leitourgia* overflowing the lip of the liturgical cup that contains it. What cult cannot contain is contained in liturgical cult, just as what heaven and earth could not contain was contained in the womb of the Theotokos. The Christian mysteries are explosions that transfigure everything that lies within their blast radius; they cannot be restrained within the walls of the temple. And my reason to trace connections between liturgy, asceticism, and theology—connections seen so naturally by the great tradition but apparently difficult for us—comes from my desire to have us understand that the true function of *leitourgia* is that it takes possession of us by a process of *askesis,* so that we are put in union with God, a state of *theologia.*

4. Alexander Schmemann, *Celebration of Faith: Vol. 3, The Virgin Mary* (Crestwood, N.Y.: St. Vladimir's Seminary Press, 1995), 64–65.

APPENDIX A CENTURY ON LITURGICAL ASCETICISM

The following article arose out of a lecture given as the Richardson Fellow at the University of Durham, U.K., in 1996. It contains this book in embryonic form. It was published in Diakonia *31, no. 1 (1998), and is reprinted here by kind permission of that journal.*

1. I am going to write about liturgical asceticism, which is a very foolish thing to do. The topic is not foolish, I mean writing about it is foolish. Although a committee produces a thousand-page report on birthday parties, it is far more important to attend the party than to read the report. Attending to asceticism is far more important than studying it, a fact repeatedly emphasized in the ascetical tradition.

> Once a brother came to Abba Theodore of Pherme, and spent three days asking him for a word. But the Abba did not answer, and he went away sadly. So Abba Theodore's disciples asked him, "Abba, why did you not speak to him? Look, he has gone away

> sad." And the old man said: "Believe me, I said nothing to him because his business is getting credit by retailing what others have said to him."[1]

> According to St. Maximos the Confessor there are three motives for writing which are above reproach and censure: to assist one's memory, to help others, or as an act of obedience. It is for the last reason that most spiritual writings have been composed, at the humble request of those who have need of them. If you write about spiritual matters simply for pleasure, fame or self-display, you will get your deserts, as Scripture says, and will not profit from it in this life or gain any reward in the life to come. On the contrary, you will be condemned for courting popularity and for fraudulently trafficking in God's wisdom.[2]

2. Aware of the disparateness between academics (where the intellect is loosed to range imaginatively through the world) and asceticism (in which one strives to enclose the intellect within the body to facilitate the descent of the mind into the heart),[3] we have elected to adopt a graphic style which might, if not duplicate the ascetical genre, at least encourage a halting read. Monastic ascetical texts frequently presented a summary of traditional wisdom in the form of paragraphs or chapters strung together, often one hundred of them and hence called a Century.

In the case of the ascetical authors this style made traditional teachings easier to ponder and assimilate; in our case, it is hoped that it will, first, impede assumptions and retard hasty conclusions, and, second, invite the reader to reflection. The thoughts in each paragraph do not lead primarily to the next paragraph, as in a traditional sequential essay, but to every paragraph. The reader thus makes connections not foreseen by the author. This further allows a point to be made without exclusivity. Centuries do not exclude the complementary angles of a thought; this style

1. Owen Chadwick, ed., *Western Asceticism* (Philadelphia: Westminster Press, 1958), 98.

2. St. Gregory of Sinai, *The Philokalia* (London: Faber & Faber, 1995), 4.251.

3. See Dumitru Staniloae, *Prayer and Holiness* (Oxford, U.K.: SLG Press and Convent of the Incarnation, 1987).

is conducive to paradox. Metaphor is the currency of the realm. Instead of merely juxtaposing one thing to another (X is to Y), relationships are compared (as X is to Y, so A is to B), and the reader becomes an active participant in perceiving the connections.

3. In the tradition, numbering the paragraphs at one hundred expressed completeness or perfection. In this case, no claim to completeness is being made. This is only a beginning sketch of the issues I judge germane to understanding liturgical asceticism. After having swirled in my mind for several years (like paint mixing), these thoughts attained some organization thanks to the University of Durham, U.K., whose award of the Richardson Fellowship permitted their synthesis, and which 1996 lecture, named for the late dean of York, makes the basis of this work. As to any perfection here, the observant reader will notice an arithmetical expression of humility at the end.

4. In *The Ladder of Divine Ascent* John Climacus writes, "It is risky to swim in one's clothes. A slave of passion should not dabble in theology."[4] This is the starting point of our investigation into what we will call liturgical asceticism. I have elsewhere defended the claim that liturgists are theologians, meaning by "liturgists" the people who do liturgy, not the people who study it or direct it or preside over it.[5] Ultimately a liturgist is one who does the liturgy like a wrestler is one who wrestles and a carpenter is one who builds. If it is risky for a theologian to swim in his or her clothes, then it behooves liturgists to think about ascetical matters.

5. There is an enterprise practiced in the academy which also goes by the name "theology" which some think is immune from

4. John Climacus, *The Ladder of Divine Ascent* (New York: Paulist Press, 1982), 262.

5. David W. Fagerberg, *What Is Liturgical Theology? A Study in Methodology* (Collegeville, Minn: Pueblo Press, 1992). A revised second edition was published as *Theologia Prima* (Chicago: Hillenbrand Books, Liturgy Training Publications, 2003.) This is also the proper understanding of Fr. Kavanagh's famous Mrs. Murphy: she is a personification of someone who does liturgy.

St. John's words of warning. This intellectual coordination of information is thought to be an exercise so rational that the passions do not impact it. Whether this is really the case will not be a subject of investigation here. Could it be possible, as claimed, to remove the heart's passions from the working of memory, imagination, intellect, insight, reason, speculation, and wit? The question will not be debated here because we have other theologians in mind, ones who would not be interested in separating mind from heart even were it possible.

6. In his organic definition of liturgical theology, Fr. Alexander Schmemann calls liturgy the ontological condition for theology.[6] Similarly, we will define liturgical asceticism as the *askesis* (discipline) which has liturgy as its ontological condition. Therefore, we could more accurately understand how liturgy and asceticism relate if we made the effort to understand how liturgy and theology relate.

7. Liturgical theology is the by-product of the theological corporation's encounter with God. A residue is left by the scrimmage between the liturgist and God's Reign, and it is this residue which a student of liturgy analyzes. However, it should be patently evident that liturgical theology materializes upon the encounter with the Holy One, not upon the analysis. Only after God has shaped the community in liturgical encounter, and the theological adjustment has settled into ritual form, can the liturgiologist dust the ritual for God's fingerprints. Liturgical theology is the faith of the Church in ritual motion—a genuine theology, but one manifested and preserved in the community's *lex orandi* even before it is parsed systematically.

8. There was a brother at Scete who was zealous for the liturgy but negligent about the rest. One day Satan appeared to one of

6. Fr. Alexander Schmemann, "Liturgical Theology, Theology of Liturgy, and Liturgical Reform," *St. Vladimir's Quarterly* 13, no. 4 (1969): 217–44.

> the old men and said, "How wonderful! This monk is strangling me in a headlock, to prevent me from leaving him. He does everything I want, and yet he says to God at every hour, 'Lord, deliver me from the Evil One.'"[7]

If our notion of liturgy is too narrow, concerned only with rubrics, and smells and bells in the chapel, then liturgy will remain isolated from both theology and spirituality. And so long as liturgy is misperceived to be nontheological and nonascetical, the widespread mistake will continue to spread even more widely that liturgical renewal has more to do with relocating furniture in the sanctuary than reallocating hearts to God.

9. Liturgical theology is inadequately conceived if liturgy is treated as a branch of esthetics and not as the root of theology.

In divinity schools, liturgy is often tucked between other pastoral "how to" courses of the practical curriculum for ecclesiastics who get a thrill out of rubrical tidiness. (This same prejudice renders liturgical studies irrelevant to secular departments of religious studies.) By this understanding, liturgy is adventitious to theology, therefore its study must be grafted onto some other branch of the academic tree. Sometimes it is treated as a branch of spirituality, that is, the doxological titillation of the otherwise stolid, impassive theological mind. Or it is handled as a branch of history, so that as historians might treat the creeds, the papacy, or Calvin, they might likewise investigate an obscure medieval psalter. Or liturgical studies is subsumed under a branch of systematics, usually sacramentology, but also under various "theologies of ..." worship, prayer, doxology, and so forth. And finally, and increasingly in vogue, liturgy is made a branch of ritual studies which tries to replicate anthropology's old ideal of producing a neutral and unbiased report, in this case a phenomenology of worship protocols practiced by a given community.

7. Cited in Irenee Hausherr, S.J., *Penthos: The Doctrine of Compunction in the Christian East* (Kalamazoo, Mich.: Cistercian Publications, 1982), 159.

10. Approaches that derive from a complex definition of liturgical theology search for ways of connecting liturgy and theology. Supposing liturgy to be ritual cliché in need of content, they are out to bond liturgy with theology, or theology with liturgy, like a chemist would bond one atom with another atom to make a complex molecule.

11. The usual approach to liturgical theology attempts to add, like parsley, a bit of liturgical garnish to the theological platter; or else to add, like red meat would, a little theological virility to a flabby ritual diet.

12. Contradicting these complex approaches, we hold that liturgical theology is simple. When we say "simple," we mean in the philosophical sense of being one; of not having many parts. Liturgical theology names one subject, not two. It is a simple concept, named by two words; it is not a complex of two subjects.

13. Liturgical theology is not conducted by mixing yellow liturgy marbles with blue theology marbles to make a jar full of yellow and blue marbles. Liturgical theology is green marbles.

14. Liturgical theology is simple in the way a human being is simple even though composed of body and soul. The Scholastics said form and matter make one substance. A human being, although both soul and body, is one substantial being, not two. Theology does not have to be added to liturgy in order to make liturgical theology. Liturgy is a substantially theological enterprise.

15. Christian asceticism is also a substantially liturgical product. Liturgical asceticism does not name two things, it names Christ's purity of heart become our own. "Then God shall be all our love, all we desire and seek and follow, all we think, all our life and speech and breath. The unity which now is between Father and Son shall be poured into our feelings and our minds."[8]

8. Abba Isaac, *The Conferences of Cassian,* in Owen Chadwick, *Western Asceticism,* 237.

16. It is not adequate to simply speak of bridging liturgy and asceticism. That is as inadequate as speaking of bridging soul and body in order to understand the human being, when the human being cannot be understood apart from soul or apart from body. Liturgy cannot be understood apart from asceticism, and Christian asceticism cannot be understood apart from liturgy.

17. Not all worship is liturgical, but there is liturgical worship. Not all prayers are liturgical, but there is liturgical prayer. Not all theology is liturgical, but there is liturgical theology. Not all assembly, space, time, service, or sacrifice is liturgical, but they each have their liturgical instances. And not all asceticism is liturgical. An athlete might be placed under discipline in order to win a prize; political *askesis* is inspired by patriotism; moral asceticism is inspired by the philosophical sense of the good. But there is liturgical asceticism.

18. Christian liturgical asceticism could not have existed before the Incarnation any more than iconography—and for the same reason.

19. Whereas liturgy is the faith of the Church in motion, and whereas this faith creates an attitude toward the world, and whereas this attitude is properly called ascetical, therefore it seems fitting that the ascetical behavior that is incumbent upon all liturgists be called "liturgical asceticism." It behooves not only monks and religious, by virtue of being professed, but all liturgists, by virtue of being baptized, to know the Christian liturgical grammar which is simultaneously (and simply) theological and ascetical.

20. Becoming a theologian involves learning the grammar of faith revealed in the economy of God which, for Christians, stems from the Trinity and manifests itself from genesis to the parousia, coming to incarnate fruition in the Paschal Mystery of Jesus. Being a theologian involves using this grammar to speak

about God. Even more, it means speaking of God. Even more, it means speaking with God. Evagrius of Pontus calls prayer *theology*. "If you are a theologian you truly pray. If you truly pray you are a theologian."[9] And before there were universities with theology faculties it was possible to learn this theological grammar.

21. Ancient Christians borrowed a word from its secular world to describe the work they did when they gathered in Christ for they meant to describe something deeper than musical tones and how the vestments were embroidered. *Leitourgia* meant a kind of public service, in such a way that paying taxes was one's *leitourgia* to the city. It meant the work of a few on behalf of the many. Our problem is that we've come to think of liturgy as the work of the clergy on behalf of the assembly, when in fact it is the work of Christ-in-his-body on behalf of the world. Getting clear about this would contribute significantly to a correct understanding of hierarchy. The work of the people of God is Christ's own work perpetuated in history. Christ is the premiere liturgist, but baptismal regeneration means that he is the firstborn of many little liturgists.

22. Liturgy is not the work of a rubricist or a worship committee or a floral arranger or a musician or a scholar or the presider; it is the synergistic work of a deified people, a race grafted by the full paschal mystery into eighth day existence. The primary agenda of liturgy is the creation of a new heavens and a new earth, not a new rite or a new altar cloth. Like a needle pulling thread through fabric to stitch up a rent cloth, the liturgist moves in and out, in and out between earth and heaven, time and eternity, the profane and the sacred, plunging into one and then the other and drawing them together by the thread of his or her life.

23. You can't taste your tongue. Why not? Because it is the organ by which you taste other things. You can't celebrate liturgy.

9. *The Praktikos and Chapters on Prayer* (Kalamazoo, Mich.: Cistercian Publications, 1981), 65.

Why not? Because it is the organ by which we celebrate the Kingdom of God. Liturgical time, then, is only partially understood by an anthropological study of human festival, because festival is how the eighth day is celebrated. Liturgical space, then, is not first a history of architecture, it is the nine square yards in front of the burning bush. Liturgical assembly, then, is only partially understood by sociology, for it is the body of Christ.

24. Two uses of the term "liturgical" must be accounted for, one thin, the other thick. In its thin sense, liturgy references ritual propriety, worship etiquette, temple decorum, rubrical protocol. If one has this thin use in mind, then it is hard to imagine liturgical theology meaning anything more than devotional affectation, and it is hard to imagine liturgical asceticism meaning anything more than austere decor, frugally performed rites, architectural minimalism, or the meritorious endurance of a painfully done liturgy. But there is a thicker grammar of the word "liturgy," and it is our overarching purpose to keep this deeper liturgical grammar before the face of liturgical studies curricula.

25. "Liturgy consists of the various means whereby the church makes it possible for the faithful to experience through their senses the mysteries of religion, that is, the sweetness of the kingdom of God."[10] These various means are material: the building, vessels, hymnody, psalmody, iconography, vestments, and the like. Therefore the study of the deep grammar cannot proceed without a study of these matters.

26. To remind ourselves of the thicker grammar, it might help to say something so outlandish, so exorbitant, that it will become immediately clear that the thicker grammar is meant, because the statement will appear ridiculous by a thin under-

10. Fotis Kontoglous, selections translated by Constantine Cavarnos, in *Byzantine Sacred Art* (Belmont, Mass.: Institute for Byzantine and Modern Greek Studies, 1985), 127.

standing. Here is such a statement, only it's not original with us: *Lex orandi statuat lex credendi* (The law of prayer establishes the law of belief). That's a perfectly ludicrous statement if *lex orandi* means human worship protocol, because devotional opinion, even magnified to a corporate level, does not determine doctrine. Therefore, we join Fr. Kavanagh in supposing that in this phrase deriving from Prosper of Aquitaine, *lex orandi* means something deeper, thicker.[11]

27. When wading around in matters liturgical, one has in fact stepped into the headwaters of a river (*lex orandi*) which can be followed downstream into any number of channels (*lex credendi*). Liturgical theology involves ecclesiology, because the Church is the people that this ritual creates; and ecclesiology involves Christology since that is whose body the Church is; and this requires triadology for an ontological Christology and soteriology for a functional Christology; and redemption outlines a doctrine of sin, which assumes knowledge of what it means to stand aright, which is a doctrine of creation.

28. The Church modifies the liturgy only in its thin sense; in its thick sense, it is the liturgy that creates the Church.

29. Liturgy in its thin sense is an expression of how we see God; liturgy in its thick sense is an expression of how God sees us.[12]

30. *Sacrosanctum Concilium* calls the liturgy the "fount from which all her [the Church's] power flows" (#10). Things flow from a summit. Because the liturgical encounter, therefore the proposition; because primary theology is transacted liturgically, therefore secondary theology. Our theological understanding of the world, of our destiny in it, and of the Trinity (which was what the fathers meant by "theology" anyway) proceeds out of our liturgi-

11. Aidan Kavanagh, O.S.B., *On Liturgical Theology* (New York: Pueblo, 1984).
12. Paul Holmer, "About Liturgy and Its Logic," *Worship* (January 1976): 18–28.

cal work. First the event, then the mystagogy. "Because there is preaching for that reason there is theology; not *vice versa*."[13]

> 31. The worship of the Church is not the liturgy of a human religious society, connected with a particular temple, but worship which pervades the whole universe and in which sun, moon, and all the stars take part.... [T]he Church is no purely human religious society. The angels and saints in heaven belong to her as well. Seen in this light, the Church's worship is no merely human occasion. The angels and the entire universe take part in it.[14]

So in a flash it becomes lucidly clear. Liturgical theology cannot be phenomenology, or comparison of religions, or sociology, or anthropology, or history of cultus and ritual, for the simple reason that Christ founded the Church, not another religion. If one wishes to speak about the Church's liturgy then one will have to speak theology.

32. *Sacrosanctum Concilium* also calls liturgy "the summit toward which the activity of the church is directed" (#10) and notes that "the sacred liturgy does not exhaust the entire activity of the Church" (#9). Persons must come to their liturgical work in faith and conversion. The Church therefore preaches, provides penance, catechizes for sacraments, teaches to observe Christ's commands, and encourages works of charity and piety. This is a strenuous discipline (*askesis*).

33. Here is another outrageous statement to arrest our customary inclination to refer liturgy to protocol. It is not original with us, either, but comes from Makarios of Egypt.

> The soul that has not yet acquired this citizenship in heaven and is not yet conscious of the heart's sanctification should be full of sorrow and should implore Christ fervently.... [The soul will then go forward,] receiving unutterable gifts and advanc-

13. Karl Rahner, S.J., "Priest and Poet," *Theological Investigations* (New York: Crossroad, 1982), 3.305.

14. Erik Peterson, *The Angels and the Liturgy* (New York: Herder & Herder, 1964), 22, 50.

> ing from glory to glory and from peace to greater peace. Finally, when it has attained the full measure of the Christian life, it will be ranged among the *perfect liturgists* and faultless ministers of Christ in his eternal Kingdom.[15]

What could it mean to say that our beatitude will consist of becoming perfect liturgists? Shall we look forward to an eternity of ringing bells and stoking incense pots? What thicker grammar of liturgy would be required to permit us to say with a straight face that the world was created to be peopled with beings whose perfection lies in their capacitation as liturgists?

34. Liturgical asceticism is the discipline that capacitates a liturgist.

35. There is an asceticism that leads to baptism: it is stimulated by agape and is called mortification, justification, conversion. We may think of it as catechumenal asceticism. However, there is also an asceticism that leads from baptism, from this conversion, and it is stimulated by charity (i.e., by the theological virtues received in the sacrament), and we shall call it liturgical asceticism because it is practiced by the baptized.

36. *Askesis* increases the measure by which we can participate in the liturgical life to which baptism initiated us. Liturgy is where the Kingdom is symbolized in its fullest capacity, and *askesis* enlarges the eyes of the perceiver; it cleanses the surface of the liturgist to reflect glory.

37. If liturgy means sharing the life of Christ (being washed in his Resurrection, eating his body), and if *askesis* means discipline (in the sense of forming), then liturgical asceticism is the discipline required to become an icon of Christ and make his image visible in our faces.

15. Makarios of Egypt, "Love," *The Philokalia* (London: Faber & Faber, 1986), 3.334; emphasis added.

38. Baptism drops the spirit of the Holy One into our veins, but there is no fire where there is not matter to burn. *Askesis* makes us combustible.

39. This asceticism is not born in the sand of the desert (although these athletes brought it to full perfection there), it is born in the waters of the font and is to be practiced by all Christians. In his foreword to *Unseen Warfare,* Nicodemus of the Holy Mountain describes the book's ascetical subject matter in this way:

> It teaches not the art of visible and sensory warfare, and speaks not about visible, bodily foes but about the unseen and inner struggle, which every Christian undertakes from the moment of his baptism, when he makes a vow to God to fight for Him, to the glory of His divine name, even unto death.[16]

If we remember that the word "sacramentum" meant the vow taken by a soldier upon enlistment in the army, then liturgical asceticism is the fulfillment of our baptismal sacrament.

40. From the beginning, God intended to share divine life with man and woman. The Kingdom is not an exception, but the flowering of the paradisial seed. A newborn child is the image of a full-grown adult, but must nevertheless itself grow up. St. Makarios says, "something similar should have happened to the soul."

> Before the fall, the soul was to have progressed and so to have attained full manhood. But through the fall it was plunged into a sea of forgetfulness, into an abyss of delusion, and dwelt within the gates of hell. As if separated from God by a great distance, it could not draw near its Creator and recognize him properly. But first through the prophets God called it back, and drew it to knowledge of Himself. Finally, through his own advent on earth, He dispelled the forgetfulness, the delusion; then, breaking through the gates of hell, He entered the deluded soul, giving

16. Nicodemus of the Holy Mountain, ed., *Unseen Warfare, Being the Spiritual Combat and Path to Paradise of Lorenzo Scupoli,* revised by Theophan the Recluse (New York: St. Vladimir's Seminary Press, 1987), 71.

himself to it as a model. By means of this model the soul can grow to maturity and attain the perfection of the Spirit.[17]

41. St. Ephrem of Syria also observed that the human person was created unfinished (a *homo viator*). Other beings were created finished, but the human being is a being-on-the-way, because the person is called to participate freely, willingly, in his or her growth into the likeness of God. What motivated God's decision?

> For this is the Good One, who could have forced us to please Him,
> without any trouble to Himself; but instead He toiled by every means
> so that we might act pleasingly to Him of our free will,
> that we might depict our beauty
> with the colours that our own free will had gathered;
> whereas, if He had adorned us, then we would have resembled
> a portrait that someone else had painted, adorning it with his own colours.[18]

42. From the beginning, man and woman were called to be royal priests. A human being is a liturgical being, *homo adorans*,[19] ruling over material creation in consort with the angelic principalities, and serving as the tongue of mute creation in the cosmic eucharist. But "there are no more singers for the cosmic liturgy because the Taboric light has no longer been seeded in the opacity of our bodies, and the glory of God has lost its place in a nature put to another and illegitimate use."[20] Although the Fall took place on a spiritual level, it affected matter, which is why asceti-

17. Makorios of Egypt, "Patient Endurance and Discrimnation," *The Philokalia*, 3.306.

18. St. Ephrem, *Hymns on Faith*, cited in Sebastian Brock, *The Luminous Eye: The Spiritual World Vision of St. Ephrem the Syrian* (Kalamazoo, Mich.: Cistercian Publications, 1985), 61.

19. "The unique position of man in the universe is that he alone is to bless God for the food and life he receives from Him. He alone is to respond to God's blessing with his blessing.... All rational, spiritual and other qualities of man, distinguishing him from other creatures, have their focus and ultimate fulfillment in this capacity to bless God, to know, so to speak, the meaning of the thirst and hunger that constitutes his life. 'Homo sapiens,' 'homo faber' ... yes, but, first of all, 'homo adorans.' The first, the basic definition of man is that he is the priest"; see Fr. Alexander Schmemann, *For the Life of the World* (New York: St. Vladimir's Seminary Press, 1973), 15.

20. Paul Evdokimov, *Art of the Icon* (Redondo Beach, Calif.: Oakwood, 1990), 76.

cism must be done to the body, through the body, by the body, for the body. "By what rule or manner can I bind this body of mine? ... He is my helper and my enemy, my assistant and my opponent, a protector and a traitor.... If I strike him down I have nothing left by which to acquire virtues."[21]

43. As the end of a watch is to tell time, the end of man and woman is liturgy. Heaven has always been our destiny. We were not expelled from the garden because God was jealous of divinity and would not share it. The Christian myth is not the myth of Prometheus. We were created for immortal happiness—and we do not mean by the modifier how long the happiness will last, but from whom it must come. Only the Immortal One can satisfy us, and happiness will elude us until we stand aright in our vocation as liturgical beings.

44. Happiness does elude us, because we have forfeited our vocation as *homo adorans*. In our fallen state, we no longer see the world as sacramental means, but as an end—our end—as if we were created for no more glory than this temporal world can confer. We are plunged into a sea of forgetfulness.

45. The sin was not that man and woman took something which God never intended them to have; the sin was that the serpent convinced them to take it prematurely.

> He deceived the husbandman
> so that he plucked prematurely
> the fruit which gives forth its sweetness
> only in due season
> —a fruit that, out of season,
> proves bitter to him who plucks it.[22]

Sin alters our humanity ontologically. We don't "look right."

21. John Climacus, *The Ladder of Divine Ascent,* 185–86.

22. St. Ephrem the Syrian, *Hymns on Paradise* (Crestwood, N.Y.: St. Vladimir's Seminary Press, 1990), 161.

46. Gregory of Nyssa notes that man and woman were created in the image of God, and that according to Scripture our prototype has wings. Hence, he concludes, human nature was also created with wings.

> It is clear, of course, that the word "wings" here will be interpreted on an allegorical level suitable for the divinity. Thus the wings would refer to God's power, his happiness, his incorruptibility, and so on. Now all these attributes were also in man, so long as he was still like God. But then it was the inclination towards sin that robbed us of these wings. Once outside the shelter of *God's* wing, we were also stripped of *our* wings.[23]

So that is what sin looks like! An eagle trudging or a falcon shuffling along, kicking up little clouds of dust; dogs in wheelchairs, or dolphins scrounging like bottom-feeders. A human being ruled by the passions looks like Pegasus crawling on his belly like a great Komodo dragon.

47. Not only is the human spirit is disordered, but by consequence matter cannot fulfill its end either, which is why creation waits with groaning anticipation for the redemption of man and woman. St. Ephrem describes the sun's reaction to human idolatry.

> The sun bellowed out in silence to the Lord against his worshippers.
> It was a suffering for him, the servant, that instead of his Lord he was worshipped.
> Behold the creation is joyful that the Creator is worshipped. . . .
> Since fools honored the sun, they diminished him in his honor.
> Now that they know he is a servant, by his course he worships his Lord.
> All the servants are glad to be counted servants.
> Blessed is he who set the natures in order!
> We have done perverse things that we should be servants to servants.[24]

23. Gregory of Nyssa, *From Glory to Glory: Texts from Gregory of Nyssa's Mystical Writings*, edited by Jean Danielou, S.J. (Crestwood, N.Y.: St. Vladimir's Seminary Press, 1979), 284.

24. St. Ephrem, "Hymns on the Nativity," in *Ephrem the Syrian: Hymns* (New York: Paulist Press, 1989), 180–81.

48. Until we fulfill our destiny as liturgical *homo adorans,* we will remain agitated, unhappy, and vaguely ill-at-ease. Sin is *dis*-ease. And our consciousness of this disease is planted deeper than doctrine. It was Chesterton who said the Fall is

> embodied in the common language talked on the top of an omnibus. Anybody might say, "Very few men are really manly." Nobody would say, "Very few whales are really whaley."
>
> If you wanted to dissuade a man from drinking his tenth whiskey you would slap him on the back and say, "Be a man." No one who wished to dissuade a crocodile from eating his tenth explorer would slap it on the back and say, "Be a crocodile." For we have no notion of a perfect crocodile; no allegory of a whale expelled from his whaley Eden.[25]

A dog cannot be any more doggy than he is, but we could be more human than we are. As we are, we are not enough. Disciplining a crocodile not to eat an explorer would make the beast less a crocodile; but disciplining a person not to eat gluttonously would make that person more human.

49. Fasting (like feasting) is a uniquely human activity. Only humans can fast, since the angels don't hunger and animals can't will to check their appetite. The Scholastics said that animals, in the presence of the delectable, cannot not desire it, for they are not masters of their inclination. And only humans need to fast. The doctrine of original sin precisely claims that it is not natural for people to sin. So while one may not be able to teach an old dog new tricks, one can teach the old Adam new tricks, the original tricks, the liturgical tricks the human race was created to celebrate.

50. In the *Chronicles of Narnia* C. S. Lewis describes the effect that eating enchanted food had upon Edmund.[26] First, "This was

25. G. K. Chesterton, "The Blatchford Controversies," in *G. K. Chesterton: Collected Works* (San Francisco: Ignatius Press, 1986), 1.385.

26. A lengthier use of Turkish delight as an illustration can be found in Fagerberg, "Liturgy, Christian Asceticism, and Turkish Delight," *New Theology Review* 9, no. 4 (November 1996): 93–101.

enchanted Turkish Delight and anyone who had once tasted it would want more and more of it, and would even, if they were allowed, go on eating it till they had killed themselves." Second, when Edmund sat down to supper at that evening, he did not enjoy the meal because, Lewis observes, "There's nothing that spoils the taste of good ordinary food half so much as the memory of bad magic food." The Christian doctrine of original sin claims that each human being is born with a spoiled appetite, and that humanity was expelled from Paradise before we killed ourselves eternally, and that the memory of this bad magic food has spoiled the taste of this good ordinary earth. Asceticism, which is the weaning of our appetites from magic food, does not make us less human, but finally human.

51. Man and woman were expelled from the garden until they got their appetites under control. They had been plunged into a sea of forgetfulness by the delectability of the world.

> In my opinion they saw that the tree was the most attractive in paradise to look at and to eat from. But the food most pleasant to the senses is not truly and in every way good, nor is it always good, nor good for everyone. Rather it is good for those who can make use of it without being mastered by it.... For only those fully established in the practice of divine contemplation and virtue can have concourse with things strongly attractive to the senses without withdrawing their intellect from the contemplation of God and from hymns and prayers to Him. Only such people can make these things the material and starting-point for raising themselves to God.[27]

52. The liturgical tradition held Baptism to be a return to Paradise. The font was the gate to Paradise. The insides of baptisteries were decorated like the Garden of Eden, the same garden where we were to have grown into full likeness of God. Would it not be the very gate before which an angel stood, with fiery sword, barring our re-entrance?

27. St. Gregory of Palamas, *The Philokalia* (London: Faber & Faber, 1995), 4.369.

53. The world's original purpose was to be raw matter for eucharist. The whole world was meant to have been an hierophany of grace and a liturgical tool, but human sin stripped matter of spirit. The whole world was meant to be sacramental encounter with God, but we took it as an end in itself, and we are barred reentrance until we have regained control of our appetites.

54. Our fall is the forfeiture of our liturgical career.[28]

55. Adam was heedless / as guardian of Paradise,
for the crafty thief / stealthily entered;
leaving aside the fruit / —which most men would covet—
he stole instead / the Garden's inhabitant!
Adam's Lord came out to seek him; / He entered Sheol and found him there,
then led and brought him out / to set him once more in Paradise.[29]

When the man and the woman hid themselves from the presence of the Lord God among the trees of the garden, the Lord God called, saying "Where are you?" (Genesis 3:9). The cry, "Adam, Eve, where are you?" sounded in the garden that first time. Angels went to the corners of the universe shouting the question, not only because bid to do so by their Lord, but because they missed the human's voice in the celestial choir. The King sent inquirers with the question through the long corridors of history: Abraham, Moses, Elijah, Isaiah—but neither did they find Adam or Eve. Then the Lord put on flesh so he could die so he could look in the last, last place: Sheol. And there he found them: deaf, mute, ashamed, dead, and the Lord brought out the man and woman and led them once more to Paradise. This dogma is written in icon, too.

28. "In our perspective, the 'original' sin is not primarily that man has 'disobeyed' God; the sin is that he ceased to be hungry for God and God alone.... The only real fall of man is his noneucharistic life in a noneucharistic world"; see Fr. Alexander Schmemann, *For the Life of the World*, 18.

29. St. Ephrem the Syrian, *Hymns on Paradise*, 135.

56. St. Mark the Ascetic says it is because of the passions that we are commanded not to love the world. "Not so that we should hate God's creation ... but so that we should eliminate the occasions for [the] passions."[30] We fast so that the Witch can't get control of us through the Turkish delight. Therefore, baptism is an act of conversion (*metanoia*), turning around, and this movement is the basis of each liturgical celebration. To understand that there is nothing wrong with the world, but that we must leave the world and bless the Kingdom of God is a very great paradox. It is the liturgical paradox.

In order to realize the Kingdom of God on earth, it is necessary, first, to *recede* from earth; in order to manifest the spiritual idea in the material world it is necessary to be free and detached from that world. A slave of the earth cannot possess it and consequently cannot make it the foundation of God's Kingdom....

The highest aim for Christianity is not ascetic detachment from the natural life but its hallowing and purification. But in order to purify it, one must, in the first instance, be pure from it. The purpose of Christianity is not to destroy earthly life, but to raise it towards God who comes down to meet it.... Only he who is free from the world can benefit it. A captive spirit is unable to rebuild its prison into a temple of light: he must first of all free himself from it.[31]

57. Baptism is not pickling someone in holy water until judgment day. Baptism is not life in a bottle of ecclesiastical formaldehyde. Baptism is deliverance. There we pass with Christ through the mystical Jordan into the wilderness of ascetical struggle. "Wrestlers are not the only ones whose occupation is to throw others down and to be thrown in turn," Evagrius observes; "the demons too wrestle—with us. Sometimes they throw us and at other times it is we who throw them."[32]

30. St. Mark the Ascetic, "On the Spiritual Law," *The Philokalia*, 1.117.

31. Vladimir Solovyof, "The Jews," in *A Solovyof Anthology*, arranged by S. L. Frank (London: SCM Press, 1950), 119–20.

32. Evagrius, *The Praktikos*, 35.

58. Life must be so simple for a hedonist.

59. Baptism is the return to Paradise from which our journey to fullness in God was to have begun. "After the Fall, human history is a long shipwreck awaiting rescue: but the port of salvation is not the goal; it is the possibility for the shipwrecked to resume his journey whose sole goal is union with God."[33] But there is this difference, now: we are in Christ, and Christ is in us (*Felix Culpa!* O Happy Fall! the Easter Vigil exults). The visible Church has Christ's liturgy to perform on behalf of the family of Adam and Eve. Liturgical asceticism is cosmological and evangelical.

60. Liturgical asceticism witnesses to the possibility of efficacious death. Remember that the monks considered themselves dead in the desert, and that the meaning of *martyria* is "witness." Asceticism is "nothing else but the anticipating grasp of Christian death understood as the most radical act of faith."[34]

61. The monks are the new martyrs: new witnesses! When Abba Poemen confessed envy, Abba Ammonas said to him, "Poemen, are you still alive? Go, sit down in your cell; engrave it on your heart that you have been in the tomb for a year already."[35] To what do both those who died, and those who die to the world, witness? That there is something worth dying for. They witness to the new creation, the Church. They witness to what gives the temporal its meaning. Paul Claudel said, "It seems as if the acorn knows its destiny and carries within itself an active idea of the oak required of it. And in the same way it seems as if memory and foresight join together in the hearts of Adam's sons to deny the immediate the right to prevail." Liturgical asceticism is denying the immediate the right to prevail.

33. Vladimir Lossky, *Orthodox Theology: An Introduction* (New York: St. Vladimir's Seminary Press, 1978), 84.

34. Karl Rahner, "The Passion and Asceticism," *Theological Investigations,* 3.73.

35. *The Sayings of the Desert Fathers,* translated by Benedicta Ward, S.L.G. (Kalamazoo, Mich.: Cistercian Publications, 1975), 164.

62. Liturgical asceticism corroborates the death of Christ in our own bodies by taming those passions that accompany life-in-the-body so that we may notarize with our hope that death has not been victorious; instead, death has been made a portal to the new age, if grasped in a radical act of faith. The pall has become a swaddling cloth, the sepulchre a birth canal.

63. There is only one way to understand the liturgical ascetic's life of renunciation: eschatologically.

64. Scholasticism distinguished between two types of goods: those ordered to an end (*bonum utile*) and those that contain meaning in themselves (*bonum honestum*). The latter type are not "good for" something; they simply are good. For example, it misses the point to treat marriage as a utilitarian good and ask "What is it good for?"

65. The monastic ascetic does not renounce a lower for a higher good. This would be an act of moral asceticism. Instead, the monk renounces highest goods—*bonum honestum*. But in a purely natural order there could be no other values for the sake of which highest goods could be sacrificed. It would be "ethically perverse" to renounce them. "A positive value can be sacrificed only for the sake of a higher value."[36] What value is higher than the highest natural good?

66. When the monk renounces the goods of freedom by vowing stability, marriage by vowing celibacy, and autonomy by vowing obedience,[37] then either such vows are (a) ethically perverse—that is, a denial of natural goods and as blatant a form of Manichaean dualism as ever snuck into Christianity—or else (b)

36. Karl Rahner, "Reflections on the Theology of Renunciation," *Theological Investigations*, 3.51–52.

37. We are aware of the difference between a monk and a member of a religious order, and insofar as these comments pertain to the latter, which they do, we also have them in mind.

there is a good higher than the highest natural good. We reiterate: liturgical asceticism could not have existed before Christ.

67. The charge that asceticism is dualistic hatred of the world has been frequently, though inaccurately, leveled against Christian monasticism. Chesterton remarks on the mistake.

> Nothing is more common ... than to find such a modern critic writing something like this: "Christianity was a movement of ascetics, a rush into the desert, a refuge in the cloister, a renunciation of all life and happiness; and this was part of a gloomy and inhuman reaction against nature itself, a hatred of the body, a horror of the material universe, a sort of universal suicide of the senses and even the self."

Not so, he replies.

> The early Church was ascetic, but she proved that she was not pessimistic, simply by condemning the pessimists. The creed declared that man was sinful, but it did not declare that life was evil, and it proved it by damning those who did.... It proved that the primitive Catholics were specially eager to explain that they did *not* think man utterly vile; that they did *not* think life incurably miserable; that they did *not* think marriage a sin or procreation a tragedy.[38]

68. Christians do not practice asceticism because they think the world ugly, but because they believe it an anticipatory reflection of the Kingdom (i.e., a sacrament). Christians do not practice asceticism because they hate this world, but because by its ordered use (i.e., as sacrament) it can become an encounter with the Kingdom. "The purpose of Christian asceticism is not to weaken the flesh, but to strengthen the spirit for the transfiguration of the flesh."[39] The sacramental life requires asceticism.

38. G. K. Chesterton, *The Everlasting Man*, in *G. K. Chesterton: The Collected Works* (San Francisco: Ignatius Press, 1986), 2.354, 356.

39. Vladimir Solovyof, *A Solovyof Anthology*, 119–20.

69. Before the Fall, holy life was lived in a garden, but now we live in the desert and the holy man is on the cross defeating the Prince of the desert. The fourth century ascetics went into the desert to engage battle with Satan. "Anchorites surround him and tear him to bits; apostles torment him with their bones."[40] And that is why our desert fathers and mothers look the way they do: mortified! All who have been to the font are mortified by the experience, having come under the hand of the holy mortician who did not die to exempt us from dying but rather to make our dying efficacious.

So the holy men and women die to the world as martyrs (witnesses). Their ministry is to go by the shorter but harder route to the same destination that awaits all who keep the commandments. They are witnesses (martyrs) to what lies ahead. Our destiny is beatitude, not monasticism, but monasticism is what it costs to prophetically display this beatitude, now, existentially, in this old age, and the monks pay that price for the Church in love. It will cost everyone the same price: death. We must die to enter the Kingdom; no one can see God and live.

70. Liturgical asceticism is a matter of faith, just as the liturgy cannot be celebrated until after baptismal conversion. Rahner says, "This higher value cannot be *experienced* in its own intrinsic reality but must be believed and hoped for." Christian renunciation is

> the giving up of a value which can be experienced in favor of a value possessed only by faith and hope.... In death, man is really asked in the most fundamental manner whether he will allow himself to be disposed beyond himself into what is hidden and incalculable, and he thereby renounces himself. Christian renunciation is therefore a training ground for death in Christ understood as the highest deed of that radical state of submitting oneself to a higher will.[41]

40. St. Ephrem the Syrian, "Hymns on Virginity," *Hymns*, 317.
41. Rahner, "Reflections on the Theology of Renunciation," 52.

71. Liturgical asceticism is a manifestation of the theological virtue of hope.

72. Not a single word of what we have written should be interpreted as debasing the excellence of the monastic vocation in the name of some pseudoegalitarianism. Yes, the tradition unhesitatingly affirms that salvation may be attained in the world, and there are several stories in which the monk is humbled by finding a person in the city who is an equal or superior (e.g., "It was revealed to Abba Anthony in his desert that there was one who was his equal in the city. He was a doctor by profession and whatever he had beyond his needs he gave to the poor, and everyday he sang the Sanctus with the angels."),[42] and, yes, Abba Silvanus explains that "Mary needs Martha. It is really thanks to Martha that Mary is praised."[43] Nevertheless, Mary has chosen the more excellent part. A Christian in the world may be equal in merit, nevertheless, "those who lead a life of silence lead a superior life, and follow a line of conduct which is more excellent than all the rules of life which are followed among brethren."[44] It is a challenge for us to grasp the grammar by which it can be said that two can be equal in merit but one's labor be more excellent.

73. We do not think that the monk is an ascetic while the layperson is not; we think that liturgical asceticism is practiced by both the desert ascetic and the secular ascetic, and we are interested in what the former can teach those living in the world about liturgical asceticism.

> [I]t is the total Church that teaches the Church, just as it is in the whole of its teaching that the Gospel is addressed to each and all. Prayer, fasting, the reading of the Scriptures and ascetic discipline are imposed on all for the same reason. That is why

42. Ward, *Sayings of the Desert Fathers*, 223.

43. Ibid., 6.

44. E. A. Wallis Budge, *The Paradise* (London: Chatto & Windus, 1907), vol. 2, "Questions and Answers on the Ascetic Rule," nos. 606 and 660.

> the laity very exactly forms the state of *interiorized monasticism.* Its wisdom consists essentially in assuming, while living in the world and perhaps on account of this vocation, the eschatological attitude of the monks, their joyous and impatient expectation of the parousia.[45]

74. "[I]n the East, monasticism was not seen merely as a separate condition, proper to a precise category of Christians, but rather as a reference point for all the baptized, according to the gifts offered to each by the Lord; it was presented as a symbolic synthesis of Christianity."[46]

75. Fr. Aidan Kavanagh used to say about Sunday, to establish its normativity, that it is not a small Easter; instead, Easter is a big Sunday. What we normally celebrate on Sunday we do in a big way on Easter. In that spirit, we suggest that a secular Christian is not a little monk; instead, a monk is a big baptized. What every liturgical ascetic normally does, the monk does in a big way.

76. When things are enlarged, they are often easier to see. A small object lit from behind can have a nearly limitless shadow if projected upon a landscape that stretches without break to the horizon. The monk's poverty in the desert is but a shadow of the baptismal liberty from avarice, cast upon the vast desert landscape that elongates and exaggerates it.

77. There are ascetics who make a vow, a profession—they are professionals. Professional ascetics live a visible life of renunciation in personification of the theological virtue of hope. The non-professionals, the layman and laywoman, exercise this virtue no less, only in different form. The ascetical way "is most appropriate for those detached from the world, for they are consecrated to God, and this union allows them continually to converse with Him with a pure mind.... As to those who live in the world, they

45. Paul Evdokimov, *The Struggle with God* (Glen Rock, N.J.: Paulist Press, 1966), 200.

46. John Paul II, *Orientale Lumen*, 9.

must force themselves to use the things of this world in conformity with the commandments of God."[47]

78. The Church accommodates many paths to holiness.

> There are many roads to holiness (and to hell). A path wrong for one will suit another, yet what each is doing is pleasing to God.... God in his unspeakable providence has arranged that some received the holy reward of their toils even before they set to work, others while actually working, others again when the work was done, and still others at the time of their death. Let the reader ask himself which one of them was made more humble.[48]

79. All vocations to holiness begin in baptism. Christ, who is the light of the world, contains, as pure white light does, all the colors of the rainbow. All the colors of the spectrum are in Christ's laser white light which can be dispersed through a prism into its various colors. What can serve as the prism? A drop of water will do. "Bless this font...." All paths to holiness are baptismal dispersions of the light of Mt. Tabor into a spectrum of vocational colors.

80. Liturgical asceticism is ecclesiological. "The whole of Christian life is only a realization of these first fruits, and as full an anticipation as possible of the glory of the time to come; monastic life is a particular form of this anticipation, a means which Scripture and ecclesiastical tradition recommend better to realize the grace of baptism, and to manifest the Kingdom to come here below."[49] Monasticism is not an alternative form of Christian communion, it is an special form, which exists in ministry to the Church. "Without the ascetic dimension, the person is inconceivable. But in the end the context of the manifestation of the person is not the monastery: it is the eucharist."[50]

47. Gregory Palamas, *The Triads* (New York: Paulist Press, 1983), 55.

48. John Climacus, *The Ladder of Divine Ascent,* 243, 241.

49. Fr. John Meyendorff, *A Study of Gregory Palamas* (Leighton Buzzard, U.K.: Faith Press, 1974), 198.

50. John Zizioulas, *Being as Communion* (Crestwood, N.Y.: St. Vladimir's Seminary Press, 1985), 63.

81. Why did the professionals go into the desert? Because "[i]f a man is entangled in the things of this world, caught by their many shackles, and seduced by the evil passions, it is very hard for him to recognize that there is another invisible struggle and another inner warfare. But, after detaching himself from all visible things and worldly pleasures, and beginning to serve God, he then becomes capable of recognizing the nature of this inner struggle and unseen warfare against the passions."[51] Remember, it is hard to keep your wits about you in the middle of a seduction. The monk's witness (martyrdom) is his or her detachment.

82. Starting in the fourth century monks went into the deserts of Egypt to carry out a radical experiment in disciplined life. They wanted to see what it took to order a life to God. In an experiment, as anyone in high school science knows, the first requirement is to isolate the object to be tested by removing any external factors that might alter the experiment. This is called a controlled environment. The desert fathers sought a controlled environment, too, but they removed the external factors by removing themselves from the external factors. They headed to the desert—away from city, family, wealth, and property—not because they thought these things were bad, and not in order to do something none of the rest of us should do, but so they could experiment on the human heart.

83. The same Church that acclaimed celibacy made marriage a sacrament.

84. It is not as though God cannot be found in the world. Charles Williams is quite right in saying the Church recognizes two ways to God, one by the negation of images, the other by the affirmation of images, and Rahner is quite right when he insists that even in the monk's flight from the world to God, he or she

51. St. Makarios of Egypt, "The Freedom of the Intellect," *The Philokalia,* 3.351.

must confess that it is also possible to reach the same transcendent God through the world.

85. The monk went into the desert to repent, and to weep Christ's tears over the death of Adam. However, they are not the only ones to grieve the curse of death that hangs heavy on the cosmos. Baudelaire wrote,

> It is this immortal instinct for the beautiful which makes us consider the earth and its various spectacles as a sketch of heaven.... It is at once through poetry and across poetry, through and across music, that the soul glimpses the splendours situated beyond the grave; and when an exquisite poem brings tears to the eyes, these tears are not proof of an excess of joy, they are rather the testimony of an irritated melancholy, a demand of the nerves, of a nature exiled in the imperfect and desiring to take possession immediately, even on this earth, of a revealed paradise.[52]

Both the monk in the desert and the layperson in the world weep over death, and both these gifts of tears draw their liquid origin and supply from the same font. Holy water can be found at the door of the nave. Holy salt water can be found at the door to the soul (which is the eye) and cleanses what comes into the heart. Both these types of tears arise from mortification. The laity, too, weep with an "irritated melancholy" over the scent of death. (It tears the eyes like onions.) Our exiled nature remembers a home it has not seen yet. Liturgists are homesick at home. That's why they practice self-discipline.

86. St. Bonaventure reminds us that Jesus "wept for us in our misery not only once but many times. First over Lazarus, then over the city and finally on the cross, a flood of tears streamed forth from those loving eyes for the expiation of all sins." If your heart is not hard, he continues, you would "consider your weeping physician and make mourning ... a bitter lamentation....

52. Charles Baudelaire, quoted in Jacques Maritain, *Approaches to God* (New York: Macmillan, 1954), 80.

Give yourself no rest, nor let the pupil of your eye be still."[53] Religious tears are ours. Liturgical tears are Christ's, wept from our eyes.

87. St. Symeon the New Theologian bids us remember "that 'the kingdom of heaven is entered forcibly, and those who force themselves take possession of it' (Mt 11:12); ... apply force to yourself."[54] Force must be used to overcome something which stands as an obstacle between oneself and a goal. If salvation and beatitude are our goal, what stands in our way? What obstacle prevents us from attaining happiness? What gates must be forced with ascetical leverage, what locks smashed by fasting, what chains broken by prayer? What must be violently overcome? Certainly not God. We do not need to do violence to the gates of heaven in order to get past them. In fact, it is ourselves. We must do violence to ourselves in order to desire to enter those gates. (Dorothy Sayers says that her friend C. S. Lewis once remarked that the joys of heaven would be, for most of us, in our present condition, an acquired taste.)

88. So long as there is a trace of ego, humility will feel like humiliation.

89. The layperson, no less than the monk, desires to take possession of paradise immediately, violently, forcibly, even on this earth. So both frequent the Eucharist. Both make community (the monastic community, and the domus ecclesiae). Evdokimov and Solovyof both write that there are two ascetical vocations: monasticism and marriage.[55] If you like, marriage is the sacramental

53. St. Bonaventure, *The Tree of Life* (New York: Paulist Press, 1978), 137.

54. Symeon the New Theologian, *The Philokalia,* 4.55.

55. Paul Evdokimov, *The Sacrament of Love* (Crestwood, N.Y.: St. Vladimir's Seminary Press, 1985), ch. 2, "Marriage and the Monastic State"; and Vladimir Solovyof, *The Justification of the Good: An Essay on Moral Philosophy* (London: Constable and Company, 1918), 411–15; see also Solovyof's work on love, *The Meaning of Love* (West Stockbridge, Mass.: Lindisfarne Press, 1985). Romano Guardini also explains possession in light of poverty in Christ, and virginity in light of marriage in *The Lord* (Chicago: Henry Regnery, 1954), 270–87.

expression of the way of affirmation,[56] as the cloister is the sacramental expression of the way of negation. Both storm the gates of heaven impatiently, living the Beatitudes now. Both ways are liturgical in that they spring from our baptismal grafting into Christ's liturgy (work) and see the world with the eye of the dove, in the light of Mount Tabor.

90. Evagrius said there were three stages: *praktike, physike,* and *theologia*. It would seem, then, that between being an ascetic and a theologian, one must become a physician. Not the medical kind; not the scientific kind, either. This physics transcends these divided disciplines because this is the kind of physics that heals (like the former) by means of knowing the world (like the latter). A true physician knows the world to be a temple. It knows what matter is for, and therefore the cure for what is the matter with the world. "Seek the reason why God created, for this is true knowledge."[57]

91. "The poverty of the monk is resignation from care," says John Climacus.[58] The amount of resignation held by a tall, narrow container can also be held by a broad, flat receptacle, as you will find by pouring water from a dinner glass onto a dinner plate. The desert ascetic excels because he or she is tall and narrow; the secular ascetic is more spread, commanded by the Creator to oversee many cares; but although the latter's resignation may not be as deep, it may be as much.

92. Sacrifice is an act of love, not disgust. In the Eucharistic sacrifice we throw everything we hold into a monument of un-

56. "Marriage is the great example, in this sense, of the Way of Affirmation. The intention of fidelity is the safeguard of romanticism; the turning of something like the vision of an eternal state into an experiment towards that state. Once that experiment has been formally begun, it cannot be safely abandoned, or so the Christian Church maintains"; see Charles Williams, *The Figure of Beatrice* (New York: Farrar, Straus & Cudahy, 1961), 49.

57. Maximus the Confessor, "The Four Hundred Chapters on Love," 4.5, in *Maximus Confessor: Selected Writings* (New York: Paulist Press, 1985), 76.

58. John Climacus, *Ladder of Divine Ascent*, 189.

fathomable thanks. Liturgical sacrifice is activated by the "discovery of an infinite debt."

> It may seem a paradox to say that a man may be transported with joy to discover that he is in debt ... [but that is] the key of asceticism. It is the highest and holiest of the paradoxes that the man who really knows he cannot pay his debt will be forever paying it. He will be for ever giving back what he cannot give back, and cannot be expected to give back.... We are not generous enough to be ascetics; one might almost say not genial enough to be ascetics.[59]

93. The attempt to understand asceticism will always end in failure unless one admits the possibility of wild, bracing divine love. At the end of his biography of Francis, Chesterton treats the story of Claire running away at the tender age of seventeen to become a nun, and suggests viewing it as St. Francis helping Claire to *elope* into the cloister, since the scene had many of the elements of a regular romantic elopement. She escaped through a hole in the wall, fled against her father's wishes, and was received at midnight by the light of torches. "Now about that incident, I will here only say this. If it had really been a romantic elopement and the girl had become a bride instead of a nun, practically the whole modern world would have made her a heroine.... The point for the moment is that modern romanticism entirely encourages such defiance of parents when it is done in the name of romantic love. For it knows that romantic love is a reality, but it does not know that divine love is a reality."[60]

94. The reason we find the extremes to which the fathers went in the desert so difficult to comprehend is because we do not know that divine love is a reality. We have become calloused to our divine lover's touch.

59. G. K. Chesterton, *St. Francis of Assisi*, in *G. K. Chesterton: The Collected Works*, 2.76.

60. Ibid., 99.

95. Monks are not the only ones who practice asceticism, because they are not the only ones who must be trained for death. I'm dead, you're dead, the monk is dead. All the little fishes in the baptismal font caught by Christ are dead. He has taken one rusty nail out of his hand and bent it into a fish hook to catch us. But some he throws back into the world! The layperson in the city is as dead to sin as the hermit in the desert, but has been thrown back into the world to complete the King's commands: to beget justice, to birth peace, to make babies, and to sit on the throne as royal *homo adorans* and gather up the cosmos into the liturgical ascent to God.

96. Liturgical asceticism lightens the load of pride and arrogance that we carry about. Chesterton quips that a characteristic of the great saints is not only their power of levitation, but their power of levity. "Angels can fly because they take themselves lightly.... But the kings in their heavy gold and the proud in their robes of purple will all of their nature sink downwards, for pride cannot rise to levity or levitation. Pride is the downward drag of all things.... It is easy to be heavy; hard to be light. Satan fell by force of gravity."[61]

97. There are two movements in the liturgy, identified in the Greek rite as anabatic and catabatic—*basis* means "to go": to go up, to go down. The anabatic is our ascent into the heavenly realm ("Lift up your hearts"), and the catabatic is the Spirit's epicletic descent upon the assembly and sacrifice.

The dictionary includes a meteorological definition for anabasis as well: "pertaining to an uphill wind produced by the affects of local heating." No, wait; that's a Pentecostal definition.

And the dictionary also gives a spatial metaphor. Anabasis, it says, is a march from the coast to the interior (where, in silence, one will find the Holy Spirit waiting) while catabasis is a march

61. G. K. Chesterton, *Orthodoxy*, in *G. K. Chesterton: The Collected Works*, 1.326.

from the interior of a country to the coast (where, in need, one will find the world waiting). Every liturgy is a two-way march: inward, then outward. Or upward, then downward.

The prefix *acro-* means "aloft." The Holy Spirit, then, restores Adam and Eve's wings, making us liturgical acrobats: tumbling, twirling, doing barrel rolls with the angels above the altar. Liturgical asceticism lightens one's gravity, increasing the measure of our liturgical capacity.

98. Anabasis, catabasis—the respiratory rhythm of the Holy Spirit. Like holding one's breath, to do one alone tends to cut down on one's pneumatic capacity. The secular ascetic does not neglect prayer any more than the desert ascetic neglected the world. If the monk was in the desert for the sake of the world, the layperson is in the world for the sake of the heavenly Jerusalem and a new humanity.

99. We are all of us royalty in exile, made for blessing, battle, and beatitude. We were made for a sacramental world in which apples illicitly obtained can curse, and bread can become the body of God. The professed ascetics are walking adventure tales of divine love who awaken our eagerness for whatever wild ascetical adventure will be required of each of us in order to go home.

BIBLIOGRAPHY

Afanasiev, Nicholas. *The Church of the Holy Spirit.* Notre Dame, Ind.: University of Notre Dame Press, 2007.

Afanasiev, Victor. *Elder Barsanuphius of Optina.* Platina, Calif.: St. Herman of Alaska Brotherhood, 2000.

Alfeyev, Hilarion. *The Spiritual World of Isaac the Syrian.* Kalamazoo, Mich.: Cistercian Publications, 2000.

Arseniev, Nicholas. *Russian Piety.* Crestwood, N.Y.: St. Vladimir's Seminary Press, 1964.

———. *Mysticism and the Eastern Church.* Crestwood, N.Y.: St. Vladimir's Seminary Press, 1979.

Athanasius. *The Life of Antony and The Letter to Marcellinus.* New York: Paulist Press, 1980.

Bamberger, John Etudes, O.C.S.O. Introduction to *The Pratikos, Chapters on Prayer.* Kalamazoo, Mich.: Cistercian Publications, 1981.

Barsanuphius and John. *Guidance for Spiritual Life: Answers to the Questions of Disciples.* Platina, Calif.: St. Herman of Alaska Brotherhood, 2002.

———. *Letters from the Desert.* Crestwood, N.Y.: St. Vladimir's Seminary Press, 2003.

Basil. *Ascetical Works.* Washington, D.C.: The Catholic University of America Press, 1962.

———. *On the Human Condition.* Crestwood, N.Y.: St. Vladimir's Seminary Press, 2005.

Behr, John. *Asceticism and Anthropology in Irenaeus and Clement.* New York: Oxford University Press, 2000.

———, ed. *Abba: The Tradition of Orthodoxy in the West: Festschrift for Bishop Kallistos Ware.* Crestwood, N.Y.: St. Vladimir's Seminary Press, 2003.

———. *The Mystery of Christ: Life in Death*. Crestwood, N.Y.: St. Vladimir's Seminary Press, 2006.
Behr-Sigel, Elisabeth. *The Place of the Heart: An Introduction to Orthodox Spirituality*. Torrance, Calif.: Oakwood Publications, 1992.
Berger, Kevin (Calinic) M. *Towards a Theological Gnoseology: The Synthesis of Fr. Dumitru Staniloae*. Ph.D. diss., The Catholic University of America, 2003.
The Blackwell Dictionary of Eastern Christianity. Oxford, U.K.: Blackwell, 1999.
Bloomfield, Morton W. *The Seven Deadly Sins*. Michigan: Michigan State University Press, 1967.
Bolshakoff, Sergius. *Russian Mystics*. Kalamazoo, Mich.: Cistercian Publications, 1980.
Bouyer, Louis. *The Paschal Mystery: Meditations on the Last Three Days of Holy Week*. Chicago: Henry Regenery Company, 1950.
———. *The Meaning of the Monastic Life*. London: Burns & Oates, 1955.
———. *The Spirit and Forms of Protestantism*. Westminster, Md.: Newman Press, 1957.
———. *The Seat of Wisdom: An Essay on the Place of the Virgin Mary in Christian Theology*. New York: Pantheon Books, 1960.
———. *The Spirituality of the New Testament and the Fathers*, vol. 1 of *A History of Christian Spirituality*. New York: Seabury Press, 1982.
Bradshaw, David. *Aristotle East and West: A Metaphysics and the Division of Christendom*. New York: Cambridge University Press, 2006.
Brakke, David. *Athanasius and the Politics of Asceticism*. New York: Oxford University Press, 1995.
Brianchaninov, Ignatius. *The Arena: An Offering to Contemporary Monasticism*. Madras, India: Diocesan Press, 1970.
Brock, Sebastian. *The Luminous Eye: The Spiritual World Vision of St. Ephrem the Syrian*. Kalamazoo, Mich.: Cistercian Publications, 1985.
Budge, E. A. Wallis. *The Paradise*. 2 vols. London: Chatto & Windus, 1907.
Cabasilas, Nicholas. *A Commentary on the Divine Liturgy*. London: SPCK Press, 1960.
———. *Life in Christ*. Crestwood, N.Y.: St. Vladimir's Seminary Press, 1974.
Cavarnos, Constantine. *The Holy Mountain*. Belmont, Mass.: Institute for Byzantine and Modern Greek Studies, 1973.
Chadwick, Owen. *Western Asceticism*. Philadelphia: Westminster Press, 1958.
Cherubim, Archimandrite. *Contemporary Ascetics of Mount Athos*. 2 vols. Platina, Calif.: St. Herman of Alaska Brotherhood Press, 1991.
Chirovsky, Andriy, ed. *Following the Star from the East: Essays in Honour of Archimandrite Boniface Luykx*. Ottawa, Canada: St. Paul University and Sheptytsky Institute of Eastern Christian Studies, 1992.
Chitty, Derwas. *The Desert a City*. Crestwood, N.Y.: St. Vladimir's Seminary Press, 1995.
Clement, Olivier. *The Roots of Christian Mysticism*. New York: New City Press, 1996.
———. *On Being Human: A Spiritual Anthropology*. New York: New City Press, 2000.

———. *Three Prayers*. Crestwood, N.Y.: St. Vladimir's Seminary Press, 2000.

The Cloud of Unknowing. Translated by William Johnston. New York: Image Books, Doubleday, 1973.

Corbon, Jean. *The Wellspring of Worship*. New York: Paulist Press, 1988.

Daley, Brian, S.J. *On the Dormition of Mary: Early Patristic Homilies*. Crestwood, N.Y.: St. Vladimir's Seminary Press, 1998.

Dawes, Elizabeth, and Norman H. Baynes, trans. *Three Byzantine Saints: Contemporary Biographies of St. Daniel the Stylite, St. Theodore of Sykeon, and St. John the Almsgiver*. Crestwood, N.Y.: St. Vladimir's Seminary Press, 1996.

Dorotheos of Gaza. *Discourses and Sayings*. Kalamazoo, Mich.: Cistercian Publications, 1977.

Driscoll, Jeremy, O.S.B. *The "Ad Monachos" of Evagrius of Ponticus*. Rome: Pontificio Ateneo S. Anselmo, 1991.

———. *Evagrius Ponticus: Ad Monachos*. Ancient Christian Writers 59. New York: Newman Press, 2003.

Elder Ephraim. *Counsels from the Holy Mountain: Selected from the Letters and Homilies of Elder Ephraim*. Florence, Ariz.: Saint Anthony's Greek Orthodox Monastery, 1999.

Elder Moses. *The Elder Moses of Optina*. Boston: Holy Nativity Convent, 1996.

Ephrem the Syrian. *Ephrem the Syrian: Hymns*. New York: Paulist Press, 1989.

———. *A Spiritual Psalter*. Excerpted by Bishop Theophan the Recluse. Liberty, Tenn.: St. John of Kronstadt Press, 1989.

———. *Hymns on Paradise*. Crestwood, N.Y.: St. Vladimir's Seminary Press, 1990.

———. *Selected Prose Works*. The Fathers of the Church 91. Washington, D.C.: The Catholic University of America Press, 1994.

Evagrius. *The Praktikos and Chapters on Prayer*. Translated, with introduction, by John Etudes Bamberger, O.C.S.O. Kalamazoo, Mich.: Cistercian Publications, 1981.

———. *The Mind's Long Journey to the Holy Trinity: The* Ad Monachos *of Evagrius Ponticus*. Translated by Jeremy Driscoll, O.S.B. Collegeville, Md.: Liturgical Press, 1993.

———. *Evagrius of Pontus: The Greek Ascetic Corpus*. Translated by Robert E. Sinkewicz. New York: Oxford University Press, 2003.

———. *Talking Back—Antirrhetikos: A Monastic Handbook for Combating Demons*. Translated by David Brakke. Collegeville, Md.: Liturgical Press, 2009.

Evdokimov, Paul. *The Art of the Icon: A Theology of Beauty*. Redondo Beach, Calif.: Oakwood Publications, 1990.

———. *The Sacrament of Love*. New York: St. Vladimir's Seminary Press, 1985.

———. *Woman and the Salvation of the World*. Crestwood, N.Y.: St. Vladimir's Seminary Press, 1994.

———. *The Struggle with God*. Glen Rock,N.J.: Paulist Press, 1966. (Republished as *Ages of the Spiritual Life*. Crestwood, N.Y.: St. Vladimir's Seminary Press, 1998.)

———. *In the World, of the Church: A Paul Evdokmov Reader.* Edited by Michael Plekon and Alexis Vinogradov. Crestwood, N.Y.: St. Vladimir's Seminary Press, 2001.

Fedetov, George P. *A Treasury of Russian Spirituality.* Belmont, Mass.: Nordland, 1975.

Florensky, Pavel. *Salt of the Earth: An Encounter with a Holy Russian Elder: Isidore of Gethsemane Hermitage.* Platina, Calif.: St. Herman of Alaska Brotherhood, 1987.

———. *Iconostasis.* Crestwood, N.Y.: St. Vladimir's Seminary Press, 1996.

———. *The Pillar and Ground of the Truth.* Princeton, N.J.: Princeton University Press, 1997.

Florovsky, Georges. *The Byzantine Ascetic and Spiritual Fathers.* Vol. 10 of *Collected Works.* Belmont, Mass.: Notable & Academic Books, 1987.

Frank, S. L., ed. *A Solovyof Anthology.* London: SCM Press, 1950.

Fry, Timothy, O.S.B., ed. *The Rule of Saint Benedict in Latin and English with Notes.* Collegeville, Md.: Liturgical Press, 1981.

George, Archimandrite. *The Deification as the Purpose of Man's Life.* Mt. Athos, Greece: Holy Monastery of St. Gregorios, 1997.

Gerasim, Archimandrite. *Abba Gerasim and His Letters to His Brotherhood.* Spruce Island, Alaska: St. Herman of Alaska Brotherhood, 1998.

Gillet, Lev. *Orthodox Spirituality: An Outline of the Orthodox Ascetical and Mystical Tradition.* Crestwood, N.Y.: St. Vladimir's Seminary Press, 1987.

———. *In Thy Presence.* Crestwood, N.Y.: St. Vladimir's Seminary Press, 1977.

———. *The Jesus Prayer.* Crestwood, N.Y.: St. Vladimir's Seminary Press, 1987.

Golitzin, Alexander. *Et Introibo Ad Altare Dei: The Mystagogy of Dionysius Areopagite, with Special Reference to Its Predecessors in the Eastern Christian Tradition.* Thessaloniki, Greece: George Dedousis Publishing Co., 1994.

———. *The Living Witness of the Holy Mountain: Contemporary Voices from Mount Athos.* South Canaan, Pa.: St. Tikhon's Seminary Press, 1996.

Gregorias, Hiermonk. *The Divine Liturgy: A Commentary in the Light of the Fathers.* Mt. Athos, Greece: Koutloumousiou Monastery, 2009.

Gregory of Nyssa. *The Lord's Prayer, the Beatitudes.* Ancient Christian Writers 18. New York: Newman Press, 1954.

———. *The Life of Moses.* New York: Paulist Press, 1978.

———. *From Glory to Glory: Texts from Gregory of Nyssa's Mystical Writings.* Edited by Jean Danielou, S.J.. Crestwood, N.Y.: St. Vladimir's Seminary Press, 1979.

———. *Ascetical Works.* The Fathers of the Church 58. Washington, D.C.: The Catholic University of America Press, 1999.

Gregory Palamas. *The Triads.* New York: Paulist Press, 1983.

———. *The One Hundred and Fifty Chapters.* Edited by Robert Winkewicz, C.S.B. Toronto: Pontifical Institute of Mediaeval Studies, 1988.

———. *Treatise on the Spiritual Life.* Minneapolis: Light and Life, 1995.

———. *The Homilies of Saint Gregory Palamas.* South Canaan, Pa.: Saint Tikhon's Seminary Press, 2004.

———. *Mary the Mother of God: Sermons by Saint Gregory Palamas.* Edited by Christopher Veniamin. South Canaan, Pa.: Mount Thabor Publishing, 2005.

———. *Saint Gregory Palamas: The Homilies.* Waymart, Pa.: Mount Thabor Publishing, 2009.

Gross, Jules. *The Divinization of the Christian according to the Greek Fathers.* Anaheim, Calif.: A&C Press, 2002.

Hausherr, Irenee, S.J. *The Name of Jesus.* Kalamazoo, Mich.: Cistercian Publications, 1978.

———. *Penthos: The Doctrine of Compunction in the Christian East.* Kalamazoo, Mich.: Cistercian Publications, 1982.

———. *Spiritual Direction in the Early Christian East.* Kalamazoo, Mich.: Cistercian Publications, 1990.

Hierotheos, Metropolitan. *Life after Death.* Levadia-Hellas, Greece: Birth of the Theotokos Monastery, 2000.

———. *The Mind of the Orthodox Church.* Levadia-Hellas, Greece: Birth of the Theotokos Monastery, 2000.

———. *Orthodox Psychotherapy: The Science of the Fathers.* Levadia-Hellas, Greece: Birth of the Theotokos Monastery, 2002.

———. *Orthodox Spirituality: A Brief Introduction.* Levadia-Hellas, Greece: Birth of the Theotokos Monastery, 2002.

———. *The Person in the Orthodox Tradition.* Levadia-Hellas, Greece: Birth of the Theotokos Monastery, 2002.

———. *The Feasts of the Lord: An Introduction to the Twelve Feasts and Orthodox Christian Theology.* Levadia-Hellas, Greece: Birth of the Theotokos Monastery, 2003.

———. *A Night in the Desert of the Holy Mountain: Discussion with a Hermit on Jesus Prayer.* Levadia-Hellas, Greece: Birth of the Theotokos Monastery, 2003.

Isaac the Syrian. *The Ascetical Homilies of Saint Isaac the Syrian.* Boston: Holy Transfiguration Monastery, 1984.

Isaac of Nineveh. *Mystic Treatises.* Amsterdam: Uitgave der Koninklijke Akademie van Wetenschappen, 1923.

———. *On Ascetical Life.* Crestwood, N.Y.: St. Vladimir's Seminary Press, 1989.

Ioannikios, Archimandrite. *An Athonite Gerontikon: Sayings of the Holy Fathers of Mount Athos.* Thessaloniki, Greece: Publications of the Holy Monastery of St. Gregory Palamas, 1997.

John Climacus. *The Ladder of Divine Ascent.* New York: Paulist Press, 1982.

———. *The Ladder of Divine Ascent.* Boston: Holy Transfiguration Monastery, 2001.

John Cassian. *The Conferences.* Edited by Boniface Ramsey, O.P. New York: Newman Press, 1997.

———. *The Institutes.* Edited by Boniface Ramsey, O.P. New York: Newman Press, 2000.

Kadloubovsky, E., and G. E. H. Palmer. *Writings from the Philokalia: On Prayer of the Heart.* Boston: Faber & Faber, 1992.

Kavanagh, Aidan. *On Liturgical Theology.* New York: Pueblo Publishing, 1984.

Kotsonis, Archimandrite Ioannikios. *An Athonite Gerontikon: Sayings of the Holy Fathers of Mount Athos.* Thessaloniki, Greece: Holy Monastery of St. Gregory Palamas, 1997.

Krivocheine, Archbishop Basil. *In The Light of Christ: St. Symeon the New Theologian: Life-Spirituality-Doctrine.* Crestwood, N.Y.: St. Vladimir's Seminary Press, 1986.

Kronstadt, Fr. John. *My Life in Christ.* Jordanville, N.Y.: Holy Trinity Monastery, 2000.

Kovalevsky, Pierre. *St. Sergius and Russian Spirituality.* Crestwood, N.Y.: St. Vladimir's Seminary Press, 1976.

Krueger, Derek. *Symeon the Holy Fool: Leontius's "Life" and the Late Antique City.* Berkeley and Los Angeles: University of California Press, 1996.

Limouris, Gennadios. *Icons: Windows on Eternity.* Compiled by Gennadios Limouris. Faith and Order Paper 147. Geneva: WCC Publications, 1990.

Lossky, Vladimir. *In the Image and Likeness of God.* Crestwood, N.Y.: St. Vladimir's Seminary Press, 1974.

———. *The Mystical Theology of the Eastern Church.* Crestwood, N.Y.: St. Vladimir's Seminary Press, 1976.

———. *Orthodox Theology: An Introduction.* Crestwood, N.Y.: St. Vladimir's Seminary Press, 1978.

———. *The Vision of God.* Crestwood, N.Y.: St. Vladimir's Seminary Press, 1983.

Louth, Andrew. *Theology and Spirituality.* Fairacres, Oxford, U.K.: SLG Press, 1978.

———. *The Origins of the Christian Mystical Tradition: From Plato to Denys.* Oxford, U.K.: Clarendon Press, 1981.

———. *Discerning the Mystery: An Essay on the Nature of Theology.* New York: Oxford University Press, 1983.

———. *Denys the Areopagite.* Wilton, Conn.: Morehouse-Barlow, 1989.

———. *Maximus the Confessor.* New York: Routledge, 1996.

———. *Wisdom of the Byzantine Church.* Columbia: University of Missouri Press, 1997.

———. *St. John Damascene: Tradition and Originality in Byzantine Theology.* New York: Oxford University Press, 2002.

Luykx, Archimandrite Boniface. *Eastern Monasticism and the Future of the Church.* Stamford, Conn.: Basileos Press, 1993.

Mantzaridis, Georgios. *The Deification of Man.* Crestwood, N.Y.: St. Vladimir's Seminary Press, 1984.

———. *Time and Man.* South Canaan, Pa.: St. Tikhon's Seminary Press, 1996.

Mascall, E. L. *The Mother of God: A Symposium.* Westminster, London: Dacre Press, 1959.

Matthew the Poor. *The Communion of Love.* Crestwood, N.Y.: St. Vladimir's Seminary Press, 1989.

———. *Orthodox Prayer Life: The Interior Way.* Crestwood, N.Y.: St. Vladimir's Seminary Press, 2003.

Maximus the Confessor. *Maximus Confessor: Selected Writings.* New York: Paulist Press, 1985.
———. *Maximus the Confessor's Questions and Doubts.* Translated by Despina Prassas. DeKalb: Northern Illinois University Press, 2010.
Meehan, Brenda. *Holy Women of Russia: The Lives of Five Orthodox Women Offer Spiritual Guidance for Today.* Crestwood, N.Y.: St. Vladimir's Seminary Press, 1997.
Mersch, Emile. *The Whole Christ: The Historical Development of the Doctrine of the Mystical Body in Scripture and Tradition.* Milwaukee: Bruce Publishing, 1938.
Meyendorff, John. *St. Gregory Palamas and Orthodox Spirituality.* Crestwood, N.Y.: St. Vladimir's Seminary Press, 1974.
———. *A Study of Gregory Palamas.* Leighton Buzzard, U.K.: Faith Press, 1974.
———. *Christ in Eastern Christian Thought.* Crestwood, N.Y.: St. Vladimir's Seminary Press, 1975.
———. *Byzantine Theology: Historical Trends and Doctrinal Themes.* New York: Fordham University Press, 1976.
Michel, Virgil. *The Liturgy of the Church, according to the Roman Rite.* New York: Macmillan, 1937.
Moore, Archimandrite Lazarus. *St. Seraphim of Sarov: A Spiritual Biography.* Blanco, Texas: New Sarov Press, 1994.
Moschos, John. *The Spiritual Meadow of John Moschos.* Translated by John Wortley. Kalamazoo, Mich.: Cistercian Publications, 1992.
Nellas, Panayiotis. *Deification in Christ: The Nature of the Human Person.* Crestwood, N.Y.: St. Vladimir's Seminary Press, 1987.
Nicodemus of the Holy Mountain. *Unseen Warfare: The Spiritual Combat and Paths to Paradise of Lorenzo Scupoli.* Revised by Theophan the Recluse. Crestwood, N.Y.: St Vladimir's Seminary Press, 1987
———. *A Handbook of Spiritual Council.* New York: Paulist Press, 1989.
Ouspensky, Leonid. *Theology of the Icon.* Crestwood, N.Y.: St. Vladimir's Seminary Press, 1978.
———. "The Meaning and Language of Icons." In *The Meaning of Icon,* edited by Leonid Ouspensky and Vladimir Lossky. Crestwood, N.Y.: St. Vladimir's Seminary Press, 1983.
Pachomius. *The Life of St. Pachomius and His Disciples.* Kalamazoo, Mich.: Cistercian Publications, 1980.
Palladius: The Lausiac History. Westminster, Md.: Longmans, Green, 1965.
Papanikolaou, Aristotle. *Being with God: Trinity, Apophaticism, and Divine-Human Communion.* Notre Dame, Ind.: University of Notre Dame Press, 2006.
Pekar, Athanasius, O.S.B.M. *The Perfect Christian: Religious Ideal of St. Basil the Great.* Warren, Mich.: Basilian Fathers Publications, 1993.
Peterson, Erik. *The Angels and the Liturgy.* New York: Herder & Herder, 1964.
Phan, Peter C. *Culture and Eschatology: The Iconographical Vision of Paul Evdokimov.* New York: Peter Lang, 1984.
Philokalia: The Complete Text. 4 vols. Edited by G. E. H. Palmer, Philip Sherrard, Kallistos Ware. Boston: Faber & Faber, 1983–1995.

Pseudo-Athanasius. *The Life of Blessed Syncletica.* Toronto: Peregrina Publishing, 1996.
Pseudo-Dionysius. *Pseudo-Dionysius: The Complete Works.* New York: Paulist Press, 1987.
Pseudo-Macarius. *The Fifty Spiritual Homilies and The Great Letter.* New York: Paulist Press, 1992.
Quenot, Michel. *The Icon: Window on the Kingdom.* Crestwood, N.Y.: St. Vladimir's Seminary Press, 1991.
Rahner, Hugo. *Man at Play.* New York: Herder & Herder, 1972.
Rahner, Karl, S.J. "Reflections on the Theology of Renunciation." In *Theological Investigations,* vol. 3. New York: Crossroad, 1982.
Rahner, Karl, S.J. "The Passion and Asceticism." In *Theological Investigations,* vol. 3. New York: Crossroad, 1982.
Romanides, John S. *The Ancestral Sin.* Ridgewood, N.J.: Zephyr Publishing, 1988.
———. *Patristic Theology.* Dalles, Ore.: Uncut Mountain Press, 2008.
Russell, Norman. *The Doctrine of Deification in the Greek Patristic Tradition.* Oxford, U.K.: Oxford University Press, 2004.
Schmemann, Alexander. *For the Life of the World.* New York: St. Vladimir's Seminary Press, 1973.
———. *Great Lent: Journey to Pascha.* Crestwood, N.Y.: St. Vladimir's Seminary Press, 1974.
———. *Of Water and the Spirit.* Crestwood, N.Y.: St. Vladimir's Seminary Press, 1974.
———. *The Eucharist.* Crestwood, N.Y.: St. Vladimir's Seminary Press, 1987.
———. *Celebration of Faith: Vol. 3, The Virgin Mary.* Crestwood, N.Y.: St. Vladimir's Seminary Press, 1995.
———. *The Journals of Father Alexander Schmemann, 1973–1983.* Crestwood, N.Y.: St. Vladimir's Seminary Press, 2002.
Sendler, Egon. *The Icon, Image of the Invisible: Elements of Theology, Aesthetics, and Technique.* Torrence, Calif.: Oakwood Publications, 1992.
Slesinski, Robert. *Pavel Florensky: A Metaphysics of Love.* Crestwood, N.Y.: St. Vladimir's Seminary Press, 1984.
Solovyof, Vladimir. *The Justification of the Good.* London: Constable and Company, 1918.
———. *Lectures on Godmanhood.* London: Dennis Dobson, 1948.
———. *A Solovyov Anthology.* Edited by S. L. Frank. London: SCM Press, 1950.
Sophrony, Archimandrite. *The Monk of Mount Athos: Staretz Silouan.* Crestwood, N.Y.: St. Vladimir's Seminary Press, 1973.
———. *Wisdom from Mount Athos: The Writings of Staretz Silouan.* Crestwood, N.Y.: St. Vladimir's Seminary Press, 1974.
———. *His Life Is Mine.* Crestwood, N.Y.: St. Vladimir's Seminary Press, 1977.
———. *We Shall See Him as He Is.* Platina, Calif.: St. Herman of Alaska Brotherhood, 1988.
———. *On Prayer.* Crestwood, N.Y.: St. Vladimir's Seminary Press, 1998.

Sorsky, Nil. *The Complete Writings*. New York: Paulist Press, 2003.
Spidlik, Tomas. *The Spirituality of the Christian East*. Kalamazoo, Mich.: Cistercian Press, 1986.
———. *Prayer: The Spirituality of the Christian East*. Kalamazoo, Mich.: Cistercian Press, 2005.
Staniloae, Dumitru. *Prayer and Holiness*. Oxford, U.K.: SLG Press and Convent of the Incarnation, 1987.
———. *Orthodox Spirituality: A Practical Guide for the Faithful and a Definitive Manual for the Scholar*. South Canaan, Pa.: St. Tikhon's Seminary Press, 2003.
Stewart, Columba. *The World of the Desert Fathers*. Fairacres, Oxford, U.K.: SLG Press, 1986.
———. *Cassian the Monk*. New York: Oxford University Press, 1998.
Symeon the New Theologian. *Hymns of Divine Love*. Translated by George A. Maloney. Denville, N.J.: Dimension Books, 1976.
———. *The Discourses*. New York: Paulist Press, 1980.
———. *The Practical and Theological Chapters and The Three Theological Discourses*. Kalamazoo, Mich.: Cistercian Press, 1982.
———. *The First Created Man*. Platina, Calif.: St. Herman of Alaska Brotherhood, 1994.
———. *On the Mystical Life: Ethical Discourses*. Vols. 1 and 2. Crestwood, N.Y.: St. Vladimir's Seminary Press, 1995.
Theophan the Recluse. *The Path to Salvation: A Manual of Spiritual Transformation*. Forestville, Calif.: St. Herman of Alaska Brotherhood, 1996.
———. *The Spiritual Life and How to Be Attuned to It*. Platina, Calif.: St. Herman of Alaska Brotherhood, 1996.
Thunberg, Lars. *Man and the Cosmos: The Vision of St. Maximus the Confessor*. Crestwood, N.Y.: St. Vladimir's Seminary Press, 1985.
———. *Microcosm and Mediator: The Theological Anthropology of Maximus the Confessor*. Chicago: Open Court, 1995.
Tikhon of Zadonsk. *Journey to Heaven: Counsels and the Particular Duties of Every Christian*. Jordanville, New York: Holy Trinity Monastery, 1991.
Vasileios, Archimandrite. *Hymn of Entry: Liturgy and Life in the Orthodox Church*. Crestwood, N.Y.: St. Vladimir's Seminary Press, 1984.
Velichkovsky, Paisius. *Little Russian Philokalia*. Platina, Calif.: St. Herman of Alaska Brotherhood, 1994.
Verdon, Timothy, ed. *Monasticism and the Arts*. Syracuse, N.Y.: Syracuse University Press, 1984.
Vivian, Tim. *Journeying into God: Seven Early Monastic Lives*. Minneapolis: Fortress Press, 1996.
Volotsky, Iosif. *The Monastic Rule of Iosif Volotsky*. Edited and translated by David M. Goldfrank. Kalamazoo, Mich.: Cistercian Publications, 2000.
Waddell, Helen, trans. *The Desert Fathers*. Ann Arbor: University of Michigan Press, 1936.
———. *Beasts and Saints*. Grand Rapids, Mich.: Eerdmans, 1995.
Ward, Benedicta, S.L.G., ed. *Sayings of the Desert Fathers: The Alphabetical Collection*. Kalamazoo, Mich.: Cistercian Publications, 1975.

———. *The Lives of the Desert Fathers.* Kalamazoo, Mich.: Cistercian Publications, 1981.
———. *Harlots of the Desert: A Study of Repentance in Early Monastic Sources.* Kalamazoo, Mich.: Cistercian Publications, 1987.
———. *The Desert Fathers: Sayings of the Early Christian Monks.* New York: Penguin Books, 2003.
Ware, Kallistos. *The Orthodox Way.* Crestwood, N.Y.: St. Vladimir's Seminary Press, 1995.
———. *The Power of the Name: The Jesus Prayer in Orthodox Spirituality.* Fairacres, Oxford, U.K.: SLG Press, 1997.
———. *The Inner Kingdom.* Vol. 1 of *The Collected Works.* Crestwood, N.Y.: St. Vladimir's Seminary Press, 2000.
———. *The Way of a Pilgrim and the Pilgrim Continues His Way.* New York: Seabury Press, 1965.
Wenzel, Siegfried. *The Sin of Sloth: Acedia in Medieval Thought and Literature.* Chapel Hill: University of North Carolina Press, 1967.
Williams, A. N. *The Ground of Union: Deification in Aquinas and Palamas.* New York: Oxford University Press, 1999.
Winkler, Gabriele. *Prayer Attitude in the Eastern Church.* Minneapolis: Light and Life Publishing Co., 1978.
———. *The Jesus Prayer in Eastern Spirituality.* Minneapolis: Light and Life Publishing Co., 1986.
Zander, Valentine. *St. Seraphim of Sarov.* Crestwood, N.Y.: St. Vladimir's Seminary Press, 1975.
Zizioulas, John. *Being as Communion.* Crestwood, N.Y.: St. Vladimir's Seminary Press, 1985.

INDEX

INDEX

On Liturgical Asceticism was designed in Scala and Scala Sans
and typeset by Kachergis Book Design of Pittsboro, North Carolina.
It was printed on 60-pound Natures Book Natural and bound
by Thomson-Shore of Dexter, Michigan.